Inventing Witchcraft

A Case Study in the Creation of a New Religion

Inventing Witchcraft

A Case Study in the Creation of a New Religion

Aidan A. Kelly

Thoth Publications
Loughborough, Leicestershire

A CIP catalogue record for this book is available from the British Library.

Cover design by Avanson Design

Published by Thoth Publications
64, Leopold Street, Loughborough, LE11 5DN

ISBN 978-1-870450-58-4
Web address: www.thoth.co.uk
email: enquiries@thoth.co.uk

Contents

Acknowledgements

I need here to thank some of the people who have made it possible for me to write this book. First and foremost, my friend and colleague, J. Gordon Melton, whose moral and practical support for me, my work, and my interests during past years kept me going through some extremely thin and discouraging periods. I am especially grateful to him for throwing open the archives of his Institute for the Study of American Religion to me, and allowing me to use first some raw materials that he had been saving for a rainy day or another book.

I wish to thank the staff of Ripley's International, especially Charles Thielen and Derek Copperthwaite, for their good opinions of me and for their courtesy that made it possible for me to see the materials in the collection in Toronto that have proved central to my reconstruction of Gardnerian history.

I need to thank other scholars whose work and direct contributions have been of immeasurable help to me, especially Chas Clifton, Philip Heselton, Ronald Hutton, and Robert Mattheissen.

I gladly thank the many Craft initiates who have helped me in this reconstruction work over the years, especially Margot Adler, Isaac Bonewits, Meredydd Harper, Judith Harrow, Fred Lamond, Melissa Seims, Valerie Voigt, and Carl Weschcke. Some friendships have cooled, unfortunately, but I remain grateful for past friendship and help.

I thank Lady Epona, Julie O'Ryan, for having typed the entire manuscript into memory in 1987 from its earlier, non-computer incarnation.

And last I thank my wife and High Priestess, Melinda Taylor-Kelly, for putting up with my obsession with Gardnerian history.

Chapter One

How This Book Came to Be Written

How old is witchcraft? There are literary references to witches and witchcraft going back to the Sumerians—but it is hard to be sure that all these are referring to exactly the same thing. Members of the current religious movement that calls itself Witchcraft, also known variously as Wicca, Gardnerian Witchcraft, or just "the Craft[1]" claim continuity with and descent from the witches of earlier times. Is this claim historically valid? This book attempts to provide an answer to that question based on the historical evidence, not on opinions.

To answer that question, we need to examine the history of Gardnerian Wicca during the lifetime of its major founder, Gerald B. Gardner. This history has been difficult to discover, because Gardnerians generally have a long-standing habit of keeping everything about themselves secret.

Since the 1954 publication of Gardner's *Witchcraft Today*, the book that launched the movement, Gardnerian Witchcraft has blossomed, carried by Gardnerian initiates and admirers throughout the Western world. Several different measures (circulation of the largest Pagan[2]

---

[1] "The Craft" is now the most common name used by the movement's members to name their religion. It is actually a Masonic term for Freemasonry, but is not in itself a clue to the origins of Gardnerian witchcraft, because the term only appears in documents late in the 1950s, perhaps influenced by Masonic works being used for reference. In the 1940s and early 1950s, as in *Witchcraft Today*, the term used is either "cult," which seems to come straight from Murray, or "the Art," which seems to come from a magical source.

[2] The term "pagan" in this context does not mean "nonreligious." Rather, it is a generic term for the current religions that make up the overall Pagan

periodicals; attendance at national festivals; number of coven contacts in the Mensa POWSIG contact list) indicated that in the early 1990s there were roughly 5,000 covens in the USA, and perhaps several hundred thousand people involved in the movement. A 1999 survey sponsored by the Covenant of the Goddess came up with an estimate of around 600,000 Witches in the United States and around six million active members of the Neopagan movement. This is no longer a tiny, timorous movement. It has been doubling in size every two years or less since the 1970s. Hence it is time for a serious history of the movement, one that can serve as a basis for theological reflection.

Within the Pagan Movement, the term "Gardnerian" usually refers to persons who can trace the lineage of their initiation back to Gerald Gardner. All other Witches are considered to belong to other Traditions[3] (called Alexandrian, Druidic, Dianic, Fairy, etc.), which are supposed to derive from ancient polytheism independently of Gardner. *Please* notice that I am not using the term in this sense. Instead, I use "Gardnerian Witches" to refer to all current Witches, because all the current activity derives from widespread imitating of Gardnerian practices and from no other source. I will later discuss the few covens that predated Gardner, but they had an utterly different theology from what the Gardnerians propose; objectively, they were not practicing the same religion.

In this opening chapter I need to explain what questions I was asking, and how I went about trying to find answers to them, so that you can evaluate for yourself how reliable those answers may be. People have been telling stories about the Gardnerians for the last five decades - Gardner himself, various Gardnerians, friends and foes, scholars and journalists - and almost all of these stories have been, in large part, fantasies. In contrast, I have been working since 1971 to ferret out the hard, verifiable facts of Gardnerian history. I need to explain how I was able to discover those facts, to let you see that what I am writing here

Movement. These religions all resemble Gardnerian Wicca to some greater or lesser degree: the greater the resemblance, the more the religion evolved by imitating Gardnerianism.

[3] I capitalise Tradition when I use it in the current sense of a family tree of covens that is more or less the equivalent of a "denomination" among Christian churches.

is history, not more guesswork. (Those with no patience at all for this sort of thing will now turn to Chapter 2 anyway, though I wish they wouldn't.)

Why couldn't I just let the facts speak for themselves? That won't work, because, contrary to our modern myths about how science works, a fact does not exist independently of theory. What you perceive as a fact depends on what theory you're operating with; your choice of a theory depends on your own personal history; and you cannot operate without a theory, or you wouldn't be able to perceive at all.[4] For this reason, I must summarise some of my own history here.

I first became curious about claims that Witchcraft had survived into modern times in 1954, when I came across a book called *Witches Still Live*, by Theda Kenyon, in the Marin County branch library in Tamalpais Valley, California. For the most part the book is a hodgepodge of Frazer and folklore, but it opens with a summary of Leland's *Aradia*. This "Gospel of the Witches of Tuscany" - with its talk of naked meetings, free love beneath the full moon, and rebellion against oppressive overlords - was very heady stuff for a repressed teenager in the 1950s, and I placed it high on my list of Fascinating Topics to Be Investigated As Soon As Possible.

I found Gardner's *Witchcraft Today* in the San Francisco Public Library in 1958. (In those innocent days, books on the occult could be left on open library shelves and yet not be stolen.) I recognized that this was a Witchcraft of the same general type as in the *Aradia*: I was intrigued by Gardner's claims that it had survived from the Middle Ages into this century, and that he had been initiated into one of the last surviving covens. I took careful notes on all the fragments of information about what was done in rituals that Gardner seemed to let slip in the book.

I was immensely interested in the topic of Witchcraft, and began searching out relevant books. This was not as easy as it sounds: most of the books on "Witchcraft" in the libraries were about medieval persecutions, and had nothing to do (as far as I could see) with the

---

[4] For an extremely readable survey of what recent psychological research has discovered about how our perceptual systems actually work, see Daniel Goleman's *Vital Lies, Simple Truths*.

survival of paganism that Leland and Gardner described. The most important books I found during the next decade were Margaret Murray's *God of the Witches*, Robert Graves' *The White Goddess* (given to me by my classmate, the poet Robert Chrisman), both in 1961, and Elliott Rose's *A Razor for a Goat* in 1965.

In the fall of 1967 my friend Sarah asked me to help her write a "Witches' Sabbath" for a class on creating ritual at San Francisco State. Thus began the work of creating what we came to call the New, Reformed, Orthodox Order of the Golden Dawn, a task that occupied me and many friends for much of the following decade. What enabled us to create the NROOGD, that is, to reinvent a very Gardnerian sort of Witchcraft for ourselves, was that more and more information about Gardnerian rituals and practices was being published in the late 1960s. Having been able to construct the NROOGD rituals out of fragments of information about Gardnerian practices, I began to wonder whether Gardner had done much the same thing: constructed his "survival" out of the fragments of data that can be gleaned from Margaret Murray and other sources.

After 1958 and on through the 1960s, there had appeared a steadily growing stream of books that dealt with Witchcraft in general and Gardnerian Witchcraft in particular. Most of these were written by Gardnerians, who accepted all of Gardner's historical claims as being simple fact. There were other Witches who disputed Gardner's authority, and who claimed to belong to similarly surviving covens, quite independent of Gardner. Until 1979, Doreen Valiente seemed (to Americans) to be one of the most important of these independent Witches. In complete contrast, most of the scholars who touched on Gardner dismissed his claims out of hand, asserted that he must have made the whole thing up, but did not present any sort of evidence to support this assertion. A few scholars, such as Elliott Rose, took a more moderate position and conceded that Gardner might have had some data from an older coven or covens, but Rose, for example, doubted that such data went back past about 1875.

As long as no independent evidence was available, any opinion about what Gardner did or did not do had to remain merely an opinion. An argument from probabilities cannot be convincing, because history is full of things that were highly improbable but happened anyway. It is not inherently impossible that a few rural British families might, as they claim, have maintained some sort of pagan religious tradition into this century; likewise, Gardner could have concocted everything out of whole cloth. Just as a sidelight on British history, it would be interesting to know what really happened.

I could think of one way that Gardner's claims might be tested. In their books, Doreen Valiente and various writers who were clearly Gardnerian (such as Raymond Buckland and Patricia Crowther) had argued that Gardner had not begun from scratch; that instead he had augmented the fragmentary traditions of the coven he was initiated into, building them up into a viable system, as recorded in the Book of Shadows, which he then used to found new covens during the 1950s; and that, despite his eclecticism, he was preserving the essential concepts and practices of an ancient religion. Hence by 1970 I was wondering what had constituted the traditions of the older coven into which Gardner said he had been initiated, and what Gardner's contributions had been. I thought it might be possible, by careful critical analysis, to distinguish Gardner's additions to the Book of Shadows from the older body of data he was working with. But exactly what might such an analysis be applied to?

The problem here is that the "Book of Shadows" is more a concept than an object. It is supposed to be handcopied by each Gardnerian Witch after she or he has been initiated, and therefore exists - even in this era of xerography - only as a family of manuscript traditions. The situation is exactly analogous to what a person faces in trying to do New or Old Testament textual criticism, since the Bible also survived into modern times in the form of many families of manuscripts whose readings differed in thousands of places. In 1971 I was already beginning the studies that would lead to my being in graduate school in Berkeley from 1974 to 1980, studying Christian origins as a historical problem; and that is why it occurred to me that I could apply the methods of textual and literary scholarship (which were actually invented by the first Neopagans, in Italy during the Renaissance) to Craft writings. But, again, to which Craft writings?

The specific problem is that the published versions of the Book of Shadows are actually only the versions (and usually rather degenerate ones at that) in specific manuscripts. Some bits and pieces of rituals are included in Gardner's own books, but they don't amount to much. Farrar (1971) contains the full text (*except* for the "Craft Laws") of the Gardnerian Book of Shadows that Alex Sanders obtained when he was initiated in 1963 by Pat Kopanski[5]. Furthermore, these published versions had surely been tampered with by the publishers' editors; so reliable historical conclusions about what materials Gardner had to start with, and what he added, could not be based on these published books. Instead, to arrive at dependable conclusions, I would have to work from the original manuscripts themselves. That is, I needed access to the "Master" copy of the Book of Shadows, and to whatever books or documents Gardner might have had from the older coven. In 1970, I had no idea whether such things existed. If they did, I thought they would probably be the very private and very secret property of a Gardnerian coven somewhere. Even if I could discover their existence, I would probably not be allowed to see them; so I thought my questions would have to remain unanswered.

However, in 1971 I first saw the document variously called the "Craft Laws," the "Old Laws," or the "Ardanes." It appeared in June Johns' *King of the Witches: The World of Alex Sanders.* The document fascinated me. Internally it purports to have been written in the mid-18th century, and to include materials dating back to the 16th. My intuition was that the document must somehow be the key to evaluating Gardner's historical claims, and this has turned out, in an odd way, to be quite correct.

In 1971 Llewellyn published *Lady Sheba's Book of Shadows*; this was the first time that an almost complete copy (it lacked the Third-Degree Elevation) of the Gardnerian Book of Shadows had been published and widely distributed. Lady Sheba claimed to be a pre-Gardnerian Witch, but knew only Gardnerianism and folk magic; it later turned out that she had gotten the BoS from an Alexandrian coven in London.

---

[5] There is a letter in Toronto from her to Gardner that gives the details of Sanders' initiation; she had been initiated by Patricia Crowther.

This book also began with a text of the Craft Laws. I had been reading Bruce Metzger's excellent *The Text of the New Testament*, which explains the principles of textual criticism; so it occurred to me to try comparing the two texts of the Craft Laws in Johns and Sheba. Doing so, I discovered that the texts differed in more that 150 places, often in ways for which no immediate explanation was obvious. I wrote up my conclusions in an essay called "Textual Criticism and the Craft Laws." At the time, this exercise led me to suspect there had been an earlier document (or set of documents) from which these two texts had been derived, and I was on the alert for any evidence of its existence.

In 1973 I still did not expect ever to see the kind of original documents that would allow me to satisfy my historical curiosity. To my surprise, all the necessary documents began to fall into my lap in 1974 and 1975. They did so, as it turned out, in approximately the reverse of the order in which they had been written; so I had to work my way back from the most recent material to the oldest. In this chapter I can explain the actual sequence in which I reached my major conclusions. The history that I begin reconstructing in Chapter 3 is like the history reconstructed from an archaeological dig: it begins with the pieces I found last, and ends with the pieces I found first. (And the only book I know which successfully tells a story in which time flows in both directions is James Michener's *The Source*.)

In March 1974, soon after I had begun my Ph.D. studies at the Graduate Theological Union in Berkeley, my friend Isaac Bonewits was preparing to leave for St. Paul to become Editor of Llewellyn's *Gnostica*. I mentioned to him the essay I had done on the Craft Laws, and he encouraged me to send it to him (it was subsequently published in *Gnostica*, in September 1974). When it arrived in May, he showed it to Carl L. Weschcke, President of Llewellyn Publications, who was thus reminded that he had a file full of Gardnerian materials which he thought I might like to see. Isaac, upon looking through the file, recognized the importance of the materials, and immediately sent me photocopies of them and of some relevant correspondence from Gardner and others.

When I read through them the evening they arrived, I felt something like Champollion contemplating the Rosetta Stone, the bilingual inscription that made it possible to translate Egyptian hieroglyphics, for I could see that these were pages for a Gardnerian Book of Shadows. I was especially delighted that two of the eighteen documents made up the oldest copy I had yet seen of the Craft Laws (and in 2006, they are still the oldest extant text of the Craft Laws, as far as I know). I was also able to deduce immediately, by comparing the documents with Gardner's letters, that the materials were typed and/or handwritten by Gardner himself; the handwriting matched, and so did the two different typewriter fonts. More importantly, that night I discovered that Gardner was marginally dyslexic. That is, despite his intelligence, which I do not propose to underestimate, and his avid reading and collecting of books, he could not spell or punctuate well enough to meet even minimal standards for being published, and his grasp of grammar was shaky at best. In other words, *Gardner could not by himself have produced the books published in his name*; he could, and almost certainly did, carry out the basic writing, but he must have had much help, almost a collaborator, to carry a book to its final draft. I began to wonder who this helper was.

Further conversations with Carl revealed that the documents had been sent to him in about 1969 by Charles Clark, who at that time requested anonymity, which I observed by calling him "Mr.Q" in the first edition of this book. Since he has passed on recently, and since his role in this story has become public knowledge (see the article by Melissa Seims in the February 2005 issue of *Circle Network News*), it seems better to give him full credit for his decisions.

The documents are a motley assortment: some originals, but mostly carbon copies; typed variously on white bond, onionskin, and foolscap; of various sizes and conditions, some whole, some torn in half, some wrinkled from many foldings, some clean and never folded at all. Some have staple marks or holes punched in them, and had been fastened together in at least three different binders, no doubt being used in Books of Shadows; others show no marks and no sign of having seen such use. (I will describe them all in detail when we examine them one by one later on.) They were certainly not produced all at once, as a "fair copy" intended to be a single Book of Shadows. Instead, they are miscellaneous drafts from various stages of the writing process, typed on whatever was handy.

There was no way to be certain what in these 18 documents might have come from an older tradition. However, I realized that I could identify most of the quotes or paraphrases of published sources, and set these aside; I could then ask whether what remained made sense as being from anything like the sort of native pagan tradition that Gardner claimed. As I carried out this procedure, I discovered some interesting facts.

First, some of the drafts were different versions of the same basic ritual, and sometimes they incorporated revisions of other pieces of writing. I could therefore establish a relative internal chronology ("A is a revision of B; hence was written after B"). I also had some absolute dates for the bits of ritual and verse that had been published in Gardner's books. I was thus able to establish that the 18 Weschcke documents were written between about 1954 and about 1960, and that most of them had probably been typed up about 1958 or 1959. This allowed me to see that many of the Book of Shadows rituals, including the most detailed forms of the initiations, did not exist in 1954 (when *Witchcraft Today* was published), but instead were still being written. If a "Gardnerian" coven is defined as one that works the basic Gardnerian rituals - and this is one of the rules by which Gardnerian covens judge the authenticity of any coven that claims to be Gardnerian - then no Gardnerian coven could have existed before 1955, because the basic Gardnerian rituals had not yet been written.

Second, the major published sources from which the rituals had been constructed included: (a) Mathers' edition of *The Greater Key of Solomon*; (b) Aleister Crowley's *Magick in Theory and Practice*; (c) Leland's *Aradia*; (d) some Masonic rituals akin to those described by Duncan and those of the Hermetic Order of the Golden Dawn (aside from those transmitted by Crowley); and (e) Margaret Murray's *The Witch Cult in Western Europe*. There were also bits and pieces from other works by Leland, Jane E. Harrison, Gilbert Murray, James Frazer, and the other great classicists and mythologists of the 19th century. That accounted for EVERYTHING in the rituals! There was nothing left that differed in any important way from what you can find in those sources - but that is NOT at all what Gardner had claimed.

Still, all that applies only to the *rituals* in the Book of Shadows; and should not be a startling conclusion, because anyone familiar with western magical traditions can see that the Gardnerian rituals derive from a magical system much like the (essentially Masonic) system of the Hermetic Order of the Golden Dawn, not from any native British religious traditions. Furthermore, the Gardnerians admit that the rituals are exactly where Gardner did the most reconstruction work. Rather, they claim that the pre-1939 stratum is one of concept, customs, traditions, laws, and, in brief, the sorts of things incorporated in the Craft Laws, which is almost the only piece of writing in the Book of Shadows that claims to be (and at least logically could be) historical.

I had suspected that the Gardnerian claim to historicity must stand or fall on "The Old Laws" ever since I had first seen it, and my analysis of the two typed parts of it among the Weschcke documents simply left the question open. Because it was typed in two parts, which exhibit some curious internal parallels, I thought both parts might have been derived from an older, common source document - and it was that hypothetical older document I hoped to find when I went to Toronto to examine the Ripley's holdings.

I knew there was another possible source of information about Craft history, in the documents and letters acquired by Ripley's International, Ltd., Toronto, when it bought the contents of Gardner's Witchcraft museum on the Isle of Man. In June 1974, before my visit to St. Paul, I had stopped by the Ripley Museum of Witchcraft at Fisherman's Wharf in San Francisco, looked over their exhibits, and introduced myself to the manager, Charles Thielen. When I had explained the purpose of my research to him, he offered to write a letter to the corporate headquarters on my behalf, and as a result I received an invitation to visit their offices in Toronto and examine their holdings.

In September 1975 I was able to visit their headquarters in Toronto for three days, to look over these books and manuscripts. In Toronto I met Derek Copperthwaite, then Ripley's Vice President for Research and Development, who had arranged the purchase of the museum in 1971 from Gardner's heirs, Monique and Campbell Wilson, and who explained the circumstances of that purchase to me. (I would like to emphasize that Derek, a good-humoured, well-educated, and cosmopolitan man, understood the history of the Craft and of modern religious studies quite well; and it was his intuitive grasp of the importance of the various manuscripts in the collection that ensured their safety and their availability for scholarly study.)

After Gardner had purchased the museum, located in a building called the "Witches' Mill" in Castleton on the Isle of Man, from Cecil Williamson in 1951, he had used it to display his accumulated curiosities. At some point, probably after Mrs. Gardner had died in the 1950s, the Wilsons came to live with Gardner, essentially to take care of the old boy and help mind the shop; and when Gardner died childless in 1964, they inherited the property. However, they could not keep up with the work of the museum, and after a few years offered to sell it to Ripley's.

When Derek and Charles Bristol, Ripley's Treasurer, arrived on the island to discuss the possibility of a transaction, they found that the Wilsons were desperate. They couldn't keep the ancient building in repair enough to protect the museum's contents from the winter rains, which come storming in from the Irish Sea almost continually from November to May. (Derek commented to me that, if Ripley's hadn't bought the museum, probably much of its contents, especially the books and manuscripts, would simply have perished. Derek emphasized that no other corporation was willing to pay anything for the collection, and that the Witches of Britain, instead of being peeved at the Wilsons and at Ripley's, might consider that Ripley's had ensured that the raw materials of their history had been preserved and given appropriate care.)

Once the sale had been agreed upon, the museum's contents had to be packed up for shipment across the Atlantic. This, Derek said, was an enormous task in itself, since items were crammed into every conceivable nook and cranny in the building. The crew had to dismantle every item of furniture, remove the wall panels, and strip the building down to its studs and rafters, in order to find everything. Hence, Derek assured me, he was quite certain that nothing could have been overlooked.

I asked if any Books of Shadows had been found among the manuscripts, since several people had published statements about Books of Shadows (including one supposedly in Crowley's handwriting) that Gardner had had on display.

He assured me there were no such books, and described some of the abusive crank mail he had received insisting that Ripley's had no right to own such books, and demanding that he turn any such books over to the writer. "These people always describe themselves as the High Priest of Muckety-Muck, or some such nonsense. I can't imagine why they think I could simply give corporate property away. The only reason we invited you to come was that Charlie Thielen said you seemed sensible and serious."

"Then I owe him thanks for that. Perhaps," I suggested, "the working copies of the Book were removed from the collection before the Wilsons called you in."

"Perhaps so," he said, "but not likely. The Wilsons had no idea what was valuable in the collection, and what was junk, and were very reluctant to let anything go; so I can't imagine their willingly turning loose such obviously valuable items. Anyway, the one thing we found that might be a Book of Shadows is this. We found it stuffed way in the back of a cabinet. I haven't been able to decide whether it's a Book of Shadows or not; it's rather odd. I'd like to know what you make of it."

And with these words he handed me the manuscript book titled "Ye Bok of ye Art Magical," which, as I will explain, has turned out to be the key to the puzzle. I was able to answer Derek's question thus: the book had not begun life as a Book of Shadows, but had become one - in fact, the very first one - by the time it was filled up and retired.

Derek assured me that he had personally selected the items sent out for display at Ripley's various local museums, and that they were either physical artifacts or things of no conceivable commercial or scholarly value, such as some of the vast horde of pamphlets on occult and fringe religious movements that Gardner had collected.[6] I was therefore able

---

[6] Actually, these are of the highest scholarly interest to J. Gordon Melton, and it would be very useful to reassemble some of them for his American Religions collection in the UCSB library.

to examine everything that Gardner's museum had contained, as far as Derek knew, that was relevant to his "reform" of the Craft. There were a few things that supplied me with useful facts.

First, I was able to look through Gardner's entire personal library. It represented a healthy selection of what had been published on witchcraft and the occult between about 1890 and 1950, and included precisely the books - Murray, Crowley, Leland, etc. - that I already knew he had used as sources for his rituals. It was mildly interesting to find that he did own these books, but there were no surprises among them. There were also about a hundred older "rare" books and manuscripts on occult topics ranging from the 16th to 19th centuries, but a close examination did not reveal them to be interesting, valuable, or relevant to the Craft.

Second, Gardner had saved correspondence from the 1940s or earlier, but there were no mentions of the Craft except in a single file of correspondence, dating from 1957 to 1962, which seemed to be complete. (I now know that Doreen Valiente took all the correspondence from before 1957 with her when the coven was divided in February 1957.) Most of these letters were from such well-known Gardnerians as Patricia Crowther, Lois Hemmings, Jack Bracelin, and the Wilsons, as well as from Charles Clark. There was also a very odd letter from "Ameth" to "Dafo"; since in 1975 I still thought "Dafo" had been Doreen Valiente's coven name, I could not imagine who "Ameth" was.

Third, there was a typescript, titled "New Light on Witchcraft," which was the carbon copy of the unedited manuscript of *Witchcraft Today*, in the form in which it went to the publisher. Glancing through it, I discovered it was in excellent shape. But obviously Gardner - who, as I said, was marginally dyslexic - had not produced this MS. by himself; he had had some very competent help, and I guessed at the time that it might have come from his wife. Doreen Valiente suggested to me that that it may have been Dolores North, or simply some hired help. I think it highly significant that the editor whom he thanks in the Preface, Ross Nichols, now turns out to have been a member of the Ancient Order of Druids, the same order that used Gardner's sword for its Stonehenge ritual; in fact, Nichols was elected Chosen Chief of the Order about the time Gardner died, and a book by Nichols on the Order, giving some of its heretofore secret rituals, has been published. Several manuscript books of the Order's rituals were also among the Toronto holdings.

Fourth, there were 18 notebooks filled with Gardner's notes on his reading, mainly in preparation for writing *The Meaning of Witchcraft*. These also contained a few passages that were first drafts of materials that later went into the Book of Shadows.

Fifth, in the file of letters about the Craft, I found a document titled "Proposed Rules for the Craft"; it could be dated to June 1957 because there was also a letter of that date from Jack Bracelin, Gardner's supposed biographer, which referred to them as "Ned's proposed rules for the Craft." These rules greatly overlapped the concerns of the "Craft Laws" document, and were, I finally realized, many months later, the first draft of the "Craft Laws." Given that hypothesis, I was able to identify an earlier draft of every passage in the "Craft Laws" somewhere else in Gardner's published or unpublished writings. Where later and earlier versions of the same passages have been published, often the later passages had been archaized by incorporation of obscure words gleaned from the *Oxford English Dictionary* - and Doreen Valiente told me that she had precisely such a list, in Gardner's writing, which he sent her along with a replacement copy of the "Craft Laws," since she and her coven had burned the first copy of the "Craft Laws" that he had sent them in their cauldron as an act of literary criticism.

When I returned home from Toronto, I had already found all the facts needed to demonstrate that nothing in the "Craft Laws," or in the entire Book of Shadows, makes sense as part of a tradition received from an older coven, although it took me many months to think it all through. When I had finished, I had identified a literary source for every detail. Also, the very ordinary bits of evidence (addresses, letters, diaries, even laundry lists) that we would expect to find for the existence of an older coven were nowhere to be found; and in scholarly history, this sort of situation almost always means that somebody is making up a tall tale. In nuclear physics, even if a particle has no charge and almost no mass, and is therefore very difficult to detect, its existence must have some detectable effects (if it has no detectable effects at all, there is no reason to suppose that it exists); if those effects cannot be detected after we have made statistically sufficient efforts to detect them, we can be sure the particle does not exist. Similarly, the existence of an older coven would have left detectable traces somewhere in the Gardnerian Book of Shadows. Since no traces at all can be found, we have no reason to think that such a coven existed - and so the organizational link with the past is broken: we have no evidence that the Gardnerian movement is in any way a survival of an earlier, secret pagan religion.

Let me emphasize here that I am not arguing from silence. I am NOT saying "There is no evidence to support such claims." I am saying that there is now a great deal of evidence, all of which I have used to reconstruct the history set forth in this volume.

Nor can it be supposed that I overlooked any evidence, because in 1975 and 1976 I still thought Gardner's claims were probably true: I *wanted* the Craft Laws to be based on traditional documents; I *wanted* there to have been some tradition behind Gardner's coven; I *wanted* there to have been an ancient religion of a Mother Goddess. It took me months to think through the implications of the evidence I had collected because I was being forced step by step to conclude that what I wanted to be true simply was not historically true. This methodological fact is an important part of my argument. Certainly if I had been an Evangelical going to Toronto to do battle with Satan and all his works, I might easily have overlooked important evidence. But that was not the situation. I was looking for facts that would support the Gardnerian claims, and I wanted to find them; if there had been any in Toronto, I would not have overlooked them. The reason I could not find any, therefore, is that they almost certainly do not exist.

I completed a first version of this book in 1976, in the form of a proto-dissertation; it was about 50 percent footnotes, and was accepted as satisfying one of my comprehensive examination topics at the Graduate Theological Union in 1977. I had written it under contract to Llewellyn Books, but Carl Weschcke decided not to publish it - it was far too difficult and scholarly for his market. I believe he also did not want to publish the verbatim transcripts of the documents; his readership would probably not have understood why he had put out a book full of spelling, grammatical, and other mistakes. I offered the book to several scholarly presses as well, but in the 1970s they were unable to believe that contemporary witchcraft could be a topic of any significance whatsoever. In addition, once past my comprehensive exams, I naturally began to concentrate on getting my dissertation completed; so rewriting this book got put on a back burner.

In 1979, I was still not satisfied with my conclusions: there were still other missing pieces, which I did not expect to be able to find - until, again, they fell into my lap. For example, in 1979 I received a letter from Margot Adler on the envelope of which she scrawled an excited note that Doreen Valiente had stated[7] that Gardner had initiated her in 1953 - and some missing pieces of the puzzle fell into place. Doreen also said[8] that in 1954-1955 she had co-authored the verse that begins "Darksome night and shining moon" and other materials used in the Book of Shadows. Since I knew from independent evidence that someone had been helping Gardner write, her claims seemed not only plausible but probable. Until then, no one in America had understood the importance of Doreen's work on the Craft; but obviously, if she had begun working with Gardner in 1953, she could have helped get that final manuscript of *Witchcraft Today* into shape. Even more importantly, hers was almost surely the competent hand that I had detected alongside Gardner's helping write the Weschcke documents. I wrote an academic paper setting forth these conclusions in 1980, and it was subsequently republished in at least three periodicals.

Late in 1981, I had the pleasure of a visit from a man generally known in the Craft as Robert, who was willing to answer many questions I had not thought I would ever get answered. He is still a member of Gardner's original coven, into which he was initiated in January 1957 by Gardner and by Dayonis, who was the Maiden of the coven at that time; Doreen Valiente was still, he said, the High Priestess of the

---

[7] In her *Witchcraft for Tomorrow*, p. 14.

[8] Ibid., p. 21.

coven, but was not there that night. (One reason I knew his statements were accurate is that he knew the names - which I knew from reading the letters in Toronto - of the utterly obscure people who had been members of the coven in 1957. It was a great pleasure to ask him "Who was Ned?" and be told, "Oh, he was someone in the City," which, of course, is British for "rich and well-connected.") The very next month, in February 1957, Fred told me, the coven split in half; Doreen and Ned, as her High Priest, took four or five others with them to form a new coven. Fred said those left in the original coven soon decided to use the circle dance, rather than scourging, as their major way to raise power; so Gardner then wandered off to begin initiating new members for another coven more to his liking.

This was the situation when the "Craft Laws" were created; Robert thought they were the work of Doreen's coven, since they had never been part of the original coven's tradition. He also assured me that all the English Gardnerians of his time knew that Doreen had written virtually everything in the Book of Shadows, and that the master copy of that book was still in her possession[9]. Fred said he believed there had been a pre-1939 coven, and said he knew several people who had met "Dafo," who had also been a member of it. However, he admitted, she had never been forthcoming with any data about that coven.

"Wasn't 'Dafo' Doreen's Craft name?", I asked.

Fred said, "No, hers was . . ."

---

[9] She said in Witchcraft for Tomorrow (p. 21), that she owns "Gardner's original Book of Shadows, which he gave to me." To leap ahead in the discussion, let me confirm that this is true: she does own "Text A" (in the set of labels devised by the Farrars, 1984, p. 3), the book of materials that Gardner copied from BAM in about 1952, as we will see in Chapter 3. She also owns "Text B," an expanded copy of Text A, that Gardner had been working on when they met, and her own copy of the BoS, "Text C," which is her rewriting of Gerald's BoS. After the original coven was divided in 1957, Gerald rewrote all her materials into yet a fourth version, which he gave to Olwen; and Olwen's copy became the master copy from which all Official Gardnerian Books of Shadows in the USA have been derived.

"Ameth," we said, almost together, as the light dawned. (And that explained the peculiar letter from Ameth to Dafo I had found!)[10]

"So Dafo was Dorothy Clutterbuck," I said.

"No, Dafo had been the Maiden of the old coven, and after Dorothy died, she became the High Priestess until Doreen took over," Fred said.

(It is now known that "Dafo" was Edith Woodford-Grimes, and that she and Gardner were the founders of the first coven.)

I should have gotten in touch with Doreen at that point - some things would have been much simpler if I had - but Craft history was not my main concern at that time; survival was, and has remained a major concern ever since. Fortunately, the communications between us were later straightened out. After I had sent her several peacemaking letters, explaining my trust in her truthfulness, she sent me a very helpful and friendly letter in 1990, just as I was finishing the final draft of *Crafting the Art of Magick, Book I*, that cleared up many long-standing puzzles. I sent a copy of the draft to her, and received several more extremely friendly and helpful letters, and was able to work the information she had sent me into the actual last draft of it.

The communication problem between us had arisen because, in fact, she hadn't realized that before 1979 no one on this side of the Atlantic knew how central she had been in the Craft, though everyone in England knew; so she did not understand why I was being sceptical about her statements. Actually, I was being sceptical about everybody - the essence of scholarship and all that - and I continue to be impressed by the fact that her story stands up to scrutiny. I have been able to test it against the documentary facts, and she checks out. She deserves credit for having helped transform the Craft from being the hobby of a handful of eccentric Brits into being an international religious movement, and I was glad to see that she was claiming that credit in her last books.

---

[10] I could have learned from Cardell's *Witch* that Ameth was Doreen's coven name, but that information was not in the ERN reprint, and I did not see a copy of the original until Margot Adler sent me a Xerox of her copy in about 1982.

Crafting the Art of Magick, Book I: A History of Witchcraft, 1939-1964, the first edition of this book, was unsatisfactory precisely because it was written as a "trade" book for Llewellyn. I promised Carl I would eliminate the scholarly details that had caused him to reject the book in 1976. In trying not to overwhelm the readers, I simplified the arguments, left out much of the technical analysis of documents, and cleaned up the texts of the documents, presenting them as they might have been written by Doreen or by Gardner IF he had not been somewhat dyslexic; so the argument in *CAMI* was actually not logically watertight. It was a report about my research, not the research itself, but this distinction was not obvious even to the brightest scholars who have dealt with *CAMI*. Here I present the book much as I had originally written it, with all the details in it, and let the Devil take the hindmost.

I also need to explain a little more about the techniques of modern religious studies, and about how I have applied them to the Craft as a case study to show how a religion is created. There is a current general perception among religious scholars that you cannot study a religion from the outside. You cannot understand how and why it works for its members unless you undergo experiences as close to theirs as you can. You cannot know what it is like to be initiated unless you are initiated. Paul Ricoeur wrote that you cannot understand a religious text unless you open yourself up to it enough to risk being changed by it. One scholar I know has spoken of "immersing" yourself in the religion, living the lifestyle of its members, in order to grasp its essential qualities.[11] Some conservative academics want to claim that no member of a religion can be truly objective about it - but this sort of attitude amounts to bigotry toward religion in general, and fails to confront the fact that all human being are religious.

Every human being has some beliefs that serve as his or her religion. It is not possible to live without experiencing life as meaningful; and whatever is meaningful is ultimately, I believe, religious, because it deals with values, which simply do not exist apart from the humans who hold them. To have no values, no meaning in one's life, is not scholarly

[11] Del De Chant, in a paper given to the Group on New Religious Movements of the American Academy of Religion, December 1986, Boston.

neutrality, but the state of anomie, which is a terminal and lethal stage of depression. Hence in religious studies we cannot reasonably define neutrality as being nonreligious, but only as being fair and having no hidden agendas. A scholar can in fact study his or her own religion, because there is a vast difference between being a simple "true believer" and being as well-informed as possible about the history, theology, etc., of the religion. An outsider cannot describe what the religion feels like from the inside, because he or she has never felt that. The current scholarly standard for phenomenological study of a religion is that the description you arrive at must be acceptable both to scholars and to liberal members of the religion as being accurate and objective. The most conservative members of any religion will typically refuse to accept any sort of mainstream scholarship as being accurate; so one cannot reasonably hope to gain their approval.

In demonstrating that the Gardnerian movement is actually a new religion, I am not debunking it. In papers I delivered to the American Academy of Religion during the 1980s, I argued that every religion begins as a new religion at a specific time and place in history.[12] As a new religion, the Craft is therefore the equal of Christianity. After all, what right-thinking Roman citizen during the reign of Domitian would have thought this illegal cult, which worshipped an executed political rebel and spread among renegade Jews and slaves, could survive, let alone come to dominate the Empire?

Furthermore, almost every new religion immediately claims to be an old religion: a reform that returns a corrupt faith to its pristine origins; a revival of a faith kept secret by a few survivors; a faith reclaimed from written records that were hidden away and have now been rediscovered; and so on. We thus always face the problem of the relationship between myth and history. More specifically, to fail to understand the difference between myth and history is to misunderstand both.

Several older members of the Craft have reacted to the first edition by saying, "I don't understand why you spend all this time mucking about with the details of rituals, when you could have interviewed

---

[12] These papers were summarized in my position paper, "Toward a General Theory of New religions," included here as Appendix A.

me and all the other old-timers. We would have told you the history!" Yes, I know that, but it wouldn't have solved the problem I faced in trying to construct a history of the Craft. The problem was that in, say, 1971, any ordinary academic scholar would have looked at the books available on the Craft and said, "This is all bilgewater, balderdash, and metaphysical hogwash! This has all been concocted out of whole cloth for obvious, nonreligious reasons! There is not a credible witness in this lot of bare-faced liars, and there is no hard data, no substance at all, anywhere! There is nothing here that could be used to construct a reliable, verifiable history."

I have not been trying to write a history that would be believed only by those who are already members of the Craft. I wanted to construct a history that would be credible to any open-minded, though sceptical, reader. If I had constructed a history out of material obtained by interviews, sceptical readers and academics alike would have looked at it and said, "Fine, you've found a hundred people who believe there are still witches, and that a witchcraft religion survived from some time in the past. You could also go out and find a hundred people who believe in the existence of flying saucers, or leprechauns, or whatever. That would prove the existence of their beliefs, but it in no way proves the existence of what they believe to exist" - and so I would have accomplished nothing.

The average academic scholar in America - say, in history or other social sciences—typically supposes that all religion is bilge and contains no hard data to which scholarly or scientific techniques could be applied. However, scholars in religious studies operate with somewhat different assumptions. First, to assume that all religion is nothing but bilge is to refuse to explain the primary datum, which is that religions do exist, always have, as far as we know, and so probably always will. Since they exist, they must be doing something positive for the societies of human beings that have these religions, and it is certainly legitimate to see if we can get an objective consensus on exactly what that something is. This argument takes us into the territory of the Society for the Scientific Study of Religion. If one is willing to suppose that human beings also have psychological needs that have nothing to do with material survival, then one is getting into the territory of the American Academy of Religion.

To leap ahead, let me say that although up to 90 percent of the Craft probably is bilge, the same is true of Judaism, Christianity, Islam, Hinduism, Buddhism, and all other religions. These religions nevertheless have objective histories that their believers and nonbelievers can agree on; so such a history should be constructible for the Craft— if some sort of hard data could be found with which to begin the construction. In asking what that might be, I realized that the existence of the Book of Shadows provided the needed parallel, since the task of recreating the histories of all religions has always begun with the task of deciphering just how, when, why, where, by whom, and to whom the sacred scriptures of these religions were written.

Here I have applied the techniques of historical and textual criticism that were developed for Biblical studies - that have enabled scholars to reconstruct the actual history of Judaism and Christianity despite all the protests of the "true believers" of those faiths - to the original documents of the Gardnerian movement. As far as I know, I was the first person to use those techniques to study a contemporary new religion - or so some colleagues have said to me. Christianity, Judaism, any other viable religion, stands up just fine under that sort of sceptical criticism, as long as you're willing to move on to an adult, sophisticated theology and not remain committed to simple-minded literalism. I find that the Craft stands up to such criticism also - one reason for thinking it far more important than anybody has yet guessed - as long as you are willing to give up a simple-minded belief that the Craft's foundational myths are in any way historical.

Gardner's claim to have been initiated into a surviving coven in the New Forest area of England in 1939 probably contains one hard fact, the locale, and one "soft" fact, the date. Certainly enough data have now been published - especially in Valiente's *Rebirth of Witchcraft* - to verify the locale, which is one that has no historical connections with witchcraft at all and so is not suspect as being theologically motivated. Dates in themselves are neutral, and are typically picked, not at random, but because something significant did happen on them; the problem is then to find out what that something was. For example, the traditional Jewish doctrine that all the canonical Hebrew scriptures were completed by 400 B.C.E. turns out to derive from the historical fact that the Pentateuch was published by about that date.

As I said, I began my investigation of Gardnerian history by wondering what data Gardner had from this older coven into which he said he had been initiated, and what he had added himself in later revising the rituals. Once the Weschcke documents in 1974, and BAM in 1975, became available to me, I was able to carry such an analysis, and found that almost everything in these documents turns out to be from identifiable, modern literary sources. What little is left over is bits and pieces of folk magic, not significantly different from folk magic the world over, and certainly not equivalent to the sort of religion whose survival Gardner claimed.

At this point the nature of my investigation had to change. Having - to paraphrase Wallace Stevens - seen the history that is not there, I needed to perceive the history that is there. For example, once one identifies the basic Christian myths as being nonhistorical, one must still discover the actual history of the founding of Christianity, since, after all, the Christian church does exist, and has existed since the first century C.E. (in our tautological notation). The fact of its existence is the historical datum that must be explained by any adequate history. One cannot give in - as scholars of the "mythological" school often unconsciously did - to the assumption that, since the Christian church is founded on myths, it is itself a myth, that is, does not really exist. Such giving in simply confuses different levels of abstraction.

It is an axiom of historical scholarship that phenomena almost invariably come into existence shortly before they first appear in the historical record, and more often than not the creating of such phenomena can itself be documented. To suppose that a phenomenon had existed without ever being detected for any significant length of time before its first appearance in the historical records violates the principle of parsimony: if it was never detected, then there is no evidence for its existence before the first historical record of it. Claims for earlier existence are a normal part of the foundational myth of most religions, and are part of the data that needs analysis.

In contrast, the creating of new religions is a ubiquitous phenomenon; that is, in fact, the way in which all religions have begun.[13] In the first edition, I hypothesized that in September 1939 the circle of occultists to which Gardner belonged purposely decided to recreate the religion described by Margaret Murray, and that may be why Gardner chose to claim that date for his initiation. Now, this was only a hypothesis. I did not have a shred of direct evidence that this group decision took place, let alone a date for it. But this hypothesis did seem to explain every piece of verifiable evidence, without requiring any other assumptions, which is what an adequate hypothesis is supposed to do; and we must have some hypothesis to explain the origin of the Gardnerian movement, which obviously does still exist.

But if this decision took place, it was only a decision; implementation of it was surely put on hold by the outbreak of World War II, and only resurrected after VE Day. As Ronald Hutton has pointed out, the paper trail stops in 1946. We have no serious historical evidence for the existence of any Gardnerian coven before then. Certainly in 1939 there was a network of people who knew one another and had similar interests in the occult; these provided the initial pool of persons from among whom members of the new coven were recruited beginning in 1946—but the network itself was not a coven, not by Gardnerian or any other Craft definition of a coven.

I continue to believe that the actual history of the Craft movement provides one of the best and best-documented examples of how a new religion was created; and, since all religions begin as *new* religions, thus provides insights into the general nature of all religion. I find it quite satisfying to have established the existence of an objective religious history in an area where, thirty years ago, most scholars would have thought that impossible.

---

[13] I would be perfectly happy to believe that God or the Gods, in their infinite power and wisdom, could create a religion for humankind out of whole cloth and promulgate it by direct inspiration. The historical pattern seems to be, however, that the Gods always inspire human beings to do the work for them, and to propagate it by the ordinary means of human communication.

Chapter Two

Sources of the Craft

All religions have at least one foundational myth as well as an actual history. The myth is not historically true, but instead transmits some of the spiritual values on which the religion is based. The history is true in fact, but, as history, cannot convey values.

All human beings, as children, believe that the foundational myth of their religion is actual history. Many people in late adolescence realize that the myth is not true as history, and begin to search for the factual history of their faith. Some of these, as mature adults, realize that the myth and the history convey different types of truth. They learn to live with the tension between the two.

So long as a person believes that the foundational myth is historical, and does not know what the actual history is, he or she will reduce the meaning of the myth to historical terms, and therefore will not understand the spiritual values that the myth was intended to convey by its creators. The purpose of this book is to set forth the actual history of modern Witchcraft as accurately as possible, so that, once known, it may liberate the foundational myths of the Craft to reveal their more profound meanings.

The Craft was founded as a distinct religion in 1947, give or take a year. Like all new religions, it was created from pre-existing raw materials that were combined in new ways and into a new overall structure. Since its elements are old, but its structure is new, it is neither entirely a survival from the past nor entirely a modern creation. Modern Witchcraft is based squarely on magical and occult traditions that go back at least to Hellenistic Alexandria, and yet it has transformed the elements from those traditions in new and often surprising ways. In explaining the origins of the Craft movement, I will both trace the sources of its elements in the older traditions and the ways in which the Craft does something new with each element.

In emphasizing that the Craft is a new religion, I am insisting on its ontological equality with every other religion, because *all religions begin as new religions,* which then survive only because they continue to evolve and adapt themselves to changing circumstances. For Islam and Buddhism, their origin as new religions is obvious. Hinduism as we now have it is a sibling of Buddhism, since it resulted from an acceptance of some, though not all, of the Buddha's reforms. Judaism as the state religion of Judah dates from 621 B.C.E. (I will return to this point); but Christianity and Judaism as we have them are siblings, arising together from the ashes of Jerusalem, which was destroyed in 69 C.E.

There has been a fair amount of media hysteria in recent years, fueled especially by Evangelical Christians, over "cults." People have been running around, saying, "Omigawd, people are starting cults. Something must be *w-r-o-n-g* with our society," and a great deal of energy has been wasted on looking for what's "wrong"—when in fact there's nothing wrong. The members of the Group on New Religious Movements of the American Academy of Religion, and most of the members of the Society for the Scientific Study of Religion, have agreed that "The word 'cult' means 'a religion I don't approve of,'" and generally try to avoid using that word. People have been starting new religions. When we look at history, we discover that people start new religions all the time, all over the world, whenever they are not forcibly prevented from doing so by an established state church. In other words, *starting new religions is the normal state.*

Current scholars regard the creating of new religions as a normal, healthy, and universal activity by which creative people (that is, the educated middle class, not the outcasts) in all societies attempt to meet their own religious needs; and as such, its existence does not need any further explanation. Furthermore, since all religions begin at some time and place as new religions, the study of new religions is not a luxury; it is not the study of fringe sects, marginal people, epiphenomena, weird hippies, and so on. Rather, it is the study of characteristics central to all religions.[1] In a free society, people vote with their feet: if their religious needs are not being met by the established churches, then they will set out to create their own religion. Furthermore, since a large bureaucratic organization cannot be all things to all people, there will always be some people whose needs are not being met; and so new religions will be founded all the time.

Of course, such an understanding of religious creativity, of religion as creative, of creativity as religion, is very recent, and rather sophisticated. It is certainly not held by all the theologians in the professional societies. It would be unrealistic to expect people in general to think about religion in this way—and, of course, they don't. What generally happens is that the founders of a new religion claim to be reforming an old religion, in order to have a counterclaim against the hoary antiquity that the established churches claim for themselves, and in order to speak in terms that ordinary people can grasp.

In claiming to be an old religion, a new religion may claim to be a revival of an all-but-defunct religion from the past; or to be revitalizing an existing religion by reaching back to its true, pure, and pristine roots; or to be a new revelation of ancient truths that had been garbled in all previous transmissions from the Powers On High; and so on. Very often this claim takes the form of a discovery of a manuscript that had been hidden away long before. The emphasis on elements from the past is the common, universal thread, and this is always an emphasis on something real; but understanding exactly what those elements are, and why they are important, always requires a great deal of work.

The confusion arises from the fact that these elements of the past are invariably understood in terms of the new religion's foundational myth, which is the story that states in some way (often quite symbolically or parabolically) the values that are central to this new religion. As Robert

---

[1] Having been trained in the techniques of New Testament scholarship, which I have applied to the documents written by Gerald Gardner and Doreen Valiente, I am intrigued and, in fact, rather amused by the light this enterprise has shed for me on the evolution of early Christianity and the formation of the New Testament collection —but those are matters I must report on elsewhere, to another audience.

Ellwood (1973, p. 32) observed, "In modern cults the functional myth is generally the story of the experience of the founder which establishes his ecstatic (shamanistic) capacity and his access to a new means of ultimate transformation, such as Madame Blavatsky's initiation by the Masters." That is, this foundational myth describes the experience that transmuted the religion's founder from an ordinary person into a living legend, a source of *baraka* (blessedness) worthy to found the movement. For the Craft, the foundational myth is the story of Gerald Gardner's initiation in 1939 into one of the very last surviving witch covens in England, from which he was able to transmit, to the covens that he founded, the elements of the pagan past which that coven had helped to preserve.

The evolution of Western society's understanding of foundational myths is paralleled by the stages of individual religious maturity. The first three of these stages were identified by the poet William Blake, who labeled them "Innocence," "Experience," and "Organized Innocence." The first is the stage of childhood, during which the myths of religion, learned from the parents and others, are believed implicitly. The second is the stage of adolescence, during which the critical intellect develops, and the objective facts of ordinary history are taken as the criteria by which to judge the plausibility or possibility of the myths, which are normally rejected as being simply false during this stage, which can last into the late twenties. The third stage is the beginnings of true maturity, in which the person realizes that the facts of ordinary history, being value-free, provide no basis for making decisions about life problems. At this stage the adult can begin to reappropriate the myths, recognizing that they are intended to be primarily statements of value, not statements of fact or of history, and recognizing also that an interpretation of the myths which is much more sophisticated than that of a child must be possible; else these myths would hardly have survived for millennia as the basis for the value systems of world civilizations. One mark of true maturity is therefore the ability to tolerate the ambiguous tension between myth and history. Another is the ability to see that the more-sophisticated understanding of myth is not possible so long as the myth is believed to be mere history.

(There are further stages of religious maturity. One begins with the radical decision in favor of the values asserted by the myths that enables a radical transformation of lifestyle. Another is typified by the ability to dedicate one's talents to the improvement of one's community and society, rather than merely to satisfying one's own wants and needs. These stages appear to be universal, and independent of any specific beliefs.)

Critical analysis of the Craft's foundational myth, and an attempt to reconstruct its ordinary history out of the available documentary and eyewitness data, are therefore tasks identical to those which scholars have carried out for all the major world religions. These religions have not then dried up and blown away—though this is precisely what their most conservative members feared might happen as the process of critical thinking got under way. I do not believe that the Craft will wither away under the impact of critical thought either; and its conservative members (who misunderstand, resent, and vow vengeance for the work I am doing here), in fearing that it might succumb, reveal that they do not believe deeply that the Craft can stand up as an equal in comparisons with other religions.

For clarity, let me set forth the foundational myths and ordinary histories of the two religions that will be most familiar to most readers. Let's begin with Judaism, which, in claiming to be the world's oldest monotheistic religion (which it is not; Zoroastrianism is), is usually the model for similar claims of antiquity.

Myth

Judaism began about 1300 B.C.E., when the one true God revealed himself to Moses, helped Moses rescue the Israelites from Egypt, and revealed the Torah to Moses on Mt. Sinai.

History

Judaism began as the state religion of the kingdom of Judah (whence its name) in 621 B.C.E., when (as set forth in *II Kings* 22-24, and the parallel passage in *Chronicles*) King Josiah persuaded the men of Jerusalem to ratify the "Book of the Law of Moses" that had just been "discovered" (that is, in fact, written) by Hilkiah, high priest of the temple, as the new constitution. After the capture of Judah by Babylon, the Second Isaiah (author of *Isaiah* 40-55) proposed about 550 B.C.E. that Yahweh had allowed this disaster to occur because the Judeans had still not realized that Yahweh was not merely the best God, but was the only God (notice that Xenocrates in Asia Minor was arriving at the concept of monotheism at just about the same time). Accepting this new theology, the Judeans began to think "Now that we know who He is, we can understand what He was doing," and began to rewrite their history in its light, as the story of God's trying to get their attention. The writing continued in Jerusalem, after Cyrus of Persia, the new Emperor, allowed those Judeans who wanted to to go home. The Torah (the first five books) was completed about 400 B.C.E., and the story of its reading to the first synagogue assembly was told in *Nehemiah* 8. (We can even logically suppose that what the people, standing in rows beneath the lectern, heard that day was the story of Moses, standing on the side of Mt. Sinai, above the rows of people, and reading them the Decalogue or other laws; that is, the experience was self-reflexive, as most experiences of sacred time are.) The scrolls of the Prophets (the major and minor prophets, and the historical books) were also largely complete by this time, though they were not added to the synagogue liturgy until around 200 B.C.E. As Joseph Campbell and other scholars have pointed out, the experience of captivity and loyalty to Yahweh that became central to the Jewish sense of self-identity did take place, but in Babylon, not Egypt.

Myth

Yahweh himself became a human being, born to the virgin Mary, in the person of Jesus of Nazareth. Jesus began preaching a new revelation at about age 30, but within a year or so was betrayed to the Roman rulers and executed by crucifixion. Three days later he arose from the dead, thus proving that he was God, and after revealing more to many of his followers, he ascended bodily into Heaven, from where he will return in triumph to inaugurate the Kingdom of God on Earth at the end of time.

History

Joshua of Nazareth ("Jesus" is just the Greek form of Joshua) was apparently a young rabbi of the House of Hillel. Nothing in his own teachings (as distinguished from later legend) differs in any significant way from the teachings of the House of Hillel preserved in the Talmud (and that is the opinion of Hans Küng, in his *To Be a Christian*). He apparently attacked the hypocrisy and lack of compassion of the Sadducees, who were the "rich men," and of the House of Shammai, the other major rabbinic house, which was politically dominant in his day. These targets of his irony and sarcasm apparently complained about him to the Romans, who arrested him and executed him summarily as a potential troublemaker. However, some of his friends believed that they had seen him alive (at least in visions, like Paul) afterward, and began to preach that he had been raised from the dead, that he had received God's special favour, that he was God's anointed (that is, *mashiach* or *christos*) agent, that he had been special all along, and so on. Thinking "Now that we know who he is, we can understand what he was doing and saying," they began to rework his stories and sayings, and stories about him, in the course of their preaching; that is, they rethought their history, as the Judaeans had done in Babylon. After the destruction of Jerusalem—which proved that Jerusalem was *not* going to be the capital city, and that Joshua was not going to be right back—some communities began to write these materials down, so that they wouldn't be lost completely, in what became the *Gospels*. All Christians had been Jews until about 85 C.E., but in the turmoil after the Roman-Jewish war, Judaism shattered into fragments, which became the separate religious communities known as Christianity, Judaism, Gnosticism, and so on. Beliefs about Joshua became the political shibboleth for all of these; so that Joshua, who should have been prominent in the history of the House of Hillel, was instead almost ignored when the Talmud was assembled.

Something similar could be done for all other religions. The foundational myth of Mormonism, for example, focuses on the "finding" of the *Book of Mormon* in Hill Cumorah, at the full moon. Critics and scholars of Mormonism have long since set forth the sources from which it was created. Such claims for rediscovered documents are particularly germane to Craft history, because in recent years many younger and/or more orthodox members of the Craft have come to regard the Book of Shadows in general, and the Craft Laws in particular, as documents preserved from the past by secrecy. As we will see, they are instead a modern creation, as the founding documents of new religions always are; so everything known about writing and creativity in general then apply to this situation.

The Western Magical Tradition

The history of the Western magical tradition could be traced far back into antiquity. Much of it focuses on Alexandria, the great university city (which therefore bears some striking resemblances to Berkeley and other modern university towns). Neopaganism, the concept of recreating the lost pagan religions of antiquity, appeared early in the Renaissance, and has been one thread in Western occultism ever since. However, it is most practical to begin around the year 1800, when Francis Barrett published *The Magus,* the first modern book that attempted to make the arcana of magic accessible to the middle class.

Fascination with the Classics had been a major theme of Romanticism, and the idea of reviving some sort of classical religion gained strength and became programmatic during the late nineteenth century, at which time attention was divided between Greco-Roman and Norse paganism. It was further strengthened as the new discipline of classical archaeology revealed civilizations in the Middle East that had predated the Greeks by millennia, and turned up pagan religious texts that had been baked in clay as palaces burned down around them.

Modern occult organizations typically claim a great antiquity for themselves, but in fact are all quite recent and are almost all highly interrelated. T. M. Luhrmann has documented the overlapping memberships in magical organizations in the London area in the 1980s; this pattern has been typical for the last two centuries. The usual scenario is that a charismatic leader begins an organization, which grows well during his or her lifetime, and usually attracts as its most prominent members people who have been or still are members of other extant occult organizations. Upon the leader's demise, the organization usually fractures into two or many factions as the other members struggle to decide who will assume the mantle of the founder, and these factions usually become independent organizations, which repeat the cycle. Richard Cavendish's *History of Magic* does an excellent job of detailing the complex interrelationships of teachers and students, founders and followers, among occult organizations, especially in France, in the late 19th century; and James Webb does the same for European occultism in general. I see no need to duplicate their work, especially since relatively few of these organizations are direct ancestors of the modern religion of Wicca. However, among the few that are direct ancestors, we can count the Hermetic Order of the Golden Dawn, the Stella Matutina, the Fraternity of the Inner Light, and the Ordo Templi Orientis.

To be fair, one must admit that not all of the Craft's central concepts can be traced to any known antecedents. Those that are *sui generis* manifest the specific ways in which the Craft is a unique religion, quite unlike anything else under the Sun—or the Moon._As an example of this, let us consider the concept of reincarnation. Like New Agers in general, most modern Witches believe strongly in reincarnation, which provides an alternative to the Christian concepts of Heaven and Hell. (However, this is not a dogma, because almost all modern Witches believe even more strongly that Witches must be free to believe whatever they choose.)

The earliest writings of the Greeks—Homer, Hesiod, the pre-Socratic philosophers—assume what has been called a "tripartite anthropology": that human beings consist of body, soul, and spirit. To be more precise, the Greek terms transliterate as *soma, psyche,* and *pneuma*, the recognizable roots of such modern words as psychosomatic and pneumatic. As is evident from its use in the word "psychology," the Greek word *psyche* meant something much more like "mind" or "personality." In order to have something like what we now mean by "soul," we must think of a compound of "mind" plus "spirit," of *psyche*-plus-*pneuma*. In the Greek view, when the body died, the *psyche*-plus-*pneuma* went to the underworld, to stand before the throne of Persephone, who sentenced the person to reward in the Elysian Fields, or to punishment in Tartarus, before he or she was reborn.[2]

Plato, in the "myths" that conclude many of his dialogues, synthesizes the beliefs of the philosophers who preceded him. He proposes that the natural home of the *psyche*-plus-*pneuma* is the world of pure idea, beyond the realm of the gods as we are able to form some concept of them, and that the *psyche*-plus-*pneuma* is sent down into the body in this imperfect world of decay and corruption as a punishment. He mentions an "Orphic" catchphrase: *soma sema*, "the body is a tomb." Plato suggests not only that a person may be rewarded for virtue in this life by being born into a better position in society in the next life, but also that the true reward is to be freed from rebirth entirely, so as to be able to return to the world of pure idea, and that each person has only so many chances (perhaps nine rebirths) to achieve this freedom.

There is no positive evidence that Christians as such ever believed in reincarnation. (Some people who happened to be Christians also happened to believe in a great many things, then as now, but data on popular beliefs do not define the essential doctrines of any religion.) On the other hand, once Christians had adopted the Greek concept of the immortal soul, it was not clear for some centuries whether they could believe in reincarnation or not. Finally, at the Council of Constantinople in 553 C.E., the theologians voted against reincarnation, largely because they could see no way that a person could be morally responsible for his or her own virtues and vices, and so earn the reward or punishment they merited, if after dying and being judged he or she was reborn as another person and then baptized. It seemed much simpler to the theologians to believe that each soul was created fresh for each person and had only one lifetime on Earth.

Hence from the sixth century through the 18th century, belief in reincarnation appeared in Western societies only when it was reintroduced from the outside. This happened with the Cathars, who had historical

[2] Apparently the whole point of being initiated at Eleusis was that you were thus adopted as a child of Demeter; hence when you stood before Demeter's daughter Persephone, she would judge you as a family member, not as a stranger —which made all the difference in Greek society.

connections with earlier Manichaean or Gnostic groups in the Middle East. The concept of reincarnation became a belief held in Western society only after Britain and other European nations had been a colonial power in India and in Buddhist countries for several centuries, during which generation after generation of European administrators had been exposed to Eastern beliefs.

Gardner asserts in *Witchcraft Today* that belief in reincarnation was preserved by the witch covens during the middle ages, and this has become part of the foundational myths of the Craft. In fact, belief in reincarnation was reintroduced into the Western world in the 19th century by Spiritualism, and was then taken up by Theosophy.

The first wave of belief in reincarnation arose in response to the strange phenomena revealed by Mesmerism, developed by Anton Mesmer in the late eighteenth century. Mesmerism was at first popularly associated more with psychic phenomena than with therapeutic utility. Only when psi became the stock in trade of Spiritualistic mediums did Mesmerism become transformed into hypnosis as a form of medical therapy. The importing of Mesmerism to America was part of what set off the Spiritualist movement, and belief in reincarnation is compatible with Spiritualism, though not necessary for it (one can believe that the soul survives after death, as Christians do, without believing that it has been or will be reborn). There have been two camps within Spiritualism, one favoring reincarnation, the other opposing it, since the mid-19th century.

The Theosophical Society was founded in New York City in 1875. Its leading figure, Helena P. Blavatsky, was the person who established "reincarnation" as the standard term for this concept, replacing "metempsychosis," "transmigration," "reimbodiment," and other terms that had been used. It was also she who first linked the concepts of karma and reincarnation firmly in the Western mind. (The two concepts are not interdependent; it is possible to believe in one without the other.) The Theosophical content defined into these terms in the West does not correspond closely with what was believed about these topics in the East, and the concept of reincarnation in the Craft is much closer to that of Theosophy than to those of the ancient world or of Asian religions.

Nevertheless, Witches do not believe what Theosophists, Buddhists, Hindus, the ancient Greeks, or almost anyone else has believed about reincarnation. In these latter systems, reincarnation is seen as the automatic result of a universal law, and as a punishment for ignorance; the goal of spiritual development is to stop the "wheel of rebirth," to no longer be reincarnated. Witches, in contrast, believe that reincarnation is *not* automatic, that it is controlled by the gods and is the *reward* of the initiates. They believe "that you will be reborn among those you love, and that you will remember them and love them again"; the reward is for being on the side of the gods. Some Witches seem to assume that there probably are two kinds of souls, both mortal and immortal; that all souls begin as mortal, but can be transformed into immortal souls by certain kinds of initiatory experiences and spiritual growth (specifically, that provided by the training and initiations of the Craft); and that when the uninitiated die, their mortal souls simply cease to exist. That is, the theological concepts of and surrounding reincarnation in the Craft movement cannot be explained in terms of the concepts in the older occult traditions.

A second way in which the Craft differs from most other new religions of modern times, and especially from those usually classified as New Age, is in rejecting many typical New Age assumptions about religion. Many New Agers assume, for example, that all religions are ultimately the *same*; that spirituality is best learned by sitting at the feet of a master teacher or guru, preferably from one of the Eastern religions; and that a new world teacher or messiah will appear to usher in the New Age. Pagans, in contrast, like the Craft specifically because it is so *different* from the Puritanical, world-hating Christianity that many of them were raised in. Most Pagans believe that they are practicing an ancient folk religion, whether as a survival or a revival; and, being focused on the pagan religions of the past, they are not particularly interested in a New Age in the future. They also generally believe that many religions are radically and irreconcilably different from each other; that the "reformed" religions (especially the monotheistic ones) established by Moses, Jesus, Mohammed, the Buddha, and similar figures were NOT an improvement over the folk religions that they replaced; and that if there were to be a single worldwide religion in the future, it might be even more repressive of human freedom than the Roman Catholic Church was in Europe during the "Burning Times." Hence Pagans are not receptive to teachers and teachings from the monotheistic religions nor to any from the East, with the possible exception of Hinduism, which is seen (whether accurately so or not) as an "unreformed" polytheism similar to that of the Greco-Roman world; Pagans tend to be especially interested in Tantric traditions, since these can easily be seen as a type of magic parallel to that developed in the Western occult tradition. Pagans also generally tend to be extremely anti-authoritarian (whatever the reasons in personal backgrounds might be), and so are not at all inclined to accept the personal authority of any guru.

Most Witches also operate with an ethic that forbids them to accept money for initiating anyone or for training anyone in the essential practices of the Craft as a religion. Although this ethic does create some organizational problems, these are minor when one considers that the Craft has so far escaped being exploited by the kinds of entrepreneurs who have created or taken over other new religions, only to use them as vehicles for self-enrichment. Pagan festivals have grown into national gatherings, often of several thousand people, since the mid-1970s, but they have remained quite inexpensive, because no one is attempting to make a profit from them. As a result of this ethic, Pagans look upon "Psychic Fairs" and "New Age Expos" with open contempt, and tend to consider most New Age gurus to be money-hungry frauds who are exploiting the public by charging exorbitant fees for spiritual practices that can be learned for free within a coven. This attitude does not, of course, encourage New Agers to look kindly upon Pagans.

There are, nevertheless, a minority among the Witches who consider themselves to be members of the New Age movement as well. These tend to be Witches who understand not only that the Gardnerian Witchcraft movement is a new religion, but also that this newness makes it the potential equal of every other religion in the world. If the Craft is a new religion, then it can be understood as contributing to the spiritual growth in the modern world that is leading up to the New Age, whenever and however that might begin.

The magical system used by the Craft is not inherited from a secret Pagan tradition of any sort. Rather, it goes back to that of The Hermetic Order of the Golden Dawn (HOGD), which was an offshoot of a Masonic-Rosicrucian organization, the Societas Rosicruciana in Anglia (SRIA), founded by Robert Wentworth Little in 1865, and based on old manuscripts supposedly found in Freemasons' Hall (old manuscripts again; they had actually been owned by a psychic named Fred Hockley). The London Lodge of the Theosophical Society was opened in 1883, and members of both these lodges were among the early members of the HOGD, which was founded in 1888 by W. R. Woodman, A. F. A. Woodford, W. Wynn Westcott, and Samuel Liddell Mathers (1854-1918).[3] All but Woodford had been members of the SRIA, and the first two had died by 1891. Westcott resigned in 1897 to concentrate on the SRIA, of which he was Supreme Magus, leaving Mathers in complete control of the HOGD. The four had claimed to have a charter and a set of rituals from the "secret chiefs" of the Rosicrucian order in Germany, but in fact it was all written by Mathers, who was one of the most brilliant amateur scholars of his generation, who also translated *The Greater Key of Solomon* and several major Kabalistic treatises, and who wrote a major book on the Tarot. The HOGD attracted a stellar cast from among Britain's middle-class intellectuals. Its members included Arthur Machen, Arthur Edward Waite, James M. Barrie, Sir E. A. Wallis Budge, Hugh Schonfield, Florence Farr (at one time a lover of George Bernard Shaw), and Maud Gonne (a lover of Yeats and mother of Sean McBride, the founder of Amnesty International).

The most famous member of the HOGD was William Butler Yeats, who joined in 1890, and remained a devout member (according to Virginia Moore's masterful biography) until 1900, when a fight over whether Mathers could bring Aleister Crowley rapidly up into the leadership of the organization shattered it into several factions. Most of the members left with Yeats to form the Stella Matutina (Morning Star), which Yeats served from 1901 to 1917 as Grand Master. Mathers and

[3] Mathers was a relative of Alice Liddell, whose father co-authored the most important Greek dictionary of the 19th century, and whose adventures in Wonderland were chronicled by the Reverend Charles Ludwig Dodgson.

Crowley kept the original name, but their minority organization soon foundered. Crowley, after "channeling" the *Book of the Law* in 1904, founded his own organization, the Astrum Argentinum ("silver star"), in 1907, and began publishing *The Equinox* in 1909. He also became a member of the Ordo Templi Orientis ("Order of the Eastern Temple") by 1912. According to the painstaking research of J. Gordon Melton, the OTO was actually based largely on the secret sex-magic teachings of P. B. Randolph, founder of a major Rosicrucian society in America. Crowley was recognized as head of the OTO by a majority of its members in 1924-25, but the organization then divided in two over the issue of accepting Crowley's *Book of the Law* as authoritative.

Violet Firth was initiated in 1919 into the Alpha et Omega, the HOGD offshoot presided over by Mathers' widow, Moina Bergson Mathers. In 1922 she organized the Fraternity of the Inner Light as an "outer court" for the AEO. She and Mrs. Mathers clashed more and more as Violet matured as a leader; when Mrs. Mathers expelled her in 1927, Firth, now using the name Dion Fortune, took the Fraternity of the Inner Light with her, and it is the parent or ancestor of many other important magical organizations now functioning in England.

The Fraternity of the Inner Light was divided into at least two autonomous inner sections, one of which was avowedly "pagan"—that is, non-Christian. The acting heads of the pagan section from the mid-1930s into the 1940s were Charles R. F. Seymour (1880-1943) and Christine Hartley, who have been ably brought to public notice by Alan Richardson's *Dancers to the Gods.* Seymour had written an essay, "The Old Religion—A Study in the Symbolism of the Moon Mysteries," in 1937, but it was not published until 1968, when it appeared in *The New Dimensions Red Book*, edited by Basil Wiltby. On the essay, Alan Richardson comments in *Dancers to the Gods*, "In many ways it is a piece of writing which is years ahead of its time, prefiguring many of the trends in magic today." In another essay, "The Ancient Nature Worship," also written in 1937, Seymour says, "The witch-hunting of the fourteenth to eighteenth centuries was an effort to stamp out an old religion surviving from pre-Christian days. Its sin was that it celebrated with joy and laughter the great nature festivals." In his diary on June 21 (summer solstice), 1938, he wrote, "I got the idea of linking the old symbolism of indigenous women's mysteries with the pagan mysteries of England right down to the present day and through the witchcraft period." That is, he had obviously been reading Margaret Murray.

Christine Hartley, who worked as Seymour's High Priestess, recorded in her diary on June 28, 1938, "Started when I walked over the threshold of the house and felt witchcraft all around me. Went upstairs extremely desirous of being a witch. When we had settled down I kept getting little pictures of Ishtar worship through the ages, the most constant being one of silhouetted witches in pointed hats and ragged skirts dancing round a fire. Then . . . I was aware of the goddess standing before us mistily veiled." As we will see, Seymour and Hartley were certainly in the occult circle surrounding Gardner, and their own ideas were obviously pointing toward the creation of a coven as well.[4]

A separate line of succession connecting earlier occultism with the Craft movement is that of Co-Masonry, an offshoot of Freemasonry which admits both women and men into membership; women are still excluded by the United Grand Lodge of England. Co-Masonry originated in France, and spread to England when its first British Lodge was formed in London in 1902. Annie Besant was initiated in this lodge, and became the national delegate for Britain. When H. P. Blavatsky died, and Annie Besant lost to Bishop Leadbeater in her struggle to succeed Blavatsky as head of the Theosophical Society, she shifted her efforts to organizing Co-Masonry in Britain, and in 1922 Co-Masonry was affiliated to the Grand Orient in France. When Annie Besant died, leadership of Co-Masonry in Britain devolved upon her daughter, Mabel Besant-Scott, who was Gerald Gardner's neighbour in Highcliffe, and a leading member of the Rosicrucian Fellowship of Crotona.

The publication of Margaret Murray's *The Witch-Cult in Western Europe* in 1921 set off a new burst of interest in paganism, since Murray proposed that the witch-hunters of medieval and early modern times were actually finding the remnants of the pagan religions of northern Europe. Murray's hypothesis (on p. 12) is that "underlying the Christian

---

[4] On Seymour and Hartley I have relied on Doreen Valiente's citations of data from Richardson.

religion was a cult practised . . . chiefly . . . by the more ignorant or those in the less thickly inhabited parts of the country. It can be traced back to pre-Christian times, and appears to be the ancient religion of Western Europe." (Murray nowhere substantiates this assertion.) The idea of recreating the kind of witch cult described by Murray was discussed by English occultists during the 1920s and 1930s. However, the first successful attempt to recreate Murray's "witch cult" was carried out by Gerald Gardner. This is the topic of the next chapter.

Pre-Gardnerian Witches

There were certainly people in America (and probably in England, although I have no hard data on that) before 1939 who called themselves witches, practiced witchcraft, and considered witchcraft to be their religion. Although there were very few of them, their existence is well-documented, and is not a problem in itself. The problems that these pre-Gardnerian traditions raise for Gardnerian history are twofold:

(1) Their beliefs were utterly unlike what Gardner describes for his "cult." The available books on American "witchcraft" before 1939, such as John George Hohman's *Pow-Wows, or The Long-Lost Friend* (1819), or *Zolar's Book of Forbidden Knowledge* (no date), focus on folk-remedies for healing. The vocabulary and concepts in them are strictly Jewish or Christian in background.

(2) Current members of these traditions, despite the contempt they sometimes feel toward the Gardnerians as "Johnny-come-latelies," have for the most part (with the ahistorical eclecticism typical of true pagans) enthusiastically adopted the Gardnerian "reforms" because of their popularity and usefulness, and so have muddied whatever historical traces there might have been.

Victor Anderson's Fairy Tradition

The most important of the pre-Gardnerian witches was certainly Victor Anderson (1917-2001), founder of the "Fairy" tradition and a major teacher of Starhawk. Victor related that he was given a sexual initiation at age 9 by an older woman, and was then initiated into the Harpy coven in Ashland, Oregon, in 1932; the High Priestess and High Priest were Maybelle and Jerome W., and other members included Jim M. and Patricia F. The coven was quite eclectic, mixing Huna with varieties of folk magic more common in the continental United States. Victor said that the group's emphasis was on practical magic; there was little concern with worship, theology, ethics, or ritual. The coven did not focus on worship of a Goddess, though they were open to polytheistic beliefs; rather, the concept of God they dealt with was of a male god opposed to Christianity. They did celebrate the Sabbats by getting together to work magic on them, but the only time they met in a circle, Victor said, was when they were eating—and yet this ordinary-looking meal was part of the celebration of the Sabbat.

Russian-Jewish Witches in L.A.

The immigrant Russian-Jewish coven in Los Angeles that the mother and grandmother of Tanya, David Farren's wife, belonged to, as described in his *The Return of Magic,* also had a theology totally different from that of the Gardnerians. Their focus was strictly on working magic; they had no rule against working black magic; and insofar as they were concerned with any concept of a deity, which was very little, it was not with a goddess but with a god, whom they often equated with "Satan." Farren says (pp. 27-28), "Tanya's grandmother claims to represent the twelfth generation in the family line to be born a witch," although she is also Jewish and from the Ukraine; "she trained first her daughter and then her granddaughter in a lore which is part Russian and part Anglo-American." Both Natasha, Tanya's grandmother, and her mother "belonged to local covens which . . . reflected the Cabalistic ceremonial magic that was popular in Victorian England [but so does Gardnerian practice] . . . Natasha's coven was composed mostly of other European emigrants anxious to keep alive some of the old ways of magic, but . . . any serious apprenticeship in magic was still kept within the family." He notes (p. 52) that Tanya has "recollections of the lore of her grandmother and mother, both of whose commitments to magic have included invocations of the demonic."

Rhea W.

J. Gordon Melton's files, in the library of the University of California at Santa Barbara, contain letters from other traditional witches who know what American witchcraft was like before the influence of Gerald Gardner was felt. One lady, Rhea W., who corresponded with Dr. Melton in the late 1970s and early 1980s, wrote to him, "I will answer what questions I can for you concerning the older groups. There are some answers which I cannot give—such as names. As I am sure you know, then, more so than now, we took an oath of secrecy—and I have not been released from it. As far as I know, two of the members of the group are still alive, and I could never violate the oath I took. However, except for the actual names, there is some information which I would feel free to relate to you." Attempting to write a coherent account of her experience was not possible, given the life problems she was dealing with, but she allowed Dr. Melton to take notes on a conversation with her on June 21, 1980, and mentioned a few other facts in her letters.

Rhea said that "There was a very active group in Louisville, Ky., in 1934 and long before that. They were my first introduction to the Old Religion." As a child in the 1930s in Louisville she was given informal training in meditation, energy uses, visualization, and herbology, by a woman named Hannah in her apartment building. Hannah spoke of "following the Old Ways," and in her apartment a group met weekly. None of the women in the group cut their hair. They believed in a divine duality, in God as mother and father; they drew energy from the sun, and were particular about natural foods and herbs. The children were allowed to hold hands, do rhythmic breathing, and send energy. She never saw an altar or ritual instruments, but there was lighting of candles and calling on the spirits of the four corners.[5]

Rhea said that she was first initiated in 1943 by a group she worked with in New York City from 1942 to 1945. Her initiation required a month of preparation, and involved a three-day fast for purification. The group

---

5. The owner of the House of Hermetic, now in Eagle Rock, CA, told me after publication of CAMI that she had known this Louisville group also, and that the description was correct.

had been together for quite some time, and she knew of others; they functioned like Communist-Party cells, in that members were recruited by invitation and sworn to secrecy. "Must admit they were a wee bit different than the ones today, but the basic similarity was still there," she said. "However, they did not call themselves 'Pagans' or 'wicca.' When asked what 'religion' they were, they just replied, 'We follow the Old Ways.' In today's perspective they would be termed eclectic. Rituals were not quite as stylized as they are today. There are similarities and differences. "We worked clothed" (and/or robed). Sex within the temple or circle was taboo; however, there was a very healthy attitude toward sex." She said that when a Priest and Priestess were "Bound together," the sexual act was used, and represented oneness. Most of the members of the group were Lebanese. They said they had brought the "tradition" with them from Lebanon, and that Kahlil Gibran had derived from their tradition there. The group was not called a coven; its numbers fluctuated, but it was tight-knit. It met weekly, and celebrated all eight Sabbats, often at a farm in New Jersey, where many of the members lived. The members worked magic in terms of the phases of the moon, but did not meet specifically at new or full moon; many attended other churches as well. They used the athame, but had no grimoires or written materials aside from personal notebooks for recipes. Basic instructions were oral, and all members of group constituted the priesthood. They believed in reincarnation, and practiced both high and low magic.

They worked in a temple room used only for ritual purposes, and no circle was cast. The altar contained male and female statuettes to represent the Lord and Lady, a sword, a chalice, an incense burner, candle of various colours, and earth. Rituals were in English. They observed the elements and corners, and taught meditation, astral travel, work on the planes, and work with elements.

Rhea's later life involved frequent moves. As a result, although she had met other folk witches, both groups and individuals, in such places as Gainesville, Nashville, and Jasper, Alabama, as well as in Georgia and California, she had not, she said, joined another group.[6] Her impression

---

[6] However, I have been informed by Lady Galadriel and Lord Athanor in Georgia that they were originally trained and initiated by Rhea W.

is that the "Old Way" witches tend to remain underground, and separate from the "new" witches.

There is no way to be absolutely sure that Rhea has not "made up" some of this information, or that it is totally free of wishful thinking, but I believe that it is probably accurate, for these reasons:

1. Rhea does not seem to have any axe to grind. She is not trying to prove that the pre-Gardnerian witches she knew were totally unlike Gardner's ideas, or that they were identical with them. She simply says there were both similarities and differences, and that is just what we would expect.

2. Insofar as these "Old Way" witches seem similar to the Gardnerians, that is because they were working from similar materials and concepts, and from just about the same books. The major differences seem to arise from the fact that Margaret Murray was not central to their thinking, and they did not use concepts from Leland's *Aradia* either.

Ozark Witches

Another group of pre-Gardnerian witches are those in the Ozarks. To some extent, the Ozark folk beliefs about witches are like those in Africa: such "witches" are actually demons, spiritual entities that could not be human in real life. However, according to Vance Randolph's data, mixed in with this is an actual society or subculture of witches who are definitely real people. Randolph says (pp. 265-6),

> *Although I have known and interviewed 24 persons who were regarded by their neighbors as witches, only three admitted that they had sold themselves to the Devil. These three were quite mad, of course; the point is that their neighbors did not regard them as lunatics, but as witches. The other 21 claim that their efforts are directed* <u>*against*</u> *the forces of evil, and that their main business is the removal of spells and curses . . . These practitioners are variously known as witch masters, white witches, witch doctors, . . . and conjure folks, and it is from them that I have obtained much of my information on the subject.*
>
> *. . . most of the genuine old-timers are agreed that to become a witch is a rather complicated matter. Anybody is free to discuss the general principles of witchcraft, but the conjure words and old sayin's must be learned from a member of the opposite sex. . . . the secret doctrines must pass only between blood relatives, or*

between persons who have been united in sexual intercourse. Thus it is that every witch obtains her unholy wisdom either from a lover or from a male relative.

Not every woman who receives this information becomes a witch... not until someone actually uses the deadly formulae does a genuine witch appear... while a knowledge of witchcraft is admitted to exist in certain families and clans, it sometimes lies dormant for a long time. A virgin may possess some of the secrets of 'bedevilment,'... but she cannot be a genuine witch ... A woman can... practice the infernal arts in a small way without any ceremony, but to attain to her full powers she must be formally initiated into the sinister sisterhood.

When a woman decides to become a witch... she repairs to the family buryin' ground at midnight, in the dark of the moon. Beginning with a verbal renunciation of the Christian religion, she swears to give herself body and soul to the Devil. She removes every stitch of clothing... and delivers her body immediately to... the man who is inducting her into the 'mystery.' The sexual act completed, both parties repeat certain old sayin's... This ceremony is supposed to be witnessed by at least two initiates, also nude, and must be repeated on three consecutive nights.... the third pledge is final. Henceforth the woman is a witch...

I am told, by women who have claimed to experience both, that the witch's initiation is a much more moving spiritual crisis than that which the Christians call concersion [my emphasis]... however,... it inevitably results in the death of some person near and dear to the witch. I once attended the funeral of a woman whose death was attributed to her daughter's participation in one of these graveyard ceremonies. The accused girl sat apart from the other members of the family and was ignored.

This last paragraph establishes the social reality of the experiences: they are actual practices, not just fantasy. Obviously there are great differences here from the Gardnerian concept of the Craft as a religion, but there are also some striking similarities. The similarities are less striking when we consider that Randolph's book appeared in 1947, that is, in plenty of time for Gardner to have used it in writing his original Book of Shadows and *Witchcraft Today*.

Thomas Giles, Olney Richmond, and the Order of the Magi[7]

Olney H. Richmond (1844-1920) is most remembered as the founder of the Order of the Magi in Chicago in 1889, one of the new astrological religions (like Thomas Burgoyne's Brotherhood of Light and Hiram Butler's Esoteric Fraternity) founded in America in the nineteenth century. Richmond became a teacher to a group of about 30 men and women, and in 1889 opened a temple on South Division Street in Chicago. In 1890 a second temple was opened, in Lansing, Michigan.

What has not been known is that the Order of the Magi was the "outer court" (as it would now be called) for a coven of Witches. This Tradition of "the Magus Olney Richmond" was passed on by his daughter, Arlene Richmond, to Donald Nelson, a Chicago bookseller and publisher, who recruited "Thomas Giles" into the Tradition in 1955. Giles was then initiated by a Priestess named Virginia. The initiation, he relates, was the traditional sexual initiation of American folk witchcraft, not very different from Vance Randolph's description.[8] This "Magi" Tradition is almost the only documented pre-Gardnerian Witchcraft tradition in America. As Giles describes it, it was based on astrology, dealt mainly with practical magic, and had little formal liturgy, as might be expected. Nevertheless, it had a fairly well-defined theology, again based on astrology. Giles became a founder of the Pagan Way movement. In his own practice, Giles began blending the folk-magic practices of his own Tradition with Gardnerian procedures as they came to light in the late 1950s and early 1960s, and moving more and more toward Gardnerianism because of its usefulness, as apparently all traditional American Witches did.

The meaning of the traditional sexual initiation is hard to see precisely because it is so obvious: it is an act of political rebellion against oppression. It is a declaration of independence, an assertion

---

[7] Much of the data here is from an unpublished autobiographical essay by Thomas Giles.

[8] Giles told me that Virginia mentioned "the Magus Olney Richmond" during his initiation, but Giles had no idea who he was. I knew, because I happened to have written the entry on Richmond for *The New Age Encyclopedia*, and so was able to fill Giles in on the origins of his tradition.

of one's autonomy against a system of social controls experienced as not only intolerable but lethal. This was the stance of the Gnostics in the classical world, and this is the message preached by the Witches of Tuscany according to Leland's *Aradia.* Understood in this way, the Craft is a modern Gnosticism, which might explain why the Gnostic writings are a source of inspiration and fascination for many Witches.

It follows that the traditional Craft was a spiritual path that demanded freedom of sexual choice, for its own sake, to be sure, but primarily so that sex could be used as a spiritual weapon to shatter the unquestioned assumptions of the dominant culture. This process of psychological reconstruction is the path of the shaman, and it can be dangerous without the guidance of someone who has already traversed it successfully. Do all current Witches undergo such a discipline? No, of course not. Most follow a far safer process in becoming members of the Wiccan religion. But knowledge of the shamanic path is always close at hand for those who choose to begin exploring it, just as Tantrism is always an option in Hinduism.

In looking in the next chapter at the origins and evolution of Gardnerian Witchcraft, we will see that Gardner did begin with the traditional concept of sexual initiation. However, Gardner, having special sexual needs, proceeded to do something quite remarkable and almost unprecedented: he created a sacramental system that not only met his needs but sanctified them.

Chapter Three

A History of the Gardnerian Movement, 1946-1964

"It would be reasonable to expect high-minded people... who were sorry to see England going to the dogs for want of a god she could believe in... to set out to supply that need according to all the best anthropological principles. And as high-minded people in all ages have a bland and total disregard for the real character and content of the religions in which they choose to interest themselves, we should expect further to find that the witch-cult as they would reconstruct it would be scarcely recognizable as a witch-cult. It would happily combine the more aesthetically tolerable motifs of several former creeds and the least controversial ethical statements of all ages. Gods with Persian names and Greek bodies would prove, on examination, to have thoroughly Bloomsbury minds... good Dianists after all their incarnations would colonize new-risen Atlantis... A revised cult such as I visualize would have no particular need to be clandestine; but it might well preserve a measure of secrecy as a matter of tradition, seeing it would be dangerously short of traditions otherwise."

Elliot Rose, A Razor for a Goat, p. 201.

Logically, at this point we should go through the original documents written by Gardner and Valiente, to present the evidence on which the history in this chapter is based. But instead of overwhelming the reader with details, I will instead provide a map of where we are going before we plunge into the woods. This chapter is the map. The reader will then be able to read the analysis of the documents in Chapters 4-8 and have some sense of where we are going and why, of what is important and what is not, and so on; and can then come back, re-read this chapter, and see that it is supported by the evidence. Some people say that you should always write a book in such a way that nothing has to be read twice. Having thought about that for 35 years now, I believe such advice is sometimes simply wrong, as it is here.

The Early Life of Gerald Gardner

Gerald Brosseau Gardner was born at Great Crosby, near Blundell Sands in Lancashire, on June 13, 1884. His father was a timber merchant and a Justice of the Peace. His education for the most part was in the hands of "Con," a governess to whom the "Bracelin" biography says he was devoted. He did not obtain a university education, but instead went to work for the commercial branch of the British Civil Service in the Far East. In 1927, at age 43, he married Donna Rosedale, a clergyman's daughter. In 1936 he retired from the civil service—he had served as overseer of a rubber plantation in Malaysia, among other posts—and settled in the south of England, in the area of Hampshire known as the New Forest. He had been fascinated by the occult for his entire life, and had accumulated an immense collection of magical implements and of pamphlets issued by a great variety of new religious movements, which he brought home with him. He had also been initiated into dozens of occult organisations.[1]

Aside from his astonishing self-education on the founding of new religions revealed by his pamphlet and manuscript collection, what is most important about Gardner's life for understanding his role in founding the modern Craft movement is that he apparently suffered from a sexual addiction. Specifically, he was addicted to being whipped. To blame him or think ill of him for that would be bigotry, ignorance, or hypocrisy, because he had not chosen to acquire this addiction. Instead, it was forced upon him, as it was upon most Englishmen of his generation, by experiences like those in the English educational system.[2] In this system, as has been ably described by Ian Gibson's *The English Vice: Beating, Sex,*

---

1. A large sampling of these documents was on display in the Ripley's museums in the mid-1970s, since the Ripley's management considered them commercially valueless.

2 Gardner's devotion to his main teacher, his governess, does not prove otherwise, since abused children often show such devotion to their abusers.

and Shame in Victorian England and After, normal practice was, until very recently, to beat little boys on their bare buttocks with a cane or birch branch, before witnesses. As a result, their sexual development was distorted and fixated on their buttocks: even as adults, they needed to be beaten on their bare buttocks (or at least to fantasize about that) in order to achieve an erection and so be capable of sexual intercourse. It is eminently clear from Gardner's sexual interests and tastes that this had been his experience, whatever the source of that experience may have been, and that apparently fantasizing was not sufficient to meet his needs. Unlike most Englishmen, however, he did not try to hide this fact or make do by patronizing prostitutes who specialized in what is now called "bondage and domination." No, what Gardner did was far more courageous: he invented a religion that would meet his needs.

In a sense, Gardner was following in the steps of Algernon Charles Swinburne, the English poet (born in 1840) who recorded his experiences of being beaten at Eton in his verse—although these verses were censored and suppressed from his collected works until very recently. The man who beat Swinburne was his tutor, James Leigh Joynes, who at that time was an Anglican deacon; Joynes was later ordained as a priest. Being beaten in the name of Christ was a major reason—and, indeed, a sufficient reason—for Swinburne's famous hatred of Christianity:

> *"Thou hast conquered, O pale Galilean,*
> *And the world has gone gray with thy Breath."*

Gardner, like Aleister Crowley, did not settle for passively hating Christianity. Instead, he set out to replace Christianity. Since Christianity condemned his sexuality, distorted in Christ's name, as "perverse," he set out to found a religion that would be based on sex as a sacramental experience, and that could therefore help him meet his needs.

A craft Priestess I know who has worked as a professional "dominatrix" has shared with me some of her insights into Gardner's personality, based on her professional experiences and Gardner's own writings. She said that the instructions in his rituals for exactly how a person is to be bound and scourged show what he himself needed to have done. Furthermore, she said, he was clearly the sort of man called a "SAM, smart-assed masochist," in her trade, because, rather than obeying the orders of the "Mistress," he wanted to tell her exactly what to do to him. That is, like Leopold von Sacher-Masoch, Gardner's fantasized ideal woman is one who would appear to dominate him, but would in actuality be manipulated by him into meeting his sexual needs. From a Jungian perspective, this pattern also arises from the unconscious search for the lost "ideal mother." We would expect that most Englishmen who had been, as little boys, turned over to a governess or a tutor or a boarding school with the authority and inclination to beat them, would very reasonably feel that they had been abandoned by their mothers, and would mourn that loss for the rest of their lives. Given all that, it seems perfectly reasonable that the archetype of the Goddess would appeal to Gardner far more than the God satirized by William Blake as "Old Nobodaddy."

One may wonder what his wife, Donna, thought of all this. The pattern for the middle-class English wife was to keep her mouth shut and find a way to live with the problem; she might regret that she was not her husband's fantasized ideal woman, yet also recognize that, as a merely real and imperfect woman, there was no way that she could live up to that fantasy. Some wives would whip their husbands' bare butts in order to have sex. Others would give their husbands permission to meet their needs however they could, and would settle for enjoying the side-effects. Others, to be sure, would give up sex entirely. I am, of course, speculating here, and generalizing from very little data—for there has never been, as far as I know, an objective attempt at a scientific study of this question. But given all this, we can reasonably suppose that after a dozen years of trying to cope with Gerald's sexual problems, Donna might have been glad, or at least relieved, to have him find another path that could meet his needs. All the evidence about her is that, although not involved in the Craft herself, she never interfered with his Craft activity during their last twenty years together.

Before the outbreak of World War II, Gardner had written a letter to the London *Times* suggesting the formation of civilian defence units in the event of war, a letter for which he was denounced in the Nazi press as a warmonger. When the Home Guard was formed—whether or not in part because of his letter—he served as a unit commander during the course of the war. Charles Clifton has written an excellent paper, "Secrecy and Historicity in the Book of Shadows," in which he points out that Gardner's experience during the war, worrying about a possible German invasion, seems to have set the mood for much of his writing about the "Burning Times" in his books and documents. Certainly the British comedy series *Dad's Army,* about a Home Guard unit, seemed to shed some light on what Gardner's state of mind might have been during the war.

In the New Forest in the late 1930s, Gardner became friends with the local occultists, who included Theosophists, Co-Masons, and others. One woman he had particularly high regard for was Dorothy Clutterbuck Fordham[3] (born January 19, 1880; died January 12, 1951), who was the daughter of Thomas St. Quintin Clutterbuck (b. 1839), a British Indian Army Officer, and of Ellen Anne Morgan (b. 1857), and was of a family long resident in the New Forest area. An article sent to me by Doreen Valiente describes the finding of Dorothy's wartime diaries, filled with verse and illustrated by a friend, which were on exhibit in London.[4] The article describes her as "the wealthy Mrs. Dorothy Fordham, who owned two magnificent houses near Chewton Glen at Highcliffe: The Mill House and Lattimers." That is, she was precisely the sort of person, slightly above Gardner in social class, with whom he would have wanted to associate. However, as Hutton has argued, their social circles did not overlap to any significant degree.

In his books, Gardner stated that Clutterbuck was the head of the Rosicrucian Theater Group (it opened on June 15, 1938), which served as a front for the coven into which he was initiated in 1939. However, Ronald Hutton, in checking the theatre's records, discovered that

---

[3] In a charming appendix to the Farrars' *The Witches' Way* (pp. 283-293), Doreen Valiente describes how she tracked down the birth and death certificates of Dorothy Clutterbuck, thus verifying her existence. (Doreen, initiated in 1953, had not known Dorothy, who died in 1951.) But Dorothy's existence was never a real issue; the issue is Gardner's claim that she was some sort of hereditary witch, for which there is still no evidence.

[4] From the Bournemouth *Evening Echo* of February 25, 1986.

Clutterbuck had headed a different theatre group. The actual head of the Rosicrucian group was, first, Alex Mathews, then, when Mathews died in 1942, the leadership devolved upon the woman whose Craft name would be Dafo, recently identified as Edith Woodford-Grimes, a woman well-known in English feminist circles. In retrospect, it appears obvious that Gerald and Edith began a romance sometime during World War II, and that it continued on well into the late 1940s, while they were founding the first coven. In contrast, recent investigation of Clutterbuck has failed to unearth any evidence that she was involved in the coven at all. Hutton suggests that Gardner played her up in order to divert attention away from Dafo, who was a very private person.

The Beginning of Gardnerian Witchcraft

The book that led to the founding of the Craft movement was Margaret Murray's *The Witch Cult in Western Europe*, published by Oxford University Press in 1922. In it Murray describes the survival of a Pagan religion that she argues was the reality behind the infamous witch hunts of early modern times. I initially suspected, as Heselton also suggests, that English occultists would have immediately begun trying to recreate this religion, but there is no direct evidence that this occurred. Murray's data is quite fragmentary, and it would not have been obvious how to carry out such a reconstruction.

It may be that in September 1939, Gerald Gardner and his friends were discussing England's perilous state, now at war with Germany. Was England in danger of perishing spiritually for want of a truly native British religion they could all believe in? Gardner, at least, had been thinking for years about how to go about creating one. Encouraged by the tension of that moment, perhaps they decided to undertake the re-creation of Murray's "witch cult." If the project of creating the coven was initiated that night, each of them may have felt that his or her own initiation had started that night; perhaps that is why Gardner chose to claim that he was initiated in September 1939. But during the war this project was put on hold. It was not until 1946 that Gardner and his lover

Edith founded the first modern coven.[5] Note that one can reasonably refer to the New Forest circle of friends and fellow occultists, but it was in no sense a coven until the late 1940s.

In order to see why Gardner and his friends succeeded (where many others may have failed) in putting together a new religion based on Murray, we need to look at who they were, and at what resources were available to them. In her *The Rebirth of Witchcraft,* Doreen Valiente provided the names of people who were in Gerald's circle of occult friends and who therefore could have been members of the coven in 1945-1946. Adding a few names from other sources, we arrive at the following list, on which Ms. Valiente commented in letters to me.

Dolores North (died in 1982), pen-name Madeline Montalban, was known to Gerald "and others as `The Witch of St Giles' because she lived in St Giles High Street, London." Ms. Valiente said that she "typed out for [Gardner] the manuscript of his book *High Magic's Aid*...[and] became well-known as a regular contributor to the popular occult magazine *Prediction*... I believe her family had some connection with the then Lord Louis Mountbatten's estate, Broadlands, in the New Forest area.... during the war... she had been wearing the uniform of an officer in the WRNS [as] a cover... Mountbatten, who knew her because of her family's connection with his estate, had retained her as his personal clairvoyant and psychic advisor.[6] A very curious account of what may be a magical working with Gerald Gardner and Dolores North appears in a book by Kenneth Grant entitled *Nightside of Eden*... this ritual... took place in 1949." She is likely to have been a member of the coven from very early on, perhaps from the very first meeting. Her friendship with Gardner was a well-known fact. She later had a coven of her own, and

---

[5] I am not going to argue the blatantly obvious fact that Gerald and Edith became lovers about 1938 or 1939, and were still lovers in 1946. I find it esthetically pleasing that the Craft originated not in a supposed resurrection, but in a very real love affair. Part of my certainty about this derives from the fact that the New, Reformed, Orthodox Order of the Golden Dawn originated in the same way.

[6] Readers of Katherine Kurtz's excellent novel *Lammas Night* will recognize this scenario.

it was she who initiated John Score, editor of *The Wiccan* and a founder of the Pagan Front. (Ms. Valiente agreed that she could have been a member of the coven.)

Louis Wilkinson, who wrote novels under the name of Louis Marlow, and contributed to Crowley's *Equinox*, was one of Crowley's literary executors. In 1947 he achieved brief notoriety by reading Crowley's funeral service at the municipal crematorium. (We know about him from Francis King's report in *Ritual Magic in England* of a meeting with him in 1953. Ms. Valiente agreed that he could have been a member of the coven.)

Next is George Watson McGregor Reid, Chosen Chief of the Ancient Order of Druids, the group that used to hold sunrise services at Stonehenge on Midsummer's Day (several manuscripts of their rituals are among the documents in Toronto), and his son, Robert McGregor Reid, who succeeded his father as Chosen Chief in 1946. (Ms. Valiente thinks he was probably not a member of the coven; but since Dorothy Clutterbuck owned the sword that these Druids used for their rituals at Stonehenge, there must have been some connection.)

J.S.M. Ward, a close friend of Gardner, a leading Freemason and author of several learned books on Freemasonry, a pioneer in rescue and conservation of ancient buildings, was the owner of the "witch's cottage" that Gardner bought and had rebuilt near St Albans. (He is also discussed by King and in the "Bracelin" biography. Ms. Valiente thought it very unlikely he could have been a member of the coven, because he was a very sincere, though very unorthodox, Christian bishop. Ward was probably the source of Gardner's own consecration as a bishop, the certificate for which is among the papers in Toronto.)

Christine Hartley, whom I discussed in Chapter 2, was, Ms. Valiente agreed, also a possibility. In fact, she wrote to me, "I wish I knew! You see, all the leading people who were seriously interested in the occult in those days tended to know each other; but this does not necessarily mean they were all involved in the same things. And also, because the whole occult scene was so secretive in those times, so furtive almost (witches were, after all, still doing something actually illegal, for which they could have been prosecuted), tracks were very well covered, I can assure you." Seymour and Hartley, who are discussed in great detail in Alan Richardson's *Dancers to the Gods*, were both active as Co-Masons from 1941 on, and may have met Gardner and Dafo in that context, if they were not already acquainted. Seymour died in 1943, but Richardson told me that Hartley had said in an interview that she had been in a coven after the war; if so, Gerald and Edith's new coven was the only one she could have meant.

Mrs. Mabel Besant-Scott, daughter of Annie Besant, Gardner's neighbour in Highcliffe, on the edge of the New Forest, and a leading member of the Rosicrucian Fellowship of Crotona. (Ms. Valiente thinks it unlikely that she could have been a member of the coven, but obviously she may have been what is now called "Pagan-friendly.")

There were probably other, non-famous, members of this circle of friends, and some have now been identified by Philip Heselton.

Reconstructing Murray

If Gardner's coven (or earlier members of the circle of friends) began to reconstruct the religion described by Murray, what would their first model have looked like? That is, what information does Murray give? What does it look like when pulled together?[7]

Murray always refers to her subject as "the religion," or "the old religion," or "the cult" (as in the title of the book). She asserts (p. 12) that "underlying the Christian religion was a cult practised chiefly by the more ignorant or those in the less thickly inhabited parts of the country. It can be traced back to pre-Christian times, and appears to be the ancient religion of Western Europe." (Murray nowhere offers any evidence to support this sweeping claim.) Hence the group would have felt that any information about pre-Christian religions might be useful for reconstructing the "witch-cult."

Murray's reconstruction focuses almost entirely on the God of the witches, and on the man whom the witches believed to be the living incarnation of that God. He often wore an animal skin or costume, and often dressed entirely in black—and hence was called the Black Man.

[7] In the following I am quoting from *Witch-Cult in Western Europe* except where I specifically cite *God of the Witches.*

To "the witches themselves... [he] was God, manifest and incarnate; they adored him on their knees, they addressed their prayers to him, they offered thanks to him as the giver of food and the necessities of life, they dedicated their children to him, and . . . like many another god, he was sacrificed for the good of his people." Because "the feminine form . . . Diana, is found throughout Western Europe as the name of the female deity or leader of the so-called Witches . . . I have called this . . . the Dianic cult"[8].

Although Murray said that a woman sometimes served as the incarnation of the God, for the most part women took a secondary role. She does not mention the concept of a goddess as the chief deity of the witches except to dismiss it. (In fact, the Craft concept of the Goddess comes primarily from Leland's *Aradia*, and then from the Classical sources that Leland points back to.)

In each district the chief appointed one or more officers, who might be either men or women, whose "duties were to arrange for meetings, to send out notices, to keep the record of work done, to transact the business of the community, and to present new members" for initiation. "At the Esbats the officer appears to have taken command in the absence of the Grand Master; at the Sabbaths the officers were merely heads of their own Covens" (p. 186).

If the coven were basing itself on Murray's concepts, then *the first coven would have kept its focus on the God and on the name High Priest.* We would expect any rituals based on this information to focus on the High Priest, and not on a priestess. Contrary to what Craft members now think, this is precisely the emphasis in the rituals until about 1957, as we will see.

Murray provides the following definition of a coven:

> *"There was among the witches a body of elders—the Coven—which managed the local affairs of the cult...The word coven is a derivative of `convene,' ... [it means] a `band' or `company' ... composed of men and women... set apart for the practice of the rites of the religion and for the performance of magical ceremonies; in short, a kind of priesthood.*
>
> *"There were two kinds of assemblies; ... the Sabbath was the General Meeting*

[8] WCWE, pp. 12, 13, 28, 33-43.

of all the members of the religion; the... Esbat was only for... [those] who carried out the rites and practices of the cult... [and was] primarily for... the practice of magic for the benefit of a client or for the harming of an enemy... Very often also the Esbat was for sheer enjoyment only.

"There was no fixed day or hour for the Esbat [though probably] one day in the week was observed... The Devil let his followers know the time, either by going to them himself or by sending a message by the officer... The Esbat had less ceremonial, and the religious service was not performed... the witches worked the spells and charms... exercised new methods... or received instructions [on] how to practise the arts of healing and... fertility... The members [of the coven had] . . . to attend the weekly Esbat; ... The rest of the villagers attended the Esbats when they could [and] attended the Sabbaths as a matter of course. ... The 'fixed number' among the witches of Great Britain seems to have been thirteen: twelve witches and their officer."[9]

Notice here that the concept of meeting at the full moon does not come from Murray; instead, it was derived from Leland's *Aradia.*

At first the coven probably did meet weekly, as a committee working on the project, and those who showed up regularly for these working sessions would have considered themselves to be the members of the coven. Given the concept that the Sabbats were for all the members of the religion, the coven would have quietly invited sympathetic friends and acquaintances from the local occult circle to them. And even aside from Murray, May Day and Hallowe'en are the two dates that European custom universally associates with witches.

"The dates of the two chief festivals, May Eve and November Eve, indicate the use of a calendar which is . . . preagricultural and earlier than the solstitial divisions of the year. . . . The cross-quarter days, February 2 and August 1, . . . also kept as festivals, were probably of later date"

(pp. 12-13).

Murray's speculations on the origins of the festivals are, in fact, completely wrong; but that merely proves that the Gardnerian Book of Shadows, which in 1953 had rituals for only the four Celtic festivals,

[9] WCWE, pp. 13, 97, 112-3, 21, 124, 190-91; and *God of the Witches*. p110.

and none for the solstices and equinoxes, was based on Murray, rather than a more accurate source.

But what might the coven have done at a Sabbat? The litany of a "Witches' Sabbath" as given by Murray included the following:

(1) worship of the incarnate deity by
- (a) renewing vows,
- (b) kissing,
- (c) turning withershins several times;

(2) the business portion, consisting of
- (a) reports of & instructions on magic,
- (b) admissions to the society, and
- (c) marriages of members;

(3) the religious service, consisting of
- (a) a ceremony that varied with the seasons,
- (b) fertility rites,
- (c) feasting, and
- (d) dancing until dawn.

"Though the Chief sometimes gave an address, in which he . . . explained the dogmas of the religion, the main ceremony was the sacred dance. After this came the feast, which was often followed by another dance." "The feasts and dances show that it was a joyous religion."[10]

In the witch-trial records, this feast often appears to be confused with the Christian Eucharist, or is claimed to be a parody of the Eucharist; or else appears to be a simple meal. Neither possibility provides much in the way of a pagan ritual.

Among the dances mentioned are a jumping dance for fertility, the round dance, a follow-the-leader dance, and a processional dance. "As the processional dance was performed by men and women side by side in pairs, or in a long line with the sexes alternately, it was liable to break up into couples who continued dancing together after the procession was ended. . . . [It] could be in itself a complete act of worship, but it was most frequently used to bring the worshippers to the holy place where the round dance or 'Ring' was to be performed."[11]

---

[10] WCWE, pp. 15, 124, and *God of the Witches*, p.76.

[11] *God of the Witches*, p. 110.

Aside from mentioning folk-magic procedures and some obvious customs, such as riding a broomstick, lighting candles, boiling a cauldron, and so on, Murray gives no other specific details of what witches might have done. Clearly, then, the coven must have exercised much creativity and ingenuity in attempting to "reconstruct" this religion.

Gardner and his friends were, in fact, faced by a dilemma: the "Old Religion" described by Murray was a religion that focused on the practice of magic; but the only systems for working magic that they could find out about—e.g., the "ceremonial" or "high" magic of the grimoires and secret societies—were inherently Judaeo-Christian in concept and in vocabulary. (The pagan section of the Fraternity of the Inner Light had evolved a pagan system of magic by 1939; knowledge of it may have been Christina Hartley's contribution to the evolution of the coven.) Not only was the theory behind these systems derived from certain special branches of Judaeo-Christian theology, but the systems were so complex that the resulting practical details were almost impossible to carry out. In the so-called Abramelin system, for example, any one working would require great expense and months of preparation to carry out, as would the procedures detailed in the Greater Key of Solomon. The magical system of the Hermetic Order of the Golden Dawn was somewhat more sophisticated, and its rituals were easier to carry out—if you had a magical lodge whose members could subscribe 100 pounds sterling a year to support it, that is, more that the annual income of the average English home at that time—so these rituals were certainly not suitable for a coven of witches.

The coven was also interested in folk magic, which is always non-denominational, and made as much use of it as they could; but the problem with folk magic is that it is all practice, no theory. To cure a wart, use this herb; to win a girl, recite this charm. From a hundred such workings, no one could deduce a hundred-and-first, since no system lies behind them; they cannot be generalized. Hence such "low magic" did not offer the sort of theological structure that Gardner and his friends wanted this new "Old Religion" to have. In order to insure the success of their "revival" of the "Old Religion," they needed to have what would in fact be a new system for working magic. To create it, they needed to use some sort of ritual other than that of Kabalistic magic as a framework for it—but since these folks were Rosicrucians, Masons, Co-Masons, and so on, and were also into theatre, they had rituals at hand that they could and almost certainly did adapt. Much in the Gardnerian Book of Shadows is Masonic in underlying structure;[12] much that now seems odd in it can be explained in terms of this set of data from Murray that constituted the jumping-off point for the reconstruction.

Gardner had been gathering notes on magical procedures for many years (there are, among the materials in Toronto, half a dozen hand-illuminated manuscript books consisting of material that Gardner had copied from various grimoires and other sources), but he had never written any rituals, because he had never before had a group to write for. Now he had a new agenda: to find out how magic could be worked by a small group. He began gathering his notes on this topic in a notebook labeled "Ye Bok of ye Art Magical" (which we will discuss in great detail in the next chapter). It consists of almost 150 large sheets, which have been folded and sewn into signatures; the resulting pages are somewhat larger than British legal size (8" x 13"). The signatures were then handbound (not very skillfully) into a leather book cover whose previous contents had been removed. On the front cover is inscribed the title (exactly as spelled above), and beneath that appears a triangle above a pentacle, the Gardnerian symbol for a third-degree witch.

Gardner may have at first intended this manuscript book to be a magical workbook, because at first he entered only information about ceremonial magic in it. However, everything copied into "Ye Bok of ye Art Magical" can be carried out by one or a few persons. He searched out and gathered together materials from many sources: Crowley's developments of the HOGD systems; the Greater Key of Solomon; Masonic and other fraternal rituals; Murray, Frazer, and the Cambridge classicists—in fact, the sources included the hundreds of books shelved in Derek's office when I made my visit to Toronto.

---

[12] My colleague David R. Jones, perhaps the most knowledgeable person on things Masonic I have ever met, assures me that the Gardnerian workings are primarily Co-Masonic in their details.

There is still a problem. One identifying characteristic of the entire Gardnerian Witchcraft movement is the basic structure of the ritual:

casting the circle;
calling the quarters;
invoking the deities;
raising and using the energy;
having a small symbolic feast of "cakes and ale";
dismissing the deities and quarters;
closing down the circle.

Where did that sequence of actions come from? It cannot be derived logically from any sort of Masonic, HOGD, Ceremonial Magick, or other published procedure—and so it looks as if it might be something genuinely peculiar to the Craft. However, Gardner was a member of the Folklore Society, whose journal is filled with accounts of Native American religion. The usual description of a Native American ritual is that it consisted of:

consecrating a circle;
invoking the spirits of the four directions;
invoking the Great Spirit;
dancing around the circle, with drumming;
sharing a small feast;
thanking and dismissing the spirits;
opening up the circle.

Let us return to Murray, who (p. 14) states that most ceremonies were for securing fertility:

> *"If the women believed that sexual intercourse with the priests would increase fertility, how much more would they believe in the efficacy of such intercourse with the incarnate God of fertility himself. They would insist upon it as their right" (p. 178).*

Given this emphasis in Murray, we can presume that sex was present in the Craft, and in Craft initiation, from the start. Sex was, and is, a major reason why people become interested in the Craft. The great emphasis on sexuality in the rituals, as we will see, is neither hedonistic nor exploitative, but genuinely sacramental, since it arises out of a search for communion and for community.

As we saw in considering the pre-Gardnerian witches in America, the one element of a Witchcraft initiation that seems to be universal is that it involves sexual intercourse. Insofar as the Craft is conceived of as a rebellion against Christianity, that rebellion would obviously focus on and emphasize the aspect of human nature to which Christianity seems (to most people) to be most opposed.

Murray states (*God of the Witches,* p. 63) that there were apparently three different "admission ceremonies," one in public, one for consecration as a priestess, and one for being made an officer of the coven—these are the logical possibilities for initiatory transitions, and reflect the practices of most covens to this day.

These could take place at either Sabbath or Esbat, and were the same for either sex; they could involve being rebaptized, being given a new name, being given a mark or tattoo, and signing one's name in a book (pp. 74-6).

As Murray comments, "the renunciation of previous errors of faith and the vows of fidelity to the new belief are part of the ceremony of admission of any convert to a new religion" (p. 77), but, as she also points out (p. 15), such a ritual would be invented only after the arrival of Christianity and in reaction to it; it would not be part of an earlier religion existing in isolation.

The coven must therefore have begun creating initiation rituals for their own use. Whether or not they did some sort of initiation at the Sabbats, they certainly must have begun creating initiation rituals for use within the coven almost immediately.

In Gardner's system there were three initiations, just as Murray said, and they incorporate elements from Murray within a framework taken from the three-degree system of the Masonic Blue Lodges; they also incorporate a great deal of "binding and scourging," all of which was Gardner's own addition to the earlier raw materials.

About a hundred pages into "Ye Bok of ye Art Magical" the First-Degree Initiation begins, and the rest of the initiations are scattered throughout the rest of the book, along with about a dozen other entries relevant to the Craft as currently practiced. Obviously, Gardner chose "Ye Bok of ye Art Magical" to be his first working Book of Shadows[13] because it looks right—at least from a few feet away—so where better to write out the initiation rituals in a form that could actually be used?

The initiation rituals (unlike all the other entries) in "Ye Bok of ye Art Magical" are writ large and clear, in calligraphy careful enough to be read from three or four feet away. These initiation rituals are designed to be worked by one person for one other person at a time. Although this would indicate that his coven was very small, Gardner was not working in isolation as he created the rituals in the "Ye Bok of ye Art Magical" manuscript, which is clearly intended for liturgical use in the circle. Rather, like all liturgy, they resulted from a lengthy group process. We now know that he, Edith, Dolores North, and probably others worked together when they had a reason to; for example, Edith helped initiate Doreen Valiente in 1953.

I also doubt that Gardner worked in isolation to create the vision of a medieval pagan religion in the novel *High Magic's Aid*, which Gardner said he wrote around 1946, and which was published in 1949; rather, it also seems to me to be the product of a group process. In fact, as we will see, Gardner was working on the novel and on rewriting the rituals simultaneously, around 1946.

The novel *High Magic's Aid* is a fanciful and rather detailed description of the beliefs and practices of an English witch cult in about the 15th century. It reveals that Gardner (and whoever else helped him write it, Louis Wilkinson being a very likely candidate) had already given much

[13] Notice that this is a change of name; if Gardner had known the term "Book of Shadows" when he put BAM together, why didn't he inscribe that term onto its cover? Valiente has suggested quite plausibly that Gardner may have gotten the term "Book of Shadows" from an article about an ancient Sanskrit manuscript that appeared in 1949 in *The Occult Observer*, a journal edited by Michael Houghton, the publisher of *High Magic's Aid.* Similarly, she suggests (in *Witchcraft for Tomorrow*, p. 78) that he may have gotten the term "athame" from "The Master of the Crabs" by Clark Ashton Smith in a 1947 issue of *Weird Tales*; Smith introduced it as a tool of magic, and spelled the name "arthame."

thought to what a medieval, magical, pagan religion might have been like, and to how it might be now "reconstructed." It also reveals how thoroughly familiar Gardner and his people were with Murray; dozens of elements from *The Witch-Cult in Western Europe* are incorporated in *High Magic's Aid*[14] , and that is one of the major clues that allowed me to realize they had begun from her data. The book includes step-by-step descriptions of the First- and Second-Degree rituals, following the text of "Ye Bok of ye Art Magical" rather closely, and explains that these "witch" initiations have to be worked within a magical circle cast by a ceremonial magician! This is quite antithetical to current Craft practice—but it is how the Gardnerian circles had been worked, and would apparently continue to be worked, until about 1957.

An article in the *Sunday Pictorial* for July 29, 1951, carried an article by Allen Andrews captioned "Calling All Covens." It announced the forthcoming opening of the Folklore Centre of Superstition and Witchcraft, founded by Cecil H. Williamson at the Witches Mill, Castletown, Isle of Man. The opening ceremony was to be performed by the "resident witch, Dr. Gerald B. Gardner." Williamson had put up a memorial to the estimated nine million people killed during the witch persecutions in Europe, for which Gardner later claimed credit.

In 1952 Gardner bought the museum from Williamson, and used it to display the magical and occult curiosities he had been accumulating all his life. (And in his customarily devious manner, he never mentions Williamson in any of his own writings, and gives the impression that he had himself founded the museum.) In 1951 the very last anti-witchcraft law—which had been enacted in 1736—was repealed because of lobbying by the Spiritualist churches, and this, Gardner later implied, made it possible for him to admit the existence of the religion.

The members of the original coven probably did not claim that they were a survival from the middle ages. Gardner's statements that the coven insisted on secrecy, and would only allow him to publish a description of their beliefs in the form of a novel, may reflect more than a desire for privacy. Edith may not have allowed Gardner to claim a continuity with

---

[14] On pp. 37-39, 67-69, 118, 229, 302, and probably others.

the past which she knew was not true. In any event, it was apparently about then that Gardner began thinking about how to write *Witchcraft Today* in a way that would present a plausible claim to such continuity.[15] Edith continued to serve as the High Priestess until about 1953. Judging from the details of the rituals as they existed before about 1953, I don't think there were ever more than half a dozen people active in the coven at any one time, although there probably continued to be an informal "Outer Court" of people in occult circles who were privileged to know of the coven's existence and who were invited to the larger Sabbat rituals. By 1953, Gardner had started a new coven in London, and the new religion that he and his friends had founded—for that is what they did—had evolved far from Murray's concepts. However, their system for working magic had not progressed much beyond the situation described in *High Magic's Aid*; there was still the uneasy amalgam of the male ceremonial magician and the female folk-magic witch.

The Reign of Doreen Valiente, 1953-1957.

Late in 1952 came what has turned out to be the turning point in the evolution of the Craft as a new religion: Gardner and Dafo met, and later initiated, Doreen Valiente (who was born in 1922). This talented young woman promptly threw herself into work on the new religion, rewriting the existing rituals and creating new ones, and some of this work was reflected in the final draft of *Witchcraft Today.*

In the September 27, 1952, issue of the English popular magazine *Illustrated* appeared an article entitled "Witchcraft in Britain" by Allen Andrews. The article quoted at length the remarks of Cecil Williamson, who had opened a witchcraft museum on the Isle of Man in 1951. Williamson described various practices of the "Old Religion of the witches," mentioned the New Forest as being the meeting place of the "Southern Coven of British Witches," and "revealed how, on the night of 1 August 1940, the Sabbat of Lammas, seventeen men and women had gathered in a clearing in the New Forest to raise a 'cone of power' to prevent Hitler from crossing the Channel and invading

[15] Some data in the preceding section has been taken from Valiente, *Rebirth of Witchcraft*, pp. 14, 30-32, 38, 40, 42, 44-45, 49-50, 56, 288-93.

Britain."[16] He had invited members of the Southern Coven of English Witches to be present at the formal opening of his museum. Gerald Gardner had accepted the invitation, and also talked to the reporter about the "Old Religion."[17]

Doreen Valiente, who said that she had walked out of her convent school at age 15 and flatly refused to return, relates that she read this article in 1952, when she was living in Bournemouth (which is fairly near the New Forest), with great excitement. She had been reading everything on magic that she could get her hands on for years, but this was her first indication that witches might still exist. She wrote to Williamson, detailing her occult studies until then, and asking if he could put her in touch with the witch cult. Williamson passed her letter along to Gardner, and after a few more letters were exchanged, Gardner invited Doreen to meet him and Dafo at Dafo's house near Christchurch. This she did late in 1952, and she liked both Gerald and Dafo from the start. At that time Dafo, since she was a teacher of music and elocution, since her daughter had married a dentist, and since her health was poor, was no longer active in the Craft. As Doreen left that day, Gerald gave her a copy of *High Magic's Aid* to read, saying that it would tell her a great deal about "the witch cult as it really was."

It was not until the summer of 1953 that Doreen was initiated. Gardner came down to Dafo's house from his home on the Isle of Man in order to attend the Druids' Midsummer ritual at Stonehenge, bringing with him the sword which the Druid Order used in their ceremony, and which had belonged to Dorothy Clutterbuck. In his brochure about the Witches' Mill, Gardner said, "She had a very fine ritual sword, which for many years was lent to the Druid Order which holds the annual Midsummer ceremony at Stonehenge, because it fitted exactly into the cleft in the

[16] It may be that this fabulous story about the 1940 working against Hitler was first concocted by Williamson, who was well-known as a teller of tall tales about the Craft and much else..

[17] Williamson, like Wilkinson, seems to have been in league with Gardner in inventing stories that would push the age of the coven back some six or more years; this is an aspect of Gardner's inventing a foundation myth for his new Old Religion. There is no objective evidence anywhere that would support any of these stories.

Hele Stone." Gardner had been a friend of both the current Chosen Chief of the Druid Order, Robert McGregor Reid, and his father, George Watson McGregor Reid, whom he had succeeded as Chosen Chief in 1946; and certainly Dorothy must also have been a friend of the latter. (The overlapping use of magical tools is almost certain proof of overlapping membership.)

At her initiation, Doreen said, the ritual was virtually identical to that in *High Magic's Aid,* except that it also contained a section called "The Charge" that Gerald read to her. She recognized passages in it as being from Leland's *Aradia*, and from Crowley's *Book of the Law* and "Gnostic Mass" in *Magick in Theory and Practice*, and said that when she later mentioned this to Gerald, he "seemed none too pleased at my recognition of its sources."

The next day Doreen went to the Stonehenge ritual with Gerald and Dafo. It felt very appropriate to her that her initiation should be sealed by her first visit to "one of the great spiritual centres of Britain." Later in the year Gerald invited her up to his London flat to meet the rest of his coven. There were about eight or ten of them, most being members also of the nudist society that Gardner belonged to, some claiming to have already been witches.

About the time that Doreen was initiated, Gardner was using two different Books of Shadows. The first and shorter one (Text A) included of the ritual documents that Gardner had copied (as we will see) out of "Ye Bok of ye Art Magical": the procedure for casting the circle, the initiation ritual, the "Lift the Veil" version of the Charge, the short "Cakes and Wine" ritual, and apparently the four Sabbats for the cross-quarter days. The second Book (Text B) consisted of these rituals and/or revisions of them, plus other, newer materials; and this was the book that Gardner actually used during Doreen's initiation.

Gardner was already being far less than forthright in his dealings with Doreen. Not only did he never tell her about the existence of "Ye

Bok of ye Art Magical,"[18] which he kept at his museum and used as a notebook, but, she wrote to me, "Gerald certainly led me to assume that the text of the Book of Shadows had been copied originally from 'Old Dorothy's' book." However, there is no evidence at all that Dorothy ever had any such book. Rather, "Ye Bok of ye Art Magical" itself, since it was obviously intended for liturgical use in the circle, was probably the only book that the original coven used.

Gardner used "Ye Bok of ye Art Magical" as a notebook for drafts of passages that would later appear in *Witchcraft Today*, as well as for drafts of new rituals that he copied into "Text B." The emphasis in these entries was on finding a stance that would lend plausibility to the historical claims: that there was an earlier coven; that there was a pagan religion; that a pagan religion could have the characteristics described in *Witchcraft Today*. Hence, although "Ye Bok of ye Art Magical" was not intended to be read, it was clearly written with an audience always in mind. But if it were what the "Warning" proclaims it to be, a "witch's book," whether an individual's notebook or a group's liturgical manual, it would focus on the content of the religious tradition. It would not be ultimately concerned with manipulating audience reaction. The fact "Ye Bok of ye Art Magical" is focused on audience reaction demonstrates that Gardner was thinking deliberately and primarily about how to found a new religious movement. Once "Ye Bok of ye Art Magical" was full, and no longer useful even as a notebook, Gardner hid it in the back of a cabinet in the museum, where it was found by the team from Ripley's in 1971; the Wilsons, who arrived after it had been retired, probably didn't even know it existed; thus it was preserved, to provide the clues to unravel the puzzle.

During this period Gardner was very busy writing *Witchcraft Today,* to which Doreen contributed a few items, such as the ritual for the

---

[18] Which is why, according to her 1985 letter to *Iron Mountain*, she was unaware of its existence until 1982, when she read a copy of an earlier draft of this book. She wrote to me, "No, Gerald never told me anything about `Ye Booke of ye Art Magical.' But I had had those typewritten scraps [e.g., of the first-degree initiation] in the old book he gave me [that is, Text A], and never knew what they were until I saw your typescript."

winter solstice (which we will look at in Chapter 5). Someone other than Gardner, who could not write even a line of verse, must have written the poems "The Witch Remembers her Last Incarnation" and "Twilight is over" in *Witchcraft Today*. In addition, "The Myth of the Goddess" (which is yet another theologizing of the scourging) and the portion of the Charge that appear in its Chapter 3 are so different in literary style from (and so much better than) the rest of Gardner's writing, that I believe someone else must have written them. I had thought this person was Doreen Valiente, but she said not—and since she admits what she did write, there is no reason not to believe her. It may also be that Ross Nichols, whom Ms. Valiente said was a schoolteacher, author, and member of a Druid Order (quite likely that headed by the Reids), did do a thorough copyediting and rewriting of *Witchcraft Today*, not just a critical review. Certainly someone other than Gardner typed the clean and correctly spelled final manuscript of "New Light on Witchcraft" that went in to the publisher, who renamed it *Witchcraft Today*. Doreen Valiente told me that it was not her who retyped it, and she does not know who else did—though it might have been Dolores North again. Or Gardner might just have hired some professional help.

In 1954 *Witchcraft Today* was published. In it Gardner claimed that Margaret Murray had been right: that the "witchcraft" of the Middle Ages had been a surviving pagan religion. He knew this, he said, because that religion had survived in secret down into this century; having stumbled upon one of the last surviving covens in England, he had been initiated into it, and was now free to write a description of its actual beliefs and practices, which went back to Elizabethan times and ultimately to the stone-age religions of Europe. Gardner may have actually told Margaret Murray that his group had begun by trying to reconstruct the religion she described. This may be why she fails to notice, in her enthusiastic Introduction, what Elliot Rose points out: that the religion Gardner describes in *Witchcraft Today* is utterly unlike what Murray had described 20 and 30 years earlier. Many current members of the Craft movement fail to see that the "Great Goddess" is NOT one of the concepts in *Witchcraft Today*, which instead presents a domesticated sort of classical polytheism.

As time went on, Doreen said, she became in practice Gerald's High Priestess, and became more vocal about her dissatisfaction with the Book of Shadows as it stood when she was initiated. Many of the rituals whose existence was asserted in *Witchcraft Today* were then only in the planning stages. If a "Gardnerian" coven is defined as one that works the basic Gardnerian rituals—and this is one of the basic rules by which Gardnerians judge the authenticity of any coven that claims to be Gardnerian—then no Gardnerian coven could have existed before 1955, because the basic Gardnerian rituals had not yet been written. In fact, none of the circle rituals in use in 1953 were based on a "pagan" theology; instead, they were all adapted from the Kabalistic procedures of the *Greater Key of Solomon*, and contained great swatches of quotation from Crowley. Doreen said that other witches were quoted in the 1952 *Illustrated* article as saying that their rituals were based on "instructions handed down from the elders, eked out with the Clavicules of Solomon," and argues that therefore "Gerald Gardner did not introduce this practice of blending witchcraft with ceremonial magic." However, all the witches known to Williamson seem to have been members of the one and only coven that we know was then in existence, the Southern Coven, and their description of the rituals exactly fits those in Gardner's Book of Shadows at that time; so there is no independent evidence here.

After Gardner had gotten over his discomfiture at realizing that Doreen had been able to spot all the Crowley quotations in his rituals, he defended their presence by telling her that the rituals he had received from the old coven were very fragmentary, and that in order to make them workable, he had to supplement them with other material. He had felt that Crowley's writings "breathed the very spirit of paganism" and were expressed in what he felt was "splendid" poetry (which provides an adequate measure of just how bad Gardner's literary taste was).

The publication of *Witchcraft Today* had brought Gardner some measure of fame, and more and more people were contacting him, asking for initiation into the "witch cult." He began to realize that he had a real chance to popularize his "Old Religion," but Doreen told him flatly that he would never do so as long as Crowley's influence was so obvious in the rituals, for the simple reason that Crowley's name and reputation stank to the heavens.

"Gerald's reaction was, 'Well, if you think you can do any better, go ahead.'" Doreen accepted the challenge and set out to rewrite the Book of Shadows, cutting out the Crowleyanity as much as she could and trying to bring it back to what she felt was a more genuinely pagan wording. She felt that the words from *Aradia* qualified in this respect, so she retained them as the basis for her new version of "The Charge," which she originally wrote in verse quatrains. However, people seemed to have some difficulty using this verse in rituals, and it was also rather short; so she later wrote what has come to be the much better-known prose version of "The Charge." She, or she and Gardner jointly, continued to work on rewriting the rituals in his Book of Shadows, ending up with the version that the Farrars labeled Text C. She notes in *Witchcraft for Tomorrow* (p. 21) that she and Gerald wrote the poem "Darksome night and shining moon" in 1954 or 1955.

For some time Gerald and she had been collaborating on a new book to follow *Witchcraft Today*. They proposed to call it *The Meaning of Witchcraft*. During 1956 she worked hard on the research and writing for it. The book did eventually appear under that title, in 1959, but by that time, she and Gerald had ceased working together. Her work was not a loss, though; much of it, transmogrified, made its way into her *Where Witchcraft Lives* in 1962, and her later books.

During 1956, two factions developed in the coven: a pro-publicity faction, consisting of Gerald and mostly newcomers; and an anti-publicity faction, consisting of Doreen and most of the other old-timers. Gerald's inability to be discreet with or even reasonably sceptical about reporters had been a long-standing problem, because the raunchiest of the tabloids sold by the checkout stands in American supermarkets are staid and scholarly in comparison with the exploitative journalism allowed in Britain; Doreen said that this was actually Dafo's major reason for ceasing to work with Gardner. These two subgroups also had somewhat different theories about how to run a coven; so in February 1957 (I was told by Robert), they divided the original coven in half, or Doreen hived a new coven off, depending on how you look at it, taking Ned and five or so others with her. At this time she also took with her all the correspondence, and all the operative Books of Shadows. (She wrote to me that, as far as she could remember, this chronology seemed to be about right.)

Robert also told me that the remaining members of the original coven soon thereafter decided to use the circle-dance-and-drop technique as their major way to raise power, rather than the bound scourging that had always been Gardner's favourite technique. As a result, Robert said, Gardner soon "wandered off" to initiate new priestesses and found new covens that would be more to his liking. The original coven has continued to exist; it was the coven studied by Tanya Luhrmann in her exceedingly scholarly *Persuasions of the Witches' Craft.*

At first the hiving off of the new coven had been a peaceful process, and the two covens continued to cooperate with one another, and to meet jointly on occasion. However, because of Gardner's publicity-seeking, tensions continued to rise; the old-timers feared the worst. As a last resort, Ned, Doreen's High Priest, drew up a set of proposals, entitled "Proposed Rules for the Craft," hoping that Gerald would agree to abide by them. Doreen typed them up, and sent them to Gerald in about June 1957. The text of these rules (which I discovered in Toronto) read as follows.

1. No member of the Craft will initiate any person unless that person has been interviewed by at least two Elders and accepted as suitable.

2. No affairs of the Craft will be discussed by members in the presence of uninitiated persons, or in places where conversation is likely to be overheard.

3. No copies of any papers relating to the Craft will be made or retained without the Elders' permission. Such papers as are permissible will be kept in a secure place.

4. As it is essential for the successful working of ritual by a group that here should be unity of purpose and an harmonious psychic atmosphere, members who create dissension and discord within the Craft will be asked to resign. Should they fail or refuse to do so they will be informed in writing by the Elders that they have been expelled.

5. No member of the Craft will give any information or interview about the Craft to any journalist or writer, or cause any such information to be

published in any way, without the approval of the Elders, nor will any of the Elders do so without the approval of the rest of the Elders.

6. If any member of the Craft feels that he or she has reason to complain of the conduct of any other member in matters affecting the Craft, or of any misdemeanour towards any member whilst on Craft premises, he or she will bring the said complaint to the notice of the elders as soon as possible. The Elders, after considering all available evidence, will, if they find the complaint justified, take appropriate action.

7. No member will be present at any meeting where the working is that of a higher Grade than he or she has attained, except by invitation of the Elders. These invitations will only be extended on very rare occasions where special circumstances exist.

8. No member will disclose the name and address or telephone number of any other member to any person whatsoever, without the said other member's previous permission.

9. Members will meet upon the traditional occasions, or as near to them as possible, and such meetings will be arranged by the Elders, or such Officers as the Elders authorise to do so. If the Elders be not present at such meetings, they will receive a report of them. Members may arrange other meetings for their private working if they so desire, but if more than two members be present at such a meeting the elders will receive a report of it. This report will take the form of a short letter to the Elders giving place and date of the meeting, names of members attending, and details of ceremonies carried out. Where convenient, verbal reports will be accepted.

10. Members will endeavour to acquaint themselves with the traditions of the Craft, and will not introduce innovations into the workings without the Elders' approval. Nor will the Elders give approval to any important innovation without first asking the approval of the rest of the Craft.

11. In the event of any member resigning from the Craft, he or she will honourably observe the Oath of Secrecy taken at initiation, and will also return to the Elders any written matter relating to the Craft which may be in his or her possession.

12. All members will receive a copy of these rules, and all new members will be given a copy of these rules upon initiation. New members, prior

to initiation, will read these rules and declare upon their honour that they will abide by them in letter and in spirit. This declaration will be made to the Elders in writing, and signed.

13. It will be understood by all members that these rules are equally binding upon all Grades of the Craft, including the Elders, and that serious and/or persistent breach of these rules will be grounds for expulsion.

Notice that here the term "Craft" must actually mean something like "coven" (in rules 4, 6, 10, and by implication, 9); that is, it is the affairs of a group not much larger than a single coven that are being dealt with here. In 1957 there was, for the first time, not a single small group, which could run by unwritten rules, but an organization, the "Craft," with at least two covens, which therefore needed written rules that all could agree on. Obviously, there were not so many members in all that the group consultations required by rules 5 and 10 would have been clumsy to carry out.

We can also suppose that some (if not all) of the things forbidden by these new rules had been happening; else why have a rule against them? That is, we can suppose that Gardner (or someone) had in fact been: initiating newcomers without having them screened; talking to the uninitiated, including reporters, about Craft business; passing out copies of the rituals; fighting with others in the circle; giving out personal information; holding secret or unauthorized rituals; introducing innovations without discussing them; refusing to abide by group decisions; and so on. In these circumstances, the Elders felt they had to insist on their authority to maintain order in the organization. It is obvious that the Elders wanted to have veto power over whom Gardner decided to initiate—which is what Rule 1 says—and that he had no intention of granting them that power.

Although Gardner did not like the Proposed Rules as such, the idea of having some sort of rules in the Book of Shadows apparently caught Gardner's fancy, and he began to work on the project. Certainly he would have felt that the new document had to be in the sort of flowery, formal, and often archaic-sounding language in which most of the other documents had been written. He would also have wanted it to look and sound traditional in itself. Furthermore, he would have wanted it to have some theological content—to be concerned with how a coven is to work magic—not be just a set of organizational rules. In order to have raw materials for writing it, he combed through his earlier writings, both the published books and various Book of Shadows documents, gathered together passages that had some connection with the concept of a traditional collection of laws that defined and governed the "Craft," and rewrote them.

Doreen writes that, after Gardner had received the "Proposed Rules," he prevaricated as long as possible, and then astonished them: from his museum in the Isle of Man he sent them a long document, with a message saying that there was no need for the proposed rules, because these "Laws of the Craft" already existed. The document, Doreen said, "was couched in mock-archaic language and ornamented with awesome threats of `So be it ardane' (meaning `ordained') and invocations of `the Curse of the Goddess' upon anyone who dared to transgress them"; so it clearly must be the same as the "Old Laws" included among the Weschcke documents. (However, it consisted, I believe, of only a first draft of the first of the two documents that make up the "Old Laws," ending with #88, and leaving out ##82 and 83, as numbered in *The Grimoire of Lady Sheba.*)

Doreen said that they were apparently supposed to be overawed. Their actual reaction was to be extremely sceptical. None of them had ever set eyes on these alleged "Laws" before, though they noticed that they incorporated the "Warning" from the Book of Shadows (see Section 3.12), which had always before been a complete document in its own right. They asked why, if these Laws were so ancient and authoritative, Gerald had never mentioned them before. The issue had become of confidence in Gardner, and the more they examined the alleged "Laws," the less confidence they felt. Doreen specifically rejected the passages (about "a man loveth a woman by mastering her" and retiring in favour of a younger woman) that she believed were sexist. Doreen believes that Ned wrote back to Gerald and told him that they regarded the alleged "Laws" as "an ad hoc invention of your own."

(I had realized in 1975 that if the "Craft Laws" had been in existence in July 1957, at least half of the "Proposed Rules" would not have been needed, and that the "Proposed Rules" therefore probably occasioned the writing of the "Craft Laws" sometime after mid-1957. I then carried out a technical analysis of the Craft Laws, included here in Chapter 8, and discovered that they had originally emphasized the authority of the Elders, just as the "Proposed Rules" did, and that the emphasis on the High Priestess had been introduced in a secondary reworking. Hence I was certain that the "Craft Laws" were based on the "Proposed Rules," and not vice versa. In her 1985 letter to *Iron Mountain*, Doreen denied that the "Proposed Rules" had anything to do with the Craft Laws, because she had not grasped that Gerald was being so devious that he had taken her and Ned's proposal, rewritten it into archaic language, and sent it back to them. I am glad that she has now confirmed my reasoning.)

Later, after Gerald was caught in a lie about yet more publicity seeking, and refused to admit he was lying, even in the face of independent proof, Doreen said that she and the rest of those who felt as she did went their own ways. Actually, during 1957 and 1958, Doreen and Ned were running their own coven independently of Gardner; it was not until some time later that she resigned from the Gardnerian Craft. In 1964 she began her period of working with Robert Cochrane, who claimed to belong to a type of "traditional" witchcraft that had existed before 1939.

Doreen was predisposed to believe Cochrane's claims because she still wanted to believe Gardner's basic claim, which serves as the Craft's foundational myth, that there had been an older coven before September 1939 that had survived from the past. She said that when she broke off from Gardner, "We had had enough of the Gospel according to St. Gerald; but we still believed that the real traditional witchcraft lived . . . that when Gerald said he had found an old coven surviving in southern England, he was telling the truth." She has repeatedly mentioned the testimony of Louis Wilkinson, and her own confirmation of the real existence of Dorothy Clutterbuck, as supporting her belief; but neither of these proves the existence of anything before 1946. Doreen Valiente continued to believe in the existence of traditional witchcraft before 1939 because that, for her, was an article of faith, and there is no evidence to disprove it. However, like the resurrection of Jesus of Nazareth, it does not qualify as an historical fact.[19]

Gardner in 1957-1960

Once Doreen had stopped working with him, Gerald began to rewrite the Book of Shadows rituals as he saw fit. It is these revised rituals, rather than Doreen's versions, that became the authoritative text of the Book of Shadows passed on to the covens in America. Gardner also proceeded to initiate a great many new High Priestesses during the last seven years of his life; these included Patricia Crowther, Eleanor "Ray" Bone, and Monique Wilson, "Lady Olwen." Some of these were well-accepted by his previous initiates; others were not. Doreen Valiente, for example, was good friends with Patricia Crowther, but never had any use for Monique Wilson. Other Gardnerian priestesses from that period whose claims can be verified have occasionally come to light as well.

Gardner's activities during these years are in some ways typified by his run-in with the Cardells, who apparently first approached the Gardnerians in early 1958, claiming to be Witches also, and proposing that they all pool their information on the Craft. The earliest reliable information I have been able to find about the Cardells and their relationship to the Gardnerian movement is in a letter in the files in Toronto. It is dated July 17, 1958, and is from Doreen Valiente (using her Craft name of "Ameth") to Dafo.

Dear Dafo,
Enclosed herewith is a copy of the latest edition of "Light", a well-known quarterly which was almost defunct, and has now been revived by Mr. Francis Clive-Ross of the Aquarian Press. You will see that it contains an article by Charles and Mary Cardell, called "The Craft of the Wiccens", and also a full-page advertisement inviting genuine members of that Craft to get in touch with the advertiser, Charles Cardell.

---

[19] Material quoted and paraphrased in this section from Valiente, *Rebirth of Witchcraft*, can be found on its pages 14, 36-40, 47, 57, 60-62, 66-72.

We are in touch with Cardell, both Ned and myself have had long talks with him, and he has asked us to forward to you a copy of his "Open Letter to Gerald Brosseau Gardner", which I do herewith. He accompanies it with a letter to yourself, which is rather dramatically expressed and calls for some explanation from us.

Firstly, he says that I will vouch for his integrity. I will vouch for the fact that I have seen him once, and had a long talk with him; further than that, I cannot say. I can only repeat what he told me on that occasion.

It appears that, according to him, his mother was a member of the genuine Craft of the Wiccens (he pronounces this word "Witchens"), and that when she died she left her Athame to him and her bracelet to his sister Mary, together with her traditions. I have seen both the Athame and the Bracelet. They are not the same as ours, but bear sufficient resemblance to be worthy of our attention.

His family came from Wales, but he is now living in Surrey, and also has a flat in London. Here he contacted Gerald, and told me that he had proposed to finance the bringing of Gerald's museum to London. However, he became disgusted with Gerald's publicity-seeking and the general behaviour of his followers. . . . He therefore broke with them and wrote to Gerald the "Open Letter" enclosed.

It appears that they [Gardner and his followers] made great play with you, as being the lady from whom originated the link with the old coven. However, when he very much wanted to be put in touch with you, they put him off repeatedly. . . .

Now, there is no doubt of Cardell's enthusiasm for the Craft. I have this morning a letter from Ned, who is a shrewd businessman and nobody's fool generally, as well as having a great deal of experience of the occult, in which Ned says he is convinced Cardell is genuine. I am never convinced of anything nor prepared to vouch for anything on the strength of one meeting; however, I personally liked Cardell, and his sister. I will go so far as to say that I have a completely open mind on the subject.

What the proposal is at the moment is that we get together with Cardell and pool our respective traditions. As you will remember, I wrote to you some time ago and told you very frankly of our feelings with regard to what we had received from Gerald. Your reply was so cautious that I could make neither head nor tail of it! So what we have been doing has been to try to get as close as we could to the spirit of the old beliefs, and try to feel intuitively what was right and real, and embody it in our rituals. We were engaged on this task when our contact came with Cardell.

Incidentally, we now have a good meeting-place which we are busy getting into the shape we want it; a matter I am very pleased about, though it will mean a lot of hard work.

Well, my dear, such are the latest developments. I trust you and yours are all well. "Blessed be ......"

Yours sincerely,
Ameth

Consider the second-from-last paragraph. The mention of traditions to be pooled reminds Doreen of her dissatisfaction with the "traditions" learned from Gerald, as well as with Dafo's cautiousness when questioned. Hence, during the 18 months since she and Ned had begun their coven, they have been trying to get close to the spirit of the old beliefs (there is a contrast implied with getting close to the letter; although Doreen believed such beliefs existed, they were unwritten), discover what was real about those beliefs by means of intuition, and them embody those discoveries in their rituals. Doreen's phrase about trying "to feel intuitively what was right and real" means that they really were trying to reconstruct and recreate what they believed to be an older religion, by means of intuition and imagination. This is typical of a search for religious authenticity.

Doreen did not believe that Gardner and the other members of the original coven had simply made up everything about the Craft; instead, she believed that there had been some sort of religious tradition preserved by an older coven. Hence her initial response, and that of the other initiates in the 1950s, to Cardell's claims was to hope that the claims were true, because they would then provide independent evidence that some sort of religious tradition had existed before 1939.

All the statements about Cardell I have seen indicate that he had used a trick common among con artists: he had simply taken the data in *Witchcraft Today*, augmented it with his own inventions, and taken it back to

Gerald and Doreen, claiming to have learned it from his mother. Doreen reported to me in a recent letter that Mary was, in fact, not Charles' sister, that they had been living together for thirty years as "brother and sister"; this shows that his story about what they had inherited from "their" mother was a fabrication. Gardner must, of course, have known that Cardell was spinning a tall tale, but he could not have said so without damaging his own credibility. Instead, he allowed Doreen and the others to believe that Cardell might indeed represent an independent witness to the existence of the Old Religion.

However, Doreen has written me:

> *"the more both Ned and I saw of Cardell, the less favourably we viewed him. I was invited to his `consulting-rooms' in Queen's Gate, London. They were quite splendidly appointed as a sort of private temple; but when Cardell showed me a bronze tripod which was obviously nineteenth-century and tried to tell me that it had been dug up from the ruins of Pompeii, I became rather unhappy. When he showed me a bronze statue of Thor and tried to tell me that it was of a Celtic horned god, I couldn't help myself pointing out that Thor was not a Celtic god—and then he became rather unhappy. There were a number of other things like this. And then Cardell crowned the performance by making a ham-handed and unsuccessfull attempt to hypnotize me. Well, I knew a trick worth two of that, and he didn't get anywhere. Now, give old Gerald his due, he never went in for that sort of 'deviousness'; so I was not favourably impressed. However, I kept on friendly terms with Cardell in order to find out what he was up to. And, of course, we eventually learned just how nasty he could be when he was thwarted."*

It thus became obvious to Doreen and the others that the Cardells had no independent information to pool, and were instead engaging in a ruse in order to get their hands on a Gardnerian Book of Shadows. When this ruse failed, the Cardells turned to another strategy, which is recorded (although in a strange way) in the pamphlet *Witch*, which is analyzed here in Appendix B. Essentially, he sent in a ringer named Olive Green who persuaded Gardner to initiate her and give her a copy of his Book of Shadows, which she took back to Cardell. Cardell then went into business teaching Witchcraft for money.

Gardner's Last Years: 1960-1964

Gardner's wife, Donna, died in 1960. Her health had been failing for some time, and so at some time in the late 1950s two of Gardner's initiates, Monique and Campbell Wilson, took over the fulltime tasks of housekeeping for him and running the Museum. (Doreen Valiente informs me that "Monique Wilson was no more old Gerald's niece than I am! . . . I don't know where the `niece' story came from.") When he died in 1964, they inherited his museum and his library of books and manuscripts.

From 1960 to 1963, now operating entirely on his own (not that Donna appears ever to have cramped his style), Gardner initiated a great many people, probably many more than have ever been publicly heard of. The most prominent of these late initiates, aside from the Wilsons, included, as I have already said, Arnold and Patricia Crowther, Eleanor "Ray" Bone, and Lois Hemmings.

Robert told me that the biography titled *Gerald Gardner: Witch* was actually written by Idries Shah, who, in addition to being a Sufi, is an expert on ceremonial magic. However, by the time he had finished the project, Shah seemed to be extremely puzzled and uncomfortable. In talking about why he had done the project, Shah said, "I have it from the highest authority [that is, on the inner planes] that this will be one of the most significant religions of this century." And then, Fred said, Shah got this bewildered look on his face, and said, "Personally, I can't see it"—and so he decided that he didn't want his name on the book, and instead let it be published under Jack Bracelin's name. (This story makes sense, since Bracelin's letters in the Toronto collection show that he was even more dyslexic than Gardner.) Perhaps another reason may be that the book is certainly not up to Shah's usual standards, since he had no way to check up on Gardner's stories.

Valiente records (1989, p. 80) that "I have to recognize that it was really the events when the old coven run by Gerald Gardner and myself split open like a ripe seed-pod and many people went their separate ways, which caused the dispersion of many new covens and many new ideas. Good therefore eventually came out of evil; and I am glad . . . that, after a period of not being on speaking terms, Gerald and I met again and were reconciled. We continued friends until his death. Gerald . . . did a great work in bringing back the Old Religion to many people. I am glad to have known him."

Gardner died while on a sea voyage in February 1964, and was buried in Tunis, Africa. Valiente (1989, p. 44) relates that some years later Eleanor Bone discovered that the cemetery he was buried in was about to be redeveloped; so she raised a collection among Britain's witches, and succeeded in having him reburied in a different cemetery, where he could "rest in peace."

In May 1964 appeared the first edition of Cardell's *Witch*, in which he published the names Aradia and Cernunnos as the secret names of the deities used by the Gardnerians. (This is certainly correct, else why would these names have been written in "Ye Bok of ye Art Magical" at the point in the third-degree initiation where the names are given?) I had thought when I first saw Cardell's *Witch* that the Gardnerians must have been forced by it to "change the locks" and so they have. Monique Wilson apparently did choose a new pair of names in 1964, and Raymond and Rosemary Buckland, who were initiated in the summer of 1964 (according to Margot Adler), were among the first to receive them. The Bucklands brought these new names back to Long Island, where they founded the New York coven, which became the centre of the Gardnerian Craft in America for the next two decades, and from which almost all Gardnerians in America are now descended. (Doreen Valiente confirmed, in a letter to Judith Harrow, that these two names were never used in the coven when she was in charge.)

Neither Gardner nor anyone else planned things to work out this way, but it is nevertheless unjust that the Craft in America traces its ancestry back, not to Doreen Valiente, but to Monique Wilson, "Lady Olwen," who contributed nothing of any importance to the Craft, as far as I can tell, and who disappeared from public view after selling the museum to Ripley's in 1971. She simply happened to be the person on duty at the museum when the Bucklands went for their initiation in 1964. The Alexandrians, we now know, trace their ancestry, via Pat Kopanski, to Patricia Crowther, who at least was one of Doreen's friends. I do not offhand know how this bit of injustice might be cleared up, but I think the Craft community ought to think about acknowledging Doreen Valiente's creative genius rather more clearly than has ever been done so far.

Chapter Four

The Book of Shadows in 1949

In this chapter I will examine what Gardner wrote in his Book of Shadows during the period between roughly 1946 and 1949. However, keep in mind that there is no single text of the Book of Shadows, because Gardner never bothered to word things the same way twice; whenever he copied something, he simultaneously rewrote it. That is how an author treats his own original material; it is not how anyone treats authoritative texts preserved from an earlier generation.

I will begin with the earliest known form of the Book of Shadows, the manuscript book labeled "Ye Bok of ye Art Magickal" that is now owned by the Wiccan Church of Canada. Its information can be supplemented by information derived from Gardner's second novel, *High Magic's Aid*, since the two were being written at the same time.

Physical description of "Ye Bok of ye Art Magical"

The manuscript book entitled "Ye Bok of ye Art Magical" which Derek Copperthwaite thrust into my hands in Toronto was not at all the sort of thing I was hoping or expecting to find. As a result, it was several days before I realized what I was looking at, and many months before I could grasp its implications.

BAM consists of almost 150 large sheets, folded and sewn into signatures; the resulting pages are somewhat larger than British legal size (8" x 13"). The signatures were then handbound (not very skillfully) into a leather book cover whose previous contents had been removed. On the front cover is inscribed the title (exactly as above); next appears a triangle above a pentacle, the Gardnerian symbol for a third-degree witch. In BAM only the first 240 pages are numbered, but i have continued the numbering system for convenience in the following description of BAM's contents, which is based on notes I took during my visit). Most of BAM consists of material from magical grimoires of a type not currently considered appropriate for the Craft; my notes on those pages were quite cursory, except for quotations from *The Greater Key of Solomon (GKS; abbreviations used in the notes are listed at the beginning of the Bibliography)."*

The contents of BAM are as follows. (The italicized numbers flag pages that are in careful calligraphy and are hand-illuminated. I will explain the asterisks later.)

1-5: a list of contents
6: blank
**7: the "warning," transcribed here as Document B.5[1]
8: a watercolor drawing of a Kabalistic talisman
9-11: quotations from Isaiah (40:21-22; 47:12-14; 62:5; 51:1)
*12-13: a note on circumambulation (perhaps from Crowley)
14-15: a passage from some work on magic
16-17: blank
18-19: another passage from a work on magic
20-21: blank
22-25: Instructions on making tools from *GKS*[2]
*26-27: "1st Oath" (that is, the oath for the first-degree initiation); included here in Document A.4
*28: the cakes and wine ritual, transcribed here in Document A.5
**29: instructions about scourging; transcribed here as Document B.3
30-33: on consecration of tools (from GKS?)
34-36: blank
*37: the words (only) for the Fivefold Kiss
38-43: quotations (II Kings 22:12-16; I Corinthians 12:23, 27-28, and 1:19; Revelation 2:26 and 21:7; a passage from Virgil; I Samuel

[1] I was able to photocopy only the pages that were most difficult to read; the rest I had to transcribe or just take notes on.
[2] I photocopied only p. 22, which gives the handle symbols from GKS; the rest I transcribed.

25:25; Hebrews 1:4; II Samuel 14:20, 23); these are largely passages that mention "witches" in the King James translation
44-45: ritual of the pentagram (from Crowley)
46-47: casting circle and beginning of the first-degree initiation; transcribed here in Document A.1
48: blank
*49: a Kabalistic seal
50-63 a long paraphrase of material from *GKS* and Crowley
*64: drawing of a magical circle
**65*: instructions for drawing a circle, adapted from GKS
66-69 on magical robes
70: blank
71-73: "Of the Ordeal of the Art Magical"
74: blank
75: a watercolor painting (pasted in) of the "Devil" card from the Waite/Smith Tarot deck; labeled "Baphomet"
76-90: a concatenation of passages from *GKS* on preparations for magical workings
*91: a revision of the first-degree oath; included here in Document A.4
*92: a watercolor drawing of the Rosy Cross
93: blank
94-99: the rest of the first-degree initiation; transcribed here in Document A.4
100: blank
101-106: the second-degree initiation; transcribed here in Document A.4[3]
107: blank
108-12: beginning of the third-degree initiation; transcribed here in Document A.4
113: blank
114-17: a passage from Crowley (?) on the scourge, dagger, and chain
118-24: passages from *GKS* on the sprinkler, and on salt and the bath
*125: unidentified; transcribed here as Document B.4

---

[3] I photocopied p. 105.

126-27: blank
128: beginning of a conjuration (continued on p. 143)
129: more Biblical passages: Judges 8:20-21; Isaiah 47:12-13 and
20:2-4:
130-31: blank
132-38: "Of the Bloody Sacrifice" (from Crowley?)
*139-40: a passage from *GKS* on wax and virgin earth
143-50: a kabalistic conjuration (continued from p. 128), in a language I do not recognize, with an interlinear translation[4]
**151-54: concerning chants, and "To Heal the Sick"; transcribed here as Documents B.1 and B.2
155-56: blank
157-61: a passage from the Lemegeton (a grimoire)
**162: some recipes
163-64: blank
165-88: sigils, painted in watercolors, from a grimoire
189-90: blank
191-93: another passage from Crowley
194: blank
195-202: notes about Kabalism
**203: on cats
204: blank
205-24: more watercolor sigils (continued from p. 188)
**225-27*: rest of the third-degree initiation (continued from p.112); transcribed here in Document A.4
228: blank
229-41: more watercolor sigils (continued from p. 224)
242: blank

---

[4] This document contains words written in Theban Script, a "magical alphabet" widely used in the Craft. Professor Robert Matheisen identified it for me as first appearing, as far as he knows, in Johannes Trithenius' *Polygraphia* (1518), from where Cornelius Agrippa borrowed it for his *De Occulta Philosophia* (1533?; Englished in 1651). It was then borrowed, with much else from Agrippa, by Francis Barrett, published in his *The Magus* in 1801, and has been reprinted often since then.

*243:	watercolor drawing of the Kabalistic tree
244-47:	blank
248-59:	a long passage on Kabalism
260-62:	blank
263-68:	"Leviter Veslis"; transcribed here as Document A.3
269-70:	blank
271-88:	rituals for the four Great Sabbats; transcribed here as Document A.6

The rest of the pages in BAM (a dozen or so) are blank, except for some pencil sketches of floor plans near the end.

Now, what can we make of this hodgepodge of ceremonial magic and Craft rituals? Is this a Book of Shadows? If not, what is it?

Looking at the preceding list of contents, from about p. 126 on I see a pattern to the way the blank pages appear: after every entry, of however many pages, there are two to four blank pages, three whenever the entry ends on a lefthand page. Probably Gardner followed this pattern (though not strictly) throughout the book at first, but later, when it began to get full, he started to use pages that had been left blank. The asterisks flag pages that would have been blank at first if this general pattern holds true.

Next, if we skip over all pages flagged with asterisks, the first place in BAM where we find material that would nowadays be included in a Book of Shadows is on page 94, a third of the way through BAM. Pages 94 to 112 (plus 225-227) are done in the most careful calligraphy in the book: not at all high art, but rather pretty. In complete contrast, the pages flagged with double asterisks not only fall into the probable pattern of blank pages, but are very carelessly written; and even on the pages of careful calligraphy, later notes are scribbled in ball pen. Page 7, for example, is almost illegible. All unflagged pages are written neatly, but not in fancy calligraphy.

How can we explain the wild differences in attitude revealed by these differences in penmanship? (The curtain is lowered and raised to signify the passage of several months in thought.) Suppose Gardner put this manuscript book together sometime during or after World War II, intending it to be a magical workbook, and at first entered only information about ceremonial magic in it. (The Toronto collection includes about half a dozen hand-illuminated manuscript books consisting of material that Gardner had copied from various grimoires and other sources.) By hindsight, I can observe that the principle of selection operating in BAM is that the procedures copied into it can be carried out by one or a few persons. That is, Gardner was thinking about how magic could be worked by a small group. Then, on pp. 94 to 112, suddenly the Craft initiation rituals appear, and are completed later in the book, where there is more room. The book looks old and impressive (from a few feet away, at least), and has obviously been put together to be used "liturgically": where better to write out the initiation rituals in a form that can actually be used? Presumably this illuminated manuscript dates from the time when Gardner had begun initiating members of his coven.

The rituals are heavily disguised by the way they are entered in BAM. For the most part, key terms are indicated only by single ornate letters. There is no indication that page 94 continues page 47, or that 225 picks up from 112; a person unfamiliar with the Craft would not easily realize that these are all parts of the same rituals. Hence these versions in BAM must precede *High Magic's Aid* (HMA), in which the first-degree and second-degree rituals were published in full, with no disguise; once they had appeared thus, there would no longer have been a reason to disguise them.

Except for the initiation rituals and the material at the end of BAM (on pages 263-288), all the data that would be considered appropriate for a current Book of Shadows (including the passages from GKS that were, as we will see, raw material for the rituals) fall on pages that had at first been left blank. As the book gets more and more full, the entries on the "blank" pages become more and more careless—by this criterion, page 7 would have been the last written. About 1952, the material appropriate for what is now the Craft was copied into a new master book (the one that Stewart Farrar labeled Text A[5]), and BAM was then used as a notebook for drafts of material that would go into *Witchcraft Today* or into Text B. Soon after Doreen Valiente was initiated,

[5] See the Farrars 1984, p. 3, on this useful terminology.

BAM, no longer appropriate for use in rituals, too full to be useful as a notebook, was pensioned off into the back of a closet, where it was found by the Ripley's team; thus it was preserved, to provide the clues to unravel the puzzle. The Wilsons, who arrived after it had been retired, probably didn't even know it existed. Doreen Valiente told me that Gardner had never mentioned its existence to her.

BAM therefore did not begin its life as a Book of Shadows, but it ended up as one; in fact, it is the prototype, the one most important for my purposes in unraveling the history of the Gardnerian movement. There were no other Books of Shadows among the Ripley's holdings.

Being unsure in the fall of 1975 what they were going to do with BAM, the Ripley's staff did not feel comfortable about my photocopying more than a small fraction of the pages in the manuscript. Most of the pages in the initiation rituals were written in a very bold hand, to be readable from a few feet away; it was not hard for me to transcribe those pages by hand. The remaining pages, too complex for such a transcription, were few enough that Ripley's allowed me to photocopy them.

Doreen Valiente does own the Books of Shadows that Gardner was using when he and Dafo initiated her in 1953. The older of them (which Stewart Farrar labeled Text A) is more or less the Book of Shadows as it stood in 1949; Gardner led Doreen to believe that he had copied it from Dorothy Clutterbuck's Book of Shadows, but the extant evidence is that Dorothy never had any such book. The second book (which Farrar labeled Text B) is much fuller, and is essentially the Book of Shadows as it stood in 1953. The inventory of their contents has provided another control on my reconstruction.

As I observed, and as Doreen Valiente also comments, Gardner habitually copied rituals into his books piecemeal, on widely separated pages, often onto pages containing other material as well. What his reasons were for doing this one can only guess, but it did provide some protection for the "secrets," since a person not already familiar with the Craft, upon picking up such a book, would not be able to make head nor tail out of it. For these reasons, I am here placing materials in an arbitrary order in order to simplify my discussion of them, although we need to remember that the passages in the most careful calligraphy are probably the earliest, and the ones least carefully written the latest. I have tried to reproduce the documents exactly—and I must admit that I find it very difficult to remember to misspell words as consistently as Gardner did. Gardner's single letters are quite ornate. Square brackets indicate my insertions, numbering of paragraphs, etc., and curly brackets {these things} flag passages written in "Theban script."

A.1. Casting the Circle

The procedure in use before 1953 for casting the circle is described in general terms in *Witchcraft Today* on p. 28. This passage says, "It is most convenient to mark [the circle] with chalk, paint or otherwise, to show where it is; but marks on the carpet may be utilised. Furniture may be placed to indicate the bounds. The only circle that matters is the one drawn before every ceremony with either a duly consecrated Magic Sword or ... [an] Athame... The circle is usually nine feet in diameter, unless made for some very special purpose. There are two outer circles, each six inches apart, so the third circle has a diameter of eleven feet." This triple circle is derived from the procedures in *The Greater Key of Solomon*,[6] and so we can be sure that the procedure for casting the ceremonial magician's circle given in *High Magic's Aid* is also the basic procedure for casting the witches' circle. The fact that there was originally a triple circle is the reason why the circle is cast, censed, or otherwise circumambulated three times at various points in these instructions. Page 65 of "Ye Bok of ye Art Magical" reads as follows:

> *[1] Having chosen a place proper, take the sickle or scimitar of Art* or a Witch's Athame, if thou mayest obtain it, *and stick it into the center, then take a cord,* and 'twere well to use the Cable Tow for this, and loop it over the Instrument, four and one half feet, and so *trace out the circumference of the circle, which* must *be* traced *either with the Sword, or the knife with the black hilt,* or it be of little avail, but ever

[6] Ronald Hutton has been able to establish that Gardner obtained a copy of *The Greater Key of Solomon* only in May 1947; so all the rituals that use or depend on it must have been written in late 1947 or 1948. However, the entries about other matters in the first 94 pages of *BAM* could be a year or more earlier than mid-1947.

leave open a door *towards the North*. Make in all 3 circles, one within the other, and write names of power between these.

This follows the instructions in *The Greater Key of Solomon* (p. 103); the italics indicate identical wording. However, the reference to the Cable Tow, which is a Masonic term for a cord used to partially tie and lead an initiate in a ritual, is Gardner's own insertion, replacing the *Greater Key of Solomon* reference to a simple piece of string used as a compass. Gardner uses the Cable Tow in his initiation rituals quite differently from the way it is used in Masonic ritual (as we will see later); and the reference to it is inserted here in order to integrate the binding and scourging that characterize his initiations more firmly into the overall ritual.

Next, page 46 of "Ye Bok of ye Art Magical" gives the procedures for charging the circle, as we would now call it. These are terse and

Text	Comments
[2] First draw circle with M[agic] S[word] or Athame.	[as in paragraph 1]
[3] Consecrate Salt and Water: Touch water with Athame, saying, "*I exorcise thee, O creature of Water, that thou cast out from Thee all the impurities and uncleannesses of the Spirits of the World of Phantasm, so they may harm me not, through the virtue of God almighty who liveth and reigneth unto the Ages of the Ages. Amen.*" [4] Touching Salt with Athame, say, "*The Blessing of the Father Almighty be upon this creature of Salt, and let all malignity and hindrance be cast forth hencefrom, and let all good enter herein, for without Thee man cannot live,*	[These formulas are from *The Greater Key of Solomon*, pp. 93 and 94. They are actually formulas for preparing the bathwater, and are given as such in *High Magic's Aid* (pp. 144, 265f). Doreen Valiente says (in the Farrars 1984, pp. 41-42) that some of the "names of power" are also written in Text A; Gardner included them by mistake, since *The Greater Key of Solomon* says that they are to be recited while disrobing or in the bath.]

wherefore I bless thee and invoke thee, that thou mayest aid me."

[5] Then put the Salt into the water.

[6] Sprinkle with exorcised water.

[7] Light candles / say, "*I exorcise thee, O Creature of Fire, by Him through Whom all things have been made, so that every kind of Phantasm may retire from thee, and be unable to harm or deceive in any way, through the invocation of the Most High Creator of all. Amen.*"

[From *The Greater Key of Solomon*, p. 106.]

8] Caution initiate (if any) warn companions; enter circle and close doors with 3 pentagrams / saying "Agla / Azoth / Adonai."

[This refers to the instructions in *The Greater Key of Solomon*, pp. 103-104, immediately after the passage that paragraph [1] is based on. The business of warning the companions is another element from GKS; for example, p. 16 says, "the Master should reassemble his Disciples . . . and exhort them to fear nothing, and to keep in the places assigned to them"—the general idea being that it is dangerous to leave the protection of the circle while evil spirits are being summoned. That is, in this earliest-known outline of the casting procedure, we still find a Christian concept of what the circle is for, not the obviously later Craft concept of the circle as a reservoir for the energy being raised.]

[9] Ritual of pentacle (p. 44).

[The reference here is to a "pentacle consecration" of the kind given by Crowley, *Magick*, pp. 379-382, or by Regardie, *Golden Dawn* (I, 106f, and III, 9-19).]

[10] Proclaim object of working

[11] Circuambulate 3 times or more before commencing work.

[12] Summon: "*I summon, stir, and Call thee up, thou Mighty Ones of the East, South, West, and North*" *saluting and* [diagram of pentacle to be drawn in the air with the magic tool, with an arrow indicating the first stroke to be from top down to left].

[A longer version of this summoning is given in *High Magic's Aid* (pp. 269f) as part of a ceremonial-magic ritual; it is based loosely on the conjurations given in *The Greater Key of Solomon,* pp. 18-35. The rule that "witches start in the East when forming the circle" (*Witchcraft Today*, p. 25) also derives from magical practice, since the sequence E, S, W, N is prescribed in *The Greater Key of Solomon* (e.g., on p. 97), by the HOGD (Regardie, *Golden Dawn*: e.g., I, 106ff), and by Crowley, *Magick*, pp. 282, 328.]

cryptic, and refer to data from *The Greater Key of Solomon* that Gardner had copied onto yet other pages. Written out in full, they read as follows.

Commentary on A.1.

The procedures here are those of Judaeo-Christian (i.e., Kabalistic) ceremonial magic, not of what is now thought of as Neopagan Witchcraft. The specific procedure given here for casting a circle to work in could come from *The Greater Key of Solomon* (e.g., pp. 14f, 96f, 103) or from almost any grimoire. The overall sequence follows closely that of *The Greater Key of Solomon*, pp. 15-17. That is, we have here precisely the situation described in *High Magic's Aid*, in which the male magician must form the circle before the female witch can work her initiation rituals.

There is no indication here of who is to carry out these procedures. Presumably the circle will be cast and charged by whoever is doing the initiating, which appears to be the sole reason for casting the circle at first. Hence the circle would be cast and charged by the Magus when he is initiating a new Witch. Further, a later draft of the casting procedure from about 1957 specifies that the Magus is to cast the circle; so we may suppose that such a rule also applied in 1949.

I have added paragraphs [3] to [5] in order to include the procedures for "exorcising" the water that are written out elsewhere in "Ye Bok of ye Art Magical"; the text on p. 46 actually leaps from [2] to [6], but logically the water must be "exorcised" before it can be sprinkled.

It could not be more obvious that Gardner has adapted the casting procedure here from *The Greater Key of Solomon*. As the Farrars (1981, p. 37 n.1) sagely comment, "That these were Gardner's own borrowings, rather than part of the traditional material he obtained from the New Forest coven which initiated him, is suggested by the fact that their English corresponds to that of Mathers, instead of deriving independently from the original Latin."

The casting procedure in "Ye Bok of ye Art Magical" shows us in miniature the origin of the Craft movement: we do not have an originally pagan ritual that has been disguised by Christian trappings; rather, Gardner began with a Judaeo-Christian ritual that he later "paganized" by removing the obviously Judaeo-Christian terms, and replacing them with terms that appear more neutral. This is also an analog for the fact that the Craft movement arises from dissatisfaction with Christianity.

Gardner obviously feels that a ritual has to be worked in a "magic circle," but the only procedures he knows for casting such a circle are from books on ceremonial magic, as is described in *High Magic's Aid.* If he had learned any "traditional" procedures for casting a circle from an earlier coven, he would have used them instead of borrowing procedures, formulas, and Judaeo-Christian terminology alike from the *Greater Key of Solomon.* That is, if there had been an earlier coven into which Gardner was initiated, its members either did not cast a circle to work in or else simply used the procedures of ceremonial magic. Either alternative flatly contradicts Gardner's claim in *Witchcraft Today* (p. 28) that whereas

> *"the magician... draws a circle... and summons... demons to do his bidding, the circle being to prevent them from doing him harm, and he dare not leave it... the Witches' Circle... is to keep in the power which... they can raise from their own bodies [so that] they can mould it to their own will. They can and do step in and out if they wish to, but this involves some loss of power, so they avoid doing so as much as possible."*

We therefore see in both *"Ye Bok of ye Art Magical"* and *High Magic's Aid* a situation in which Judaeo-Christian magic—which at least has a coherent theology, if its underlying assumptions are granted—provides a framework, a circle, within which non-Christian folk magic can be worked. The trend that we can see beginning with these early documents, and that is still continuing, was to find concepts that could both "explain" folk magic and be used to replace the obviously Judaeo-Christian concepts that came from the tradition of ceremonial magic.

Looking at how Neopagan Witchcraft actually functions these days, we can see that the purpose of the circle is not to keep anything in or out, but (using Eliade's concepts) to define a "sacred space" within which "worship"—something other than ordinary, workaday activities—can take place. The Craft term for this, already stated in *Witchcraft Today*, is that "the circle is between the worlds." The Craft circle is a far more portable "sacred space" than a church building.

It seems appropriate to also discuss the origin of "athame," which here appears for the first time. It is the name that Gardner uses for the black-handled "Knife of the Art" described in GKS, p. 98. The white-handled knife that Gardner says is also a "witch tool" likewise comes from GKS. The symbols that go on the Athame (given by GLS, p. 10; by Farrar 1971, p. 39; or by Huson, p. 52) as part of its "consecration"—currently "charging"—come from the diagram on p. 99 of GKS, which is reproduced on the endpapers of HMA. The "traditional Gardnerian sword," drawn on p. 59 of Buckland, comes from p. 100 of GKS.

The etymology of the word Athame seems to be unknown. It does not appear in de Laurence's American edition of GKS. Valiente (1973, p. 43) says that a 1572 MS. of GKS in the British Museum gives it as "Arthana"—but presumably such a MS. would be in Latin; she does not mention this in discussing the origin of the term in 1978 (pp. 78-79).

Professor Robert Matheisen suggests that a more likely source is Grillot de Givry's *Witchcraft, Magic and Alchemy* (1931, translated from a slightly earlier French original; it was also reprinted by University Books in the 1960s), which uses the term *"Arthame"* in several places. De Givry has derived the term from an eighteenth-century manuscript of the Key of Solomon, no. 2350 in the Bibliothèque de l'Arsenal in Paris, and even gives a photo (fig. 74) of a page on which the term can be read. Matheisen says further, "I think that 'Arthame' is the oldest term, and that Gardner's `Athame' and Leek's 'Athalme' represent attempts to spell what was heard by them, but not seen in writing."

Arkon Daraul suggested an Arabic source, from adh-dhamme, "the bloodletter," but this seems farfetched, especially since he also suggests that "coven," a perfectly ordinary English word, might be derived from an Arabic word that means "shroud"! Still, Professor Matheisen's learned colleague David Pingree came up with the same possible etymology, though translating it as "the bloody [thing]."

It is possible that the word might have some connection with the Greek athanatos, "immortal," or with the name Athamas (with which it is identical, save for the case ending), the legendary husband of Leukothea, whose name means literally "the white goddess" (whence the name that Graves used for an entirely different concept).

A.2. Drawing Down the Moon[7]

The invocation of the Goddess appears in "Ye Bok of ye Art Magical" only buried within one of the Sabbat rituals, and in very terse form. Spelled out, it would read as follows.

High Priestess stands in front of Altar, assumes Goddess position (arms crossed).
Magus, kneeling in front of her, draws pentacle on her body with Phallus-headed Wand, invokes,

> *"I Invoke and beseech Thee, O mighty Mother of all life and fertility. 'By seed and root, by stem and bud, by leaf and flower and fruit, by Life and Love, do I invoke Thee' to descend into the body of thy servant and High Priestess [name]."*

The Moon having been drawn down, i.e., link established, Magus and other men give Fivefold Kiss:

(kissing feet) *"Blessed be thy feet, that have brought thee in these ways";*
(kissing knees) *"Blessed be thy knees, that shall kneel at the sacred altar";*
(kissing womb) *"Blessed be thy womb, without which we would not be";*
(kissing breasts) *"Blessed be thy breasts, formed in beauty and in strength";*
(kissing lips) *"Blessed be thy lips, that shall speak the sacred names."*
Women all bow.

[This would then be followed by some instruction: If there be an initiation, then at this time the High Priestess in Goddess position (Arms Crossed) says the Charge while the Initiate stands outside the circle, or else the Magus reads it if the Initiate be a girl].

A.3. "Lift Up the Veil" [The Charge]

The following gives Gardner's original wording of the Charge, from pp. 263-68 of "Ye Bok of ye Art Magical." This is the text that Doreen Valiente rewrote into verse, then later into a new prose version.

---

[7] The Fivefold Kiss is only referred to by name in BAM, although the words (with no stage directions) are written out on its p. 37; all of which shows that it was an established ritual procedure by the late 1940s. The version here is from HMA, p. 293, where it is described in full detail.

Leviter Veslis[8]

List to the words of the Great Mother who of old was also called among men Artimis: Astarte: Dione: Melusine: Aphrodite and by meny other names[9].

At mine Altars the youth of Lacedmonia and Spala made due sacrifice.

'Whenever ye have need of anything, once in the month, and better it be when the moon is full. They ye shall assemble in some secret place and adore the spirit of me who am Queen of all Witcheries.

'There ye shall assemble, ye who are fain to learn all Sorcery, yet have not won to its deepest secrets, to those will I teach things that are yet unknown.

'And ye shall be free from slavery, And as a sign that ye be realy free, ye shall be naked in your rites, both men and wemen, And ye shall dance, sing, feast make music, and love, all in my praise.'[10]

For ecstasy is mine, and joy on earth.

For 'love is my law.' 'Keep pure your highest ideal: strive ever toward it.[11] Let naught stop you or turn you aside.

There is a Secret Door that I have made to establish the way to taste even on earth the elixir of immortality. Say "Let exstacy be mine, and joy on earth even to me, To Me"[12] For I am a gracsous Goddess. `I give

---

[8] This title is garbled Latin, apparently intended to mean something like "Lift up the robe."

[9] This speech (and a later one) are not in the first-person voice of the goddess who speaks all the rest. Nowadays, when the Charge is read aloud during a Craft liturgy, these two lines (which have not been changed much) are read by a Priest, whereas the rest is read by a Priestess. The double quotes appear in the text in BAM; I have introduced single quotes to flag material whose sources I have identified.

[10] These three paragraphs are a close quote from Leland's *Aradia*.

[11] The first phrase here is, of course, from Crowley's motto, "Love is the law . . .," and the Farrars (1981, p. 42-48) identify the rest as being from Crowley's essay "The Law of Liberty."

[12] These are Gardner's quote marks but I have not identified what he is quoting; it is probably from Crowley.

unimaginable joys, on earth certainty, not faith while in life! And upon death, peace unutterable, rest, and ecstacy, nor do I demand aught in sacrifice.'[13]

Hear ye the words of the Star Goddess.[14]

'I love you: I yearn for you: page or purple, veiled or volupluous.

'I who am all pleasure, and purple and drunkenness of the innermost senses, desire you, put on the wings, arouse the coiled splendour within you, "Come unto me."

'For I am the flame that burns in the heart of every man, and the core of every Star.'[15]

Let it be your inmost devine self who art lost in the constant rapture of infinite joy.

'Let the rituals be rightly preformed with joy and beauty.'[16] Rember that all acts of love and pleasure are my rituals. So let there be beauty and strength, leaping laughter, force and fire be within you.

And if thou sayest, I have journied unto thee, and it availed me not, Rather shalt thou say, I called upon thee, and I waited patiently, and Low, Thou wast with me from the begining For they that ever desired me, shall ever attain me, even to the end of all desire."[17]

[This would be followed by a short paragraph of instruction such as the following: this much of the rites must ever be performed to prepare for any initiation, whether of one degree or of all three].

Commentary on A.2 and A.3.

It seems simplest to comment on A.2 and A.3 together, since they normally fall together in a ritual. In A.3 we have the original draft of the

---

[13] This sentence is from Crowley's *Book of the Law* (Regardie, 1974, p. 82), no. 58. It made more sense the way Crowley punctuated it.

[14] Again, to be spoken by the Priest or Magus.

[15] The preceding three paragraphs (from "I love you" on) are strung-together quotes from *CGM*, p. 351. Gardner seems to intend to indicate he is quoting, since there is a double quote just before "I love you."

[16] *CGM*, p. 351.

[17] Some of the other lines in the second half of Document A.3 may also be quotes from Crowley that I have not been able to track down, but even if they are, we've already reached overkill.

liturgical element usually called the "Charge of the Goddess." Since it is in careful calligraphy in "Ye Bok of ye Art Magical," it is probably an early entry. It was probably written about the same time as the initiation ritual (which it follows, and which we will look at next), that is, before 1948, and it was certainly written before 1953, when Gardner read it during Doreen Valiente's initiation.

Since Document A.3 is in careful calligraphy, it is probably an early entry in BAM, especially since it follows immediately after Document A.4. It certainly must have been written before 1953, when the manuscript of *Witchcraft Today*, which contained a rewriting of it, went to the printer. All the various rewritings of the Charge from 1953 on were, we now know, the work of Doreen Valiente.

What about content? The quotation in A.2 is from Crowley's "Gnostic Mass" in *Magick in Theory and Practice*. The first long quotation in A.3 is from Leland's *Aradia*, and the rest are from Crowley: first a sentence from the *Book of the Law*, no. 58, then the rest from the "Gnostic Mass." If Gardner had received anything comparable to this material from an older coven, why would he need to lift material wholesale from published sources? Notice that the line about Lacedaemon and Sparta is Gardner's own insertion, not a quotation from anything. He adds it as an attempt to claim a classical precedent for the scourging in the ritual: the allusion is to the whipping of youths before the altar of "Upright" Artemis—which was not done for "ecstasy"! All the rest of the material is a homily validating the Great Rite; hence the Charge does not make a great deal of sense if it is recited when the Great Rite (or something equally powerful) is not going to be worked. That is, the Charge was written in order to create a framework for the binding and scourging in the initiation, and as a theological justification for the Great Rite.

A.4. The Initiation

The earliest known text of the Craft initiation rituals appears in "Ye Bok of ye Art Magical," on pp. 46-47, 91, 94-99, 101-106, 108-112, and 225-27. I have augmented the text for the first two degrees from the full script in *High Magic's Aid*, pp. 290-303; these additions are enclosed in <these> brackets.

[First Degree][18]

<Magus leaves circle by the doorway, goes to Postulant, and says, "Since there is no other brother here, I must be thy sponsor, as well as priest. I am about to give you a warning. If you are still of the same mind, answer it with these words: `Perfect Love and Perfect Trust.'">

P[riest] O thou who standeth on the threashold between the plesent world of men and the Dread Lords of the Outer Spaces, hast thou the courage to make the Assey? (places sword point on the postulants heart) ffor I say verrly / it were better to rush on my Sword and perish misrably / than to attempt it with fear in thy heart/

Postulant. I have the Pass words. P[erfect] L[ove] and P[erfect] T[rust]

P[riest] <drops the sword point, saying> All who approach with p[erfect] l[ove] and p[erfect] t[rust] are doubly welcome/ (Assumes position of enterer) <Going around behind her, he blindfolds her, then putting his left arm around her waist and his right arm around her neck, he pulls her head back, says> And I give you the 3rd p[ass] w[ord] a K[iss] to pass through this dread Door/<and pushes her forward with his body, through the doorway and into the circle. Once inside, he releases her saying, "This is the way all are first brought into the circle."> (They pass through in position of Enterer)[19]

M[agus] and W[itch] enter in position of enterer. M[agus] places W[itch] in N[orth, fforms C[ircle], preforms Ritual of Pentagram. <Magus closes the doorway by drawing the point of the sword across it three times, joining all three circles, saying, "Agla, Azoth, Adonai," then drawing three pentacles to seal it.>

[Magus] summon Guids W[itch] to C[enter], Ajjusts C[able] T[ow], <Magus guides Postulant to south of altar, and whispers, "Now there is the Ordeal." Taking a short piece of cord from the altar, he ties it around

---

[18] The text of the "first-degree" ritual is from pp. 47 and 94-99 of *BAM*.

[19] "Enterer" probably refers to one of the "ritual gestures" of the HOGD system or some other Masonic ritual. Here p. 47 ends; the next line begins p. 94. The opening instructions on p. 94 duplicate most of those on pp. 46-47, which apparently constitute a later rewriting of the beginning of the ritual, and were inserted into some blank pages earlier in the book.

her right ankle, saying, "Feet neither bound nor free." Taking a longer cord, he ties her hands together behind her back, then pulls them up, so that the arms form a triangle, and ties the cord around her neck, leaving the end dangling down in front as a Cable Tow.>

[Magus] Circuambulats, Proclaims to 4 quarers. <With the Cable Tow in his left hand and the sword in his right hand, the Magus leads her sunwise around the circle to the east, where he salutes with the sword and proclaims> Take heed O Lords of the Watch Towers of the C[ircle], 'n' properly prepared Will be iniated P[riestess] and W[itch]

<Magus leads her similarly to the south, west, and north, making the proclamation at each quarter.>

[Magus] Returus to A[ltar].[20] Strike Bell/

<Next, clasping Postulant around the waist with his left arm, and holding the sword erect in his right hand, he makes her circumambulate three times around the circle with a half-running, half-dancing step. He halts her at the south of the altar, and strikes eleven knells on the bell.>

M[agus then kneels at her feet, saying,] In other religions the postulant kneels, as the Priests claim supreme power, but in Art Magic, we are taught to be humble, so we kneel to welcome them. 5S [Fivefold Kiss] Blessed be, etc.[21]

Take measure[22] [thus: height, around forehead, across the heart, and across the genitals.]

---

[20] Or perhaps the symbol here is an S (for South?). Note that to this point the initiation has covered the same eight steps as the circle casting (in A.1), but in the order 3, 1 (+2), 4 & 5, 8, 7, 6. Hence the initiation as such begins here, and the preceding business would be used to begin the second or third-degree rituals if they were worked separately.

[21] That is, the Fivefold Kiss is worked here, and so would not have been worked earlier if there is to be an initiation.

[22] "Take measure" is squeezed in between two lines, that is, added later. It refers to a magical procedure of measuring someone with a cord, then keeping the cord as a magical hostage.

[Magus says], Be pleased to kneel, Ajjusts to Alter[23] [drawing of circles] [Magus helps her kneel before the altar. He ties the end of the Cable Tow to a ring in the altar, so that the postulant is bent sharply forward, with her head almost touching the floor. He also ties her feet together with the short cord.]

M[agus] <strikes three knells on the bell and says>, Art ready to swere that thou wilt always be true to the Art?

W[itch]. I am. 7 Knells, [bell] Take measure[24]

<Magus strikes seven knells on the bell and says> Thou must first be purified. <"Before ye are sworn, art willing to pass the ordeal and be purified?"

Witch: "I am.">

11 Knells [drawing of bell, scourge, circles]

<Magus strikes eleven knells on the bell, takes the scourge from the altar, and gives a series of three, seven, nine, and 21 strokes with the scourge across the postulant's buttocks, and then says, "Ye have bravely passed the test.> Art alwaws ready to help, protect, and defend, thy Brothers and Sisters of the Art?

W[itch] I am.

[omitted nowadays][25]

M[agus] Art armed?

W[itch]. With a knife in my hair.

M[agus]. Then on that knife wilt thou swear absolute secrecy[?]

---

[23] "Adjusts Cable Tow" or "Adjusts to Altar" always means that the postulant is tied down in a full crouching position, head on floor, with the cable tow tied to the altar, as is spelled out in Farrar 1971, p. 15, or *HMA*, p. 293.

[24] "Take measure" was squeezed in between the lines here. There is obviously some rewriting going on.

[25] This is actually written one line higher up, in between "the Art" and "I am." But it clearly refers to the following three lines of dialogue, which do not appear in any of the printed versions, including *HMA*, and are flagged by curved lines in a thin point in the margin. On the significance of these three lines, see the commentary.

W[itch] swears.[26]I, 'n' in the presence of the mighty ones of the outer spaces do of my own free will most solomly swear that I will ever keep secret and never reveal the secrets of the Art, Except it be to a worthey person / proper prepared within a circle such as I am in now / and that I will never deny these Secrets to such a person if they be vouched for by a brother or Sister of the Art / Also, under no circumstance whatever will I ever reveal to anyone not of the Art / the names of any brother or sister of the Art / This I swear by my hopes of a future life and my weapons turn against me if I break this my solom oath / And I am mindfull that my measure has been taken.

M[agus] Asists to rise. <Magus now unbinds her feet, unties the Cable Tow from the altar, removes the blindfold, and helps her up to her feet.>

M[agus]. With O[il], W[ine], and k[isses] I hereby Sign and Concecrate Thee.

<Magus says, "I hereby sign thee with the triple sign. "I consecrate thee with oil." (He anoints her with oil on the womb, the right breast, the left breast, and the womb again.) "I consecrate thee with wine." (He anoints her with wine in the same pattern.) "I consecrate thee with my lips" (he kisses her in the same pattern), "Priestess and Witch.">

[Magus] Removes C[able] T[ow].[27] <Magus now unbinds her hands and removes the last cord, saying>, Now I Present to thee the Working Tools, ffirst the M[agic] S[word]. With this, as with the Athame thou canst form all M[agic] C[ircles], dominate, subdue and punish all rebelious S[pirits] and D[emons], and even persuade the A[ngels] and

---

[26] Here, judging from *HMA*, occurs the first-degree oath that *BAM* records on pp. 26-27 and (somewhat expanded) on p. 91, which is what I have inserted here.

[27] The next line in *BAM*, before "Now," begins with an illuminated drawing of a point-down triangle, representing the breasts and genitals, the points to be consecrated by oil, wine, and kisses; to its left has been written in a thin point "Priest & Witch." In Duncan, after the oath, the blindfold and cable tow are removed.

G[eniuses]. [Kiss][28] With this in your hand you are the ruler of the C[ircle] [Kiss].

Next I present the A[thame], this is the true W[it]ch's weapon and has all the powers of the M[agic] S[word] [kiss].

Next I present the W[hite] H[andled] K[nife]. Its use is to form all instruments used in the Art. It can only be properly used in a M[agic] C[ircle] [Kiss].

Next I present the W[and]. Its use is to call up and control certain A[ngel]s and g[eniuse]s, to whom it would not be mete to use the M[agic] S[word] [Kiss].

Next I present the [drawing of pentacle]s.[29]These are for the purpose of calling up approprite S[pirit]s [Kiss].

Next I present the Censer of Insense. This is used to encourag and welcome G[ood] S[pirits] and to banish E[vil] S[pirits].

Next I present the [drawing of scourge], this is the sign of power and dominance, it is also to cause suffering and purification, for it is written, to learn you must suffer and be purified. Art willing to suffer to learn?

---

[28] I translate Gardner's ornate S by "[Kiss]" throughout. Despite *HMA*'s clear interpretation of this as meaning that the Priest (or Priestess) kisses the Witch being initiated, some variations on this ritual have the initiate kiss each tool. Notice that the concept of magic in the preceding sentence, and throughout this speech, is precisely that of Judaeo-Christian ceremonial magic: that magic is controlling spirits.

[29] The symbol here is an illuminated pentacle in a circle.

W[itch]. I am. [Kiss]

M[agus]. next, and lastly I present the C[ords], they are of use to bind the s[igils] in the A[rt], also the material basis, to enforce thy will. Also they are necessary in the oath.[30] I Salut thee in the name {of the gods}[31] Newly made P[riestess] and W[itch]. 7 Knells [Bell] [Kiss]. Circuambulate and proclaim to 4 Quarters, Hear, ye Mighty Ones, 'n' hath been consecrated P[riestess] and W[itch] of the GG.[32]

Note, if ceremony ends here add [drawing of pentacle, with arrow indicating first stroke to be from lower left to top], Hail and farewell. If not go to next degree[33].

---

[30] The cords are needed for the binding and scourging that precedes the oath, as described in detail in *HMA*, pp. 292-294. In *Witchcraft Today*, pp. 134-5, we find, "There are three working tools which are essential and nothing can be done without them; that is, something to cut and stab with, something to strike with, and something to bind with. There are five others, all of which have their special uses and are only needed if that particular kind of work is being done. For an initiation all eight must be present and the initiate is told the use of, and holds, each in turn."

[31] Here is written "V, V, V, V, V," then "of the Gods" in Theban Script. The secret names of the Horned God and Goddess that are the passwords of the initiated Gardnerian Witch are not recorded here in BAM. Professor Robert Matheisen informs me that such a use of V's goes back to Crowley also, e.g., Book Four, p. 101

[32] "Of the GG" was added later; it probably means "of the Gods" also.

[33] Here a curious symbol is drawn: a point-down triangle, containing a Venus symbol at the top, and a rectangular box divided by crosslines into four quadrants at the bottom. The note is written surrounding it. It is probably just decoration.

[Second Degree][34]

Form C[ircle] and preform Ritual of Pentagram around celebrants.[35] P[riestess] asumes Oisrus position. [36] usualy dispensed with now[37].

M[agus], Ere we proceed with this sublime degree, I must beg purification from thy hands. 5S [Fivefold Kiss], Blessed Be.

P[riestess] ajjusts C[able] T[ow], Circuambulates 3 [drawing of scourge][that is, the Priestess scourges the Magus]

M[agus] Ajjusts C[able] T[ow], Cir[cumambulates], Proclaims <Magus binds Witch as before, but does not blindfold her, and circumambulates with her, proclaiming to the four quarters> Hear ye Mighty Ones, 'n' Duly consecrated P[riestess] and W[itch], is now properly prepared to be consecrated H[igh] P[riestess] and W[itch] Q[ueen].

Return to South, Ajjust to Altr. <Magus now leads her thrice around the circle with the half-running, half-dancing step, halts south of the altar, has the Witch kneel, and ties her down to the altar as before.>

M[agus]. To atain this sublime degree, it is nesscery to suffer and be purified. Art ready to suffer to Learn?

P[riestess] W[itch], I am.

M[agus] Be pleased to Kneel.

P[riestess] kneels at Altar.

M[agus], I prepare the to take the great oath.

Striks 3 Knells on bell [drawings of bell and scourge] 3, 7, 9, 21

---

[34] This document comprises pages 101 to 106 of BAM.

[35] Notice that this line "calls the subroutine" for casting the circle, and so it applies only when this initiation is being worked by itself.

[36] The "Osiris" position means "with arms crossed over chest," and usually with scourge in one hand, wand in the other. The descriptions of it in Gardnerian writings are vague about it (see, e.g., *WT*, pp. 29, 84, 92; Farrar 1971, p. 64), but it derives conceptually from the ritual positions of the HOGD magical system.

[37] This comment was written later, off to the right. It applies not to the preceding line, but to the following one, about the initial scourging of the Magus by the Priestess. If dropped, what remains is the bit of ritual described on p. 92 of *WT*: the Fivefold Kiss is given to the Priestess as she stands in the Osiris position.

[circles].[38] <That is, he strikes three knells on the bell, and again gives the series of three, seven, nine, and 21 strokes with the scourge as before.>

<Magus: "I now give thee a new name: _______. [kiss]>

Repeat thy new name after me, I, 'n,' sweare upon and by mine honour among men and among my brothers and sisters of the Art, that I will never reveal to any at all, any of the secrets of the Art, except it be to a worthy person, properly prepared, in the centre of a M[agic] C[ircle], such as I am now in, This I swere by my hope of Salvation, my past lives, and my hopes of future ones, and I devote myself to utter distruction if I break this my solome oath.

M[agus] kneels, placing left hand under 'n's knees and right hand on head, thus forming magic link.

M[agus] I hereby will all my power into you. Wills.[39] [circles] Asists to rise. <Magus now unties her feet, unties the Cable Tow from the altar, and helps the Witch to her feet.>

M[agus] I hereby sign and consecrate you with the great M[agic] S[ign] [here appears a drawing of a point-down pentacle in a circle]. Rember how it is formed and you will always recognize it. [kiss] ["I consecrate thee with oil." (He anoints her with oil on her womb, right breast, left hip, right hip, left breast, and womb again, thus tracing a point-down pentacle.) "I consecrate thee with wine." (He anoints her with wine in the same pattern.) "I consecrate thee with my lips" (he kisses her in the same pattern), "High Priestess and Witch Queen."[40]

Removes C[able] T[ow]. [Magus now unbinds Witch's hands and removes the cord, saying] Newly made H[igh] P[riestess] and W[itch] Q[ueen] [kiss] you will now use the working tools in turn.

First the M]agic S[word] with it you will scribe the M][agic] S[ircle] [circles; kiss]

---

[38] This is forty strokes, as emphasized in later versions of this initiation. Most references to the number 40 in Gardner's writings have something to do with scourging.

[39] This bit of folk magic comes from *WCWE*, p. 78.

[40] Consecration added here from *HMA*, p. 302, and, e.g., Farrar 1971, p. 86.

Secondly the Athame,[41] [kiss] [circles]

Thirdly, the W[hite] H[andled] K[nife] [kiss] [circles]

ffourthly the W[and] [kiss] [circles]

ffifthly the P[drawing of pentacle] [kiss] [circles]

Sixthly the C[enser] of I[ncense] [kiss] [circles]

Seventhly the [drawing of scourge] S [kiss] [circles] You must use this now in token that in the Art you should ever give as you receive, threefold, So where you received 3, return 9, where you received 7, return 21, where you received 9, return 27, where you received 21, return 63.

Eightly the C[ords]. [kiss]

H[igh] P[riestess] Ajjusts C[able] T[ow][that is, Witch binds Magus and ties him to Altar.] Circuambulates 3. [drawing of scourge and circles][42]

[Magus] Tho hast obeyed the Law. <But mark well, when thou receivest good, so equally art bound to return good threefold."

Witch now unbinds Magus and helps him to his feet.

Magus, taking the new Initiate by the hand and holding the Athame in the other, passes once round the Circle, proclaiming at the Four Quarters, "Hear, Ye Mighty Ones, (name) hath been duly consecrated High Priestess and Witch Queen.">

(Note, if ceremony ends here, close circle with "Hail and farewell." If not go to next degree.)

[Third Degree][43]

It is well to take cakes and wine first. As in previous Degrees, form Circle around celebrants.[44] H[igh] P[riestess] assumes Osirus position.

---

[41] The initiate uses the Athame and the next four tools to complete the casting and charging of the circle, as described in *HMA*, p. 302.

[42] Here the Priestess actually gives 120 strokes with the scourge, as described in *HMA*, p. 303.

[43] This appears on pages 108-112 and 225-227 of *BAM*.

[44] Here again appears the odd "asterisk" symbol; these sentences are written around it, and so were added later. Again, all this is needed only if the "third degree" is being worked by itself.

M[agus] kneels 5S [Fivefold Kiss] Blessed Be.[45]

M[agus] Ere we proceed with this sublime degree, I must beg purification at thy hands.

H[igh] P[riestess] Ajjusts C[able] T[ow] [circles]. Circuambulates 3 [drawing of scourge]. [That is, High Priestess binds Magus and ties him down to the altar. She circumambulates three times, and scourges Magus with three, seven, nine, and 21 strokes. She then unbinds him and helps him to his feet.]

M[agus] Ajjusts C[able] T[ow] [binds the High Priestess and ties her down to the altar]. Cir[cumambulates] [Magus scourges High Priestess with three, seven, nine, and 21 strokes.] Proclaims. to 4 Quarters. Hear ye mighty Ones, the twice consecrate and Holy 'n', H[igh] P[riestess] and W[itch] Q[ueen] is properly prepared and will now proceed to erect the Sacred Alter.

Cir[cumambulate] 3 Ajjusts to Alter. It is better to be again purified. [drawing of scourge and circles] Cakes and wine may be taken.[46]

M[agus] Now I must reveal to you a great Mystery. [kiss]. (note: if H[igh] P[riestess] has preformed this rite before, omit these words.)

H[igh] P[riestess] Asumes Osirus position.[47]

M[agus] Assist me to errect the Ancient Altar, at which in days past all worshiped, the Great Altar of all things. for in the old times [here we see an illuminated Star of David] was the Alter. Thus was the alter made and so placed and the sacred place was the point within the centre

---

[45] After the Fivefold Kiss, the symbols written here appear to me to be a heart, a T, and a heart. Doreen Valiente pointed out to me that this was Gardner's way of writing "O.T.O.", which was his flag for the cakes and wine ritual, which had come directly out of Crowley's Gnostic Mass; and the "Blessed Be" is attached to the Cakes and Wine, being the response upon passing or receiving the cup. The first line was then added later to make the point clear to some other reader.

[46] Except for the scourge symbol, everything from "it is better" to "taken" has been added later. That is, Gardner later added yet another scourging of the Magus, i.e., himself.

[47] To the right of this line appears a set of illuminated concentric triangles, point down. These probably represent the female genitalia.

of the circle, as we of old times have been taught,[48] that the point within the centre is the origin of all things. Therefore should we adore it. [kiss] 'Therefore, whome we adore, we also invoke, by the power of the lifted lance.'[49] Invokes.

'O circle of stars [kiss], whereof our Father is but the younger brother [kiss]. Marvle beyond imagination, soul of infinate space, before whome time is ashamed, the mind bewildered and understanding dark, not unto thee may we atain unless thine image be love [kiss]. Therefore, by seed and root, and stem and bud and leaf and flower and fruit do we invoke thee,' 'O, Queen of space, O dew of light, O continuous one of the Heavens' [kiss]. 'Let it be ever thus, that men speak not of Thee as one, but as none, and let them not speak of thee at all, since thou art continuous,' for thou art the point within the circle [kiss], which we adore [kiss], the fount of life without which we would not be [kiss]. And in this way, truly are errected the Holy Twin Pillars B[oaz] and jj[achin] [kiss]. In beauty and strength were they erected, to the wonder and glory of all men. [Eightfold Kiss: 3 points, Lips, 2 Breasts and back to lips; 5 points]

M[agus] 'O, Secrets of secrets that art hidden in the being of all lives. Not thee do we adore, for that which adoreth is also thou. Thou art that and That am I [kiss]. I am the flame that burns in evry man, and in the core of every star [kiss]. I am Life and the giver of Life, yet therefore is the knowledge of me the Knowledge of Death [kiss]. I am alone,' the 'Lord within ourselves whose name is Mystery of Mysteries' [kiss]. 'Make open the path of intelligance between us.' For these truly are the 5 poinst of fellowship,[50] {feet to feet, knee to knee, groin to groin,

---

[48] Do notice that an *old* ritual could not contain any such line.

[49] From here to the middle of p. 226, the Magus' speech is a pastiche of quotations (indicated by single quote marks) from *CGM*. This line is from p. 349; the following five are from pp. 350-352.

[50] Here from "Make open" to "Fellowship" is written to the left, and on the right appears an illuminated diagram of the point-up triangle above the pentacle, which is the Gardnerian symbol for the third degree. What follows is written in the form "F X F, K X K," etc. The Five Points of Fellowship are from a Masonic Blue-Lodge initiation; see Duncan, p. 121.

breast to breast, arms around backs, lips to lips}. By the Great and Holy Name V, V, V, V, V, {Abracadabra, Airdia & Cenvnnos}.[51]

M[agus] and H[igh] P[riestess]: 'Encourage our hearts, Let thy Light chrystalise itself in our blood, fulfilling of us Resurection.' 'For there is not part of us that is not of the Gods.'[52]

Closing the Circle

H[igh P[riestess] Circuambulate. Proclaime. The twice consecreate H[igh] P[riestess] greets ye Mighty Ones, and dismisseth ye to your pleasant abodes, Hail and Farewell. [Here again is the diagram of the pentacle to be drawn, the first stroke being from lower left up to the top.][53]

Commentary on A.4.

The First-Degree Initiation is now the most widely published of all the Gardnerian rituals, having been described in more or less complete detail by Glass, Johns, Holzer, Huson, the Farrars (1971 and 1984), and *The Grimoire of Lady Sheba.* Its first full publication, however, was in *High Magic's Aid* (pp. 290-296) in 1949; so 1948 is the latest date at which it could have been written.

The text in "Ye Bok of ye Art Magical" is actually the draft on which the expanded and cleaned-up version in *High Magic's Aid* is based. Many revisions made in a narrow point in "Ye Bok of ye Art Magical" were also made in the version in *High Magic's Aid*; and passages marked "not

[51] The second and third names are written in ball pen, above and to the right of the five Vs. Professor Robert Matheisen also points out that "Abrahadabra" is given in Crowley, *Magick*, p. 329; and Judy Harrow tells me that it can be construed as Hebrew.

[52] Again, quotations form *CGM*, pp. 352 and 360. In the first, Crowley actually wrote, "fulfilling us of ..." Farrar 1971 (p. 93) reproduces Gardner's reversal of the two words here, which shows that Sanders' version is based on Gardner, and not directly on Crowley.

[53] The final formula, for closing...Closing the circle, is based on the "license to depart" of ceremonial magic (e.g., on pp. 38 and 52 of *The Greater Key of Solomon*). A different version of this formula appears on p. 296 of *High Magic's Aid*

used" (or some such) in "Ye Bok of ye Art Magical" are not reflected in *High Magic's Aid*. On the other hand, some changes in "Ye Bok of ye Art Magical"— for example, those about taking the measure — were not made in *High Magic's Aid* at all, and yet they appear in later versions of the ritual; so they must have been entered in "Ye Bok of ye Art Magical" after *High Magic's Aid* had gone to the printer in about 1948. And since this initiation ritual is apparently the earliest of the "Craft" entries in "Ye Bok of ye Art Magical", it follows that the rest of the "Craft" entries in "Ye Bok of ye Art Magical" must postdate 1948. Given a book with no dates in it at all, this is a good beginning for a chronology for the Gardnerian rituals.

Next, let's consider whether anything here probably comes from a native British non-Christian religious tradition (or something like that). Much light can be shed on this question by considering a ritual with a similar purpose, the Neophyte ritual of the Hermetic Order of the Golden Dawn, as given by Regardie, *Golden Dawn* (II, 12-43). For the most part, the Golden Dawn rituals seem quite unlike current Craft rituals, since they consisted mainly of long set speeches full of metaphysical moral uplift. However, the Neophyte ritual contains so many similarities to the Gardnerian first-degree initiation that we must suppose Gardner used something like it as a source (indeed, at this time we can suppose that he specifically used rituals from the Society of the Inner Light). Let us list these similarities, in order.

1. An Officer purifies by sprinkling the temple, East, South, West, North.
2. Another Officer censes the temple, in the same pattern.
3. All the Officers circumambulate the temple three times.
4. The candidate (C) is led in, blindfolded, and with a threefold Cord about his waist.
5. C is given a new name.
6. C is purified by being sprinkled, consecrated by being censed.
7. C is made to kneel and repeat an oath of secrecy, from which we can pick out phrases: "I... in the presence of ... do of my own free will... most solemnly promise to keep secret... Furthermore, if I break this, my Magical Obligation, I submit myself... " and there are some relevant

phrases in later oaths: "never to reveal the secrets... save in" (p. 165) and "if I fail... may... my power in Magic cease" (p. 215).

8. C is led sunwise around the circle 1.5 times from North to South, where he is stopped, challenged, and sprinkled and censed again. He is then led sunwise 1.25 circuits to the West, where he is stopped, is threatened with a sword, and has to give a password, which his guide supplies for him. He is then led 1.25 times around to the North, and 1.25 times around to the East, where the two procedures are repeated, but in the East the threat is made with a scepter. He is then led to the altar at the centre.

9. All including C kneel, and the Hierophant invokes the "Mighty One."

10. C is raised to his feet, has the blindfold removed, and is formally accepted into membership.

11. C is then shown various secrets.

12. C is sprinkled and censed again, has the Threefold Cord removed, and is given the badge of his degree.

13. C is proclaimed a new initiate to all present.

14. The temple is then "closed" by a withershins circumambulation.

We can also find some exact correspondences with Masonic rituals as described by Duncan, pp. 29-34:

> *"the Senior Deacon... presents one point of the compasses to the candidate's naked left breast... The Deacon... puts a rope, called a cable-tow, once round his neck, letting it drag behind... Senior Deacon asks if candidate is "duly and truly prepared, and properly vouched for." ... The candidate, having been brought in, is conducted once around the Lodge, in the order east, south, west (and presumably ending in the north)...The candidate takes an oath containing the words, "I ... of my own free will... in the presence of [God and saints] most solemnly... swear that I will always... conceal, and never reveal, any of the arts... of the hidden mysteries... except to a true and lawful brother... in a regularly constituted Lodge... All this I most solemnly... swear...without any mental reservation ... binding myself under no less penalty that of [gruesome details]... should I ever knowingly violate this my... obligation."*

P. 41 of Duncan says: "it is necessary that you should have the working tools of an Entered Apprentice." The ruler and hammer are then shown and explained to the new Apprentice. The homilies on the "emblems" are even more similar to what follows here. Almost all the Masonic symbols are referred to as "working tools." Furthermore, the third degree in the Blue Lodges is referred to repeatedly as a "Sublime degree".

To reinforce all this, let us notice two passages from Dewar's article on "Masonic Ceremony": "The drama of the third initiation ceremony is the most powerful of the craft degrees" (p. 101); in the "third-degree working," a death and rebirth are enacted, then "the candidate is read a charge," and is asked to "demonstrate the secret signs of their degrees" (p. 103).

Now, it cannot be claimed that these similarities are fortuitous, that all initiations into secret societies will be more or less similar in general. The similarities here are both specific and numerous, occur in the same order, and include the almost identical phrases in the oaths. The only element actually needed for a "mystery initiation," after all, is an oath of secrecy. Many of the other elements here—the blindfold, the new name, the censing and sprinkling, challenge with a sword and password given by guide, the showing of "secrets," the formal proclamation-are perfectly obvious as possible elements for such a ritual. But that all should happen to occur, and in the same order, in the two rituals is quite outside the bounds of probability. Hence Gardner must have used some such Masonic ritual as his major source for this initiation ritual. If he had been initiated into an earlier coven by means of some other sort of ritual, why would he not have used that ritual here?

Now that we have identified the Masonic and Golden Dawn elements in this ritual, let us consider Gardner's own additions.

1. The triangle binding of the arms behind the back is Gardner's own addition. It is simply the way he liked to be bound while being scourged.

2. The scourging of forty strokes is Gardner's addition. There is no reference to scourging in any Masonic or magical ritual that I have yet seen.

3. The integrating of the scourging into the oath-taking is Gardner's addition.

4. The presenting of the scourge and the cords as magical tools is Gardner's addition. The presenting itself is Masonic, and all the other tools come from *The Greater Key of Solomon*, but not the scourge or cords.

5. In the second-degree ritual, Gardner would have given the woman initiate forty strokes, but she would then give him 120.

6. In the third-degree ritual, after having some cakes and wine, Gardner and the new High Priestess again give each other forty strokes, and this leads to sexual intercourse, at the words "groin to groin."

"Hear a plain truth:" does it not seem obvious that Gardner included all this scourging because he could not "work the Great Rite" without it? As Gibson says (p. 269), "the whole point of the exercise is to overcome impotence and, having been whipped to erection, the 'victims' are as a rule only too happy to effect penetration of the nearest complacent vagina." Furthermore, Gardner created a type of "witchcraft" that usually proceeds by "working a script" because that was the situation demanded by his sexual needs. Gibson goes on to say, "The beatings... are, invariably, ritualistic in character. Nothing unforeseen is ever allowed to happen, and the ceremony, carried out with great solemnity, proceeds according to a set plan, any variation in which would result in a loss of meaning, power, and effectiveness: the spell would be broken, the magic dispersed. Spontaneity is totally absent from these performances." Gibson is here describing a prostitute beating a client—but any "orthodox" Gardnerian will immediately recognize this description as being typical of Gardnerian circles as well.

Let me draw a corollary: anyone who can have sex without being scourged has no reason to include scourging in the initiation or any other ritual.

Leaving the scourging aside, we can see that in this third-degree ritual we are dealing with a genuinely sacramental attitude toward sexuality, not an exploitative one. This heightening of significance, from "mere sex" to sacrament, is the reason for all the quotes from Crowley's "Gnostic Mass" in the third section of the initiation. Gardner does not include this third-degree ritual in *High Magic's Aid*, but he does hint at it when he has Morven say (p. 300), "after that, there is what is called a degree. There is no oath, and all who have taken the second degree are qualified to work it, but 'tis the quintessence of Magic, and 'tis not to be used lightly, and then only with one whom you love and are loved by, may it be done, all else were sin."

Unlike all the Masonic ritual, the concept of sexual intercourse as initiation actually might come from a genuinely pagan tradition. Sex magic has long been used to promote fertility of crops and flocks (and I beg off from providing references on this point). Fertility magic and initiation overlap in the concept of the "sacred marriage," where the King (embodying the people) and the Queen (embodying the homeland) consummate their marriage for the benefit of the cosmos. We find this concept reflected in the Irish coronation ritual, in the Akitu Festival of Babylon (as described by Gaster), and, of course, in the vision of the Marriage of the Lamb and the New Jerusalem in the Apocalypse of John, which is the particular source of the marriage imagery in the Liturgy of the Eucharist.

In fact, where sexual intercourse occurs as part of a "pagan" or non-Christian religious initiation, it is always used during the first initiation that the person undergoes (as among the Ozark witches), not the second or third; hence the procedure here, in which the new witch is taken through all three stages at once, is actually much closer to what is known of pagan or witch initiations in general than the later pattern (of initiations separated by a year and a day) would be. However, the historical probability is that Gardner had the concept from Crowley, who in turn had it from P.B. Randolph.

It is clear from the way this initiation procedure is written in BAM that it was originally intended to be worked as a single initiation, all in one evening, as some of Gardner's earliest priestesses have described. English Gardnerian covens have only two degrees in practice, one upon beginning training, one upon graduating as a High Priestess. The "third degree" was and is worked as an independent form of sex magic. However, having the training process begin with a sexual initiation is far truer to folk-magic witchcraft and pagan religions in general than is the present Gardnerian system, in which the sexual initiation is delayed for years or sometimes forever.

Professor Robert Matheisen of Brown University first pointed out to me the significance of the three lines flagged by note 24. Consider: how would one normally "swear on" a physical object? Obviously, by placing one's hands on it. The implication is that the witch would swear by placing at least one hand on the knife in her hair. But she could do so only if, at that point in the ritual, her hands are free. This contradicts the earlier instruction that the witch had to be bound. So what is going on here? It looks as if Gardner must be rewriting an earlier version of this initiation in order to work in the binding and scourging, and had not realized at first that this business about the knife in the hair conflicted with that. It could be argued that this change is evidence that Gardner was rewriting an earlier ritual—but was it from an earlier coven? Since there is no other evidence for the existence of such a coven, it would violate parsimony to assume its existence. Rather, it is far more probable that Gardner is here revising a ritual that he himself wrote, and that he simply had not realized at first that the dramatic business with the knife in the hair would interfere with his real agenda of introducing scourging whenever possible.

What about those names? In Toronto, as I leafed through "Ye Bok of ye Art Magickal," when I reached the point in the Third-Degree ritual where the names would be given, what I saw was a name written in Theban script in gold, outlined in red, with some additional writing in Theban script entered in ballpen above it and to the right. It looks most impressive—and my heart sank. "Oh, my God!" I thought. "He did write the secret names in here." I thought I might be able to find a copy of the Theban script somewhere in Gardner's library — but time was short; so I just transcribed the Theban letters.

That evening, in writing a note to Derek Copperthwaite about what I had discovered in looking over the holdings, I included a warning that, if my suspicion about these names were correct, allowing the book to be published in full would do the Gardnerians a great disservice, since their "quality control" in their tradition depends primarily on their being able to keep these names secret, and thus being able to tell who has genuinely been initiated into their tradition and who has merely made use of some of their Book of Shadows.

When I had returned home again, in my first spare minute I grabbed a book with the Theban script, sat down with my notes, and set to work decoding. In a few minutes, the name lay before me, and it was...

(I had the great pleasure one evening of telling this story to two Gardnerian High Priestesses, Alison Harlow and Margot Adler. By the time I reached this point, they were, naturally, on the edge of their chairs, mouths wide open, ready for the worst.)

The name was: Abracadabra!

I fell back in my desk chair, and roared with laughter. It is an incredible experience to have your leg so thoroughly pulled by a "booby trap" set thirty years ago.

(Likewise, Margot and Alison, when they heard "The Name," simply collapsed, and rolled on the floor, shrieking with laughter. Finally Alison recovered enough to say, "Oh, Aidan, yes, you've discovered the truly secret name! Abracadabra!" and they were off again, howling. Now, these two ladies are my friends, and I know they weren't pulling my leg — their glee was too heartfelt — but the part of me that appreciates a good practical joke insists that "Abracadabra" might not be a bad choice for a secret name. It was a magical name for the Gnostics. It would be easy to keep secret, because who would want to admit it in public? And even if someone did, who would believe it?)

I was glad to be able to write to Derek Copperthwaite, calling off my "red alert" — but the story's not finished. There were also those Theban entries in ballpen on the page in question, and these, when decoded, turned out to read "AIRDIA & CENVNNOS," that is, the names given out by "Rex Nemorensis." Had he, in fact revealed the secret names? I asked Alison and Margo about this also — when they had calmed down — and they assured me that these were similar to one pair of the lesser names, but not the truly secret ones. I still wonder, however, if these were not the names then being given as the third-degree passwords, why were they written on this crucial page, in code?

T.C. Lethbridge thought he knew the secret name used for the Goddess. On page 62 of his *Witches*, he wrote,

> *"I happen to have been told the name under which the modern witches adore Diana, but since they are not supposed to divulge it, I think it would be unfair to mention it here. Their reticence, however, seems to me to be unnecessary, for it does not appear to be the secret name of the goddess. It seems to translate without difficulty from a garbled Celtic into 'The Lady of the Summer Pasture.' No one could use it to work magic against her."*

Now, in the Ripley's files is a letter from Lethbridge to Gardner dated June 15, 1959. It reads in part as follows.

> *"Is not this the Gaelic 'Airaidheach,' or something similar, meaning 'The Lady of the Summer Pastures'? In the same way that Cailleach is the 'Lady of the Woods'? She would be the same as the Irish Macha, who must have been 'The Lady of the Fertile Plain.' In the highlands and islands the people moved up to the airaidh for the summer grazing... The difficulties all hinge on the danger of using the real names for fear of hostile magic. Isis had 10,000 names, and Macha over 30. But if this explanation is correct, the witches need have no fear in mentioning [it], for it is not the goddess' real name, but just a roundabout way of saying who they are talking about."*

Perhaps Lethbridge misunderstood the import of a hypothetical question— but I doubt it. More likely Gardner approached Lethbridge, a Cambridge don and one of the few scholars in the world then inclined to be friendly toward the Craft, in order to get an expert opinion on the meaning of an obscure name, and had to take him into confidence in order to do so. Hence these probably were the secret names until "Rex" destroyed their usefulness as shibboleths, and they had to be replaced.

A.5. Cakes and Wine

[This consists of p. 28 of "Ye Bok of ye Art Magical." It is in a penpoint and calligraphy almost identical to that on p. 47 of BAM, and hence is fairly late.]

Of the Wine[54]

M[agus], Kneals / ffills C[up]/ Offrs to W[itch] /[55]
W[itch] / Holding A[thame] betwen palms, places point in C[up]/
M[agus] As the a[thame] is the M[ale]/ So the C[up] is the ff[emale]/ So, conjoined they bring blessedness /
W[itch],/ lays aside A[thame], and takes C[up] in both hands drinks / and gives drink/
M[agus] Holds Paten to W[itch], who blesses with A[thame] / then eats and gives to Eat /

The sources of this consecration are Judaeo-Christian. Placing the athame in the cup comes from Crowley's "Gnostic Mass" in *Magick in Theory and Practice*, pp. 356f, 359f (though it comes from the Grail legends). Crowley'wanted to attack the orthodox Catholic Mass, but the concern here is to emphasize the similar and inherent goodness of wine, cake, and sex. In the Magus' speech, sex is glorified as the greatest sacrament. The phrase in the Sabbat rituals about "the Great rite . . . in token" refers to this consecration, as is common knowledge in the Craft.

A.6. The Sabbat Rituals

On pages 271-288 in BAM are outlines of rituals for the four Great Sabbats, that is, the four Celtic festivals. I did not copy these four rituals by hand during my visit to Toronto in 1975, since it is obvious they are not traditional. Instead, I took only some notes on some interesting points. In giving the text here, I am working from photographs of the pages taken by Professor Robert Matheisen, and from a transcript of BAM done by a member of the Wiccan Church of Canada, a copy of

54 This appears on p. 28 of *BAM*. To the left of this title appear the symbols heart, T, heart, which Doreen Valiente told me was Gardner's way of writing O.T.O.

55 As we will see later, the "things done" left undescribed here are that the Priestess is seated on the altar, holding her athame, and the Priest kneels before her, holding up the cup.

which was sent to me by Professor Mathiesen in 1991. The transcript was carefully done, but the transcriber could not resist the temptation to correct some of Gardner's misspellings.

November Eve Halloween

H[igh] P[riest] leads H[igh] P[riestes]s. He carries a pirapus, or broom, head up to represent one, walk or slow dance, torches + bonfire if possible.

Bazabi lacha bachaba.[56]
Lamach cahi Achaba
Karrelos
Lamach Lamach Bachaous
Cabahagy Sabalyous
Baryolas
Lazoth Athame[57] *Cabyolas*
Samahac et Famyolas
Harrahya

Form [circle symbol] H P assumes position
H P says B[l]essed be [the feet . . .] [scourge symbol][58]
[High Priestess:] 'Dread Lord of the Shadows, God of Life + the Giver of Life. Yet is the Knowledge of Thee the, the Knowledge of Death. Open wide I pray Thee Thy Gates through which every man must pass, Let our dear ones who have gone before return this night to

---

[56] This "Bazabi lacha" chant appeared in *HMA,* p. 291, at the beginning of the initiation ritual. It seems to have been lifted from a fifteenth-century play about witches in Spain, I think, via Grillot de Givry's *Magic, Witchcraft and Alchemy*, whose errors Gardner has reproduced, as Professor Matheisen points out to me. Michael Harrison, best known as a Baker Street Irregular, exercises far more ingenuity than the topic is worth in *The Roots of Witchcraft* in trying to demonstrate that the poem is a bit of Basque folk poetry.

[57] The appearance here of "Athame" is suspicious; I suspect it does not appear in the original text.

[58] Since "H P" is used twice, it is strictly a matter of interpretation as to who works the Fivefold Kiss, and who scourges whom. However, it must be the priestess who here "draws down the Sun" on the priest.

make merry with us, + When our time comes, As it must. O Thou, the Comforter, the giver of Peace + rest, we will enter Thy domains gladly + unafraid, for we know that when rested + refreshed Among our dear ones, we are reborn Again into this life, with sturdier limbs + keener brains, by Thy Grace + by the Grace of the Great Mother. Let it be in the same place + time as our beloved ones, + may we meet + know + remember + love them again. Descend we pray Thee upon Thy Servent + Priest[59]

5S [Fivefold Kiss]

Initiations if any. Others are purified.

Note. Coupels may purify each other if they will.

Cakes + Wine.

The Great Rite if possible. either in token or truely.

Dismiss [the guardians, and close down the magic circle; the people then stay to] feast and dance.

Feb Eve

Dance step, Waving brooms, Torches if possible.

Volta dance

Form [circle]

H[igh] P[riest] enters [circle] S[word?] in right [hand], Phalus or broom in left.

H[igh] P[riestes]s invokes. "Dread Lord of Death + Resurection, of Life + the Giver of Life Lord within ourselves, whose name is Mystery of Mysteries. Encourage our hearts. Let the light chrystalise itself in our blood, fulfilling of us resurection. For there is no part of us that is not of the Gods. Descend we pray Thee upon Thy servent + Priest . . . .

Initiations if any. Others should be purified.

Cakes + Wine.

If possible, Great Rite, in token, or truly

Dismiss [the guardians, and close down the magic circle; the people then stay to] feast and dance.

---

[59] This speech is given in full in the later set of eight Sabbats, where I point out the various quotes from Crowley.

May Eve

If possible ride brooms, staves etc quick dance step, to site H[igh] P[riestes]s leading, sing.

O do not tell the Priest of our flight
For he would call it sin.
But we will be in the woods all night,
A conjouring summer in.
We bring you good news by word of mouth
for Woman, cattle & corn
The sun is coming up from the south
with Oak + Ash + Thorn[60]

Meeting Dance
fform [circle]
H[igh] P[riestes]s Assumes position
Blessed be. Officers 5S [Fivefold Kiss]
[scourge]. position[61]
H[igh] P[riest] invokes. I invoke thee, O mighty Mother of us all, Bringer of all fruitfulness, By Seed + Root, By stem + Bud, By leaf + flower + fruit, By life + love, do we invoke thee. Thee to descend upon the body of Thy servent + Priestess . . . here
5.S. [fivefold kiss]
Initiations if any others purified
Cakes + Wine.
If possible Great Rite
Dismiss [the guardians, and close down the magic circle; the people then stay to] feast and dance.

---

[60] This is Kipling.

[61] I am not entirely sure what actions are being notated here; so I transcribed with some care. Apparently all the "Officers" (however defined) give the fivefold kiss to the High Priestess and are then scourged before the invocation of the Mother.

August Eve

If possible ride brooms. Quick dance step. H[igh] P[riestes]s leading.
[Kipling verses are repeated.]
Meeting Dance
Form [circle]
H[igh] P[riestes]s position.
Blessed be. Officers 5S. [scourge symbol]
H[igh] P[riestes]s Asumes position.
H[igh] P[riest] invokes. O Mighty Mother, of us all, Giver of All Fruitfulness. Give us fruit + Grain, Flocks + Heard + Children to the Tribe (or Cult) that we be mighty. By they Rosey Love do Thou descend upon upon [dittography] thy servent + Priestess here . . . .5.S.
Initiations if any. Others purified.
Cakes + Wine
Great Rite should be celebrated if possible, in token or truely.
Dismiss [the guardians, and close down the magic circle; the people then stay to] feast and dance.

Commentary on A.6

The four rituals in "Ye Bok of ye Art Magical" are virtually identical in content with those included in the Weschcke documents, even though they are separated by ten years; obviously there was little rewriting of them. These Sabbat rituals mostly incorporate the basic procedures for all rituals, with some rather minor variations. The invocations are compounded of quotations from Crowley (from the "Gnostic Mass" in *Magick in Theory and Practice*, pp. 351-360, exactly the same passages used in the Charge, which immediately precedes these Sabbat rituals in "Ye Bok of ye Art Magical") and of bits of liturgy already used in the initiation rituals. The verse for May Eve is from Kipling, of course (though perhaps relatively few Americans can recognize Kipling, or any other poetry, these days). There is nothing new here, nothing that might come from pagan celebrations of the seasons.

The calligraphy here is plain, but very neat; by this criterion, these pages might have been written fairly early, about 1949 or so. However, the rituals are rather sketchy, as if "Ye Bok of ye Art Magical" were being used merely as a notebook, and seem to be addressing a situation in which perhaps a dozen people (at least, more than two or three) are meeting, though perhaps this is still wishful thinking. These indications point toward a date when the group had been growing for a few years, that is, around 1952.

However, "Ye Bok of ye Art Magical" does not contain any rituals for the Lesser Sabbats at the solstices and equinoxes, whereas *Witchcraft Today* contains a Yule ritual. If "Ye Bok of ye Art Magical" had been in use by a coven when that ritual was being written in 1953, then very likely the ritual would have been copied into it. Since it was not, we must deduce that "Ye Bok" was not being used by a coven in late 1953, when *Witchcraft Today* was being written, and was already or soon to be retired from service.

The "meeting dance" at the beginning of the Lammas ritual is probably the double-spiral dance described in *Witchcraft Today* (p. 167). Many have failed to notice its significance (Farrar 1971 did not describe it at all) or have confused it with a whirling dance given by Crowley (Magick, p. 80); it is discussed by the Farrars (1984). It is actually a British folk dance, often called "Troytown." In the NROOGD, we combined it with the "Thout, tout a tout tout, throughout and about" words of the Somersetshire witches (*Witch-Cult in Western Europe*), set to a simple tune; and it quickly became, and remains, one of NROOGD's biggest crowd pleasers.

If Gardner had received any information about traditional ways to celebrate these Celtic festivals from the coven he claimed initiation into, why did he not use it for these rituals? And if that coven did not celebrate the Sabbats, then what in the world did it celebrate? Obviously, if Gardner had known any traditional rituals for the Sabbats, he would have used them, instead of piecing these rituals together from bits of folklore, quotes from Crowley, and parts of the workings intended to be used at almost any meeting. It will not do to argue that "pagans" would have gone for the "Great Rite" (by another name), feasting, and dancing, and would not have bothered with drawing magic circles. The human need for meaningful, periodic rituals seems to be as deep and as ancient as any other need, and all religious ritual sets apart some sort of "sacred time" and "sacred space" to distinguish it from ordinary time and space. Hence an earlier coven would have had some way of doing that.

If we ask just what structural principle underlies these rituals, the answer becomes fairly obvious: they are focused on scourging. In fact, they generally reproduce the pattern of the initiations exactly; remember that here "purify" is code for "scourge with forty strokes".

November Eve: the High Priest is scourged with forty strokes; then all are bound and scourged with forty strokes; then follows either initiations or purifications of all with forty strokes; then cakes and wine; then the Great Rite "if possible."

February Eve: all are purified with eighty strokes; then all are purified before the High Priest with forty strokes; then he purifies others with forty strokes; then comes cakes and wine; and then the Great Rite "if possible."

May Eve: all are purified with forty strokes; then the High Priestess purifies all with forty strokes; then all are purified before her with forty strokes; she purifies the High Priest and others with her own hands (rather than the scourge?); then come cakes and wine; then the Great Rite "if possible."

August Eve: Here the pattern is reversed; there is only the purification at the beginning, and the Great Rite is not called for—because without all the scourgings it was not possible.

Most current members of the Craft, not being obsessed with scourging, find these rituals to be quite uninteresting, as well as unsuitable for the large public gatherings at the Sabbats that have become fairly common since the late 1960s. As a result, they have been replaced by much more elaborate and much more carefully researched reconstructions of what various sorts of European pagan festivals might have been like.

A.7. Consecrating Tools

"Ye Bok of ye Art Magical" contains, on pp. 22-25, 30-33, the following procedures from *The Greater Key of Solomon* for consecrating tools; these have been incorporated into later drafts of the Book of Shadows.

"In order to carry out the greatest and most important Operations of the Art, various Instruments are necessary, [such] as a Knife with a white hilt, another with a black hilt, [etc.]...With this Knife [with the white hilt] thou mayest perform all the necessary operations of the Art, except the Circles... the Knife with the black hilt [is] for making the Circle.

Swords are also frequently necessary for use in Magical Arts. Thou shalt therefore take a new sword which thou shalt clean and polish...; sprinkle and cense it, and repeat over it the following conjuration: "I conjure thee, O Sword, by these names ... that thou servest me for a strength and a defence in all Magical Operations, against all mine enemies, visible and invisible... I conjure thee anew... O Sword, that thou servest me for a protection in all adversities... I conjure thee, O Instrument of Steel, by God the Father Almighty... that thou receive such virtue that thou mayest obtain without deceit the end which I desire in all things where I shall use thee. [GKS, pp. 98, 101, 118]

It was the material in these first seven sections, plus some other materials from The Greater Key of Solomon, that Gardner copied about 1952 into the first Book of Shadows as such, the one owned by Doreen Valiente that the Farrars (1984, p. 3) label "Text A." In 1976 I had already deduced from the internal evidence in "Ye Bok of ye Art Magical" that these materials had been copied into a new book about 1952. Hence it was a pleasure to find from the discussion of "Text A" in Chapters 1-4 of the Farrars' 1984 book that its contents exactly matched what I had deduced. But this also proves that Text A, "Gerald Gardner's own Book of Shadows," as Valiente referred to it, was in fact copied from "Ye Bok of ye Art Magical," not from any hypothetical book ever owned by Dorothy Clutterbuck or anyone else.

Chapter Five

The Book of Shadows in 1953

Given the rest of the data in "Ye Bok of ye Art Magical," which we will cover here, plus that in *Witchcraft Today, High Magic's Aid*, the Weschcke manuscripts, and the data in the Farrars 1984, we can pretty well deduce what was in the Book of Shadows by about 1953. We will see that it was very close to Text B, the second Book of Shadows owned by Doreen Valiente, and the one that Gardner was actually using when he and Dafo initiated Doreen in 1953. However, Gardner continued using Text B for the next year or two, so that some of its contents were not made final until about 1955 or 1956.

Documents B.1 and B.2

Documents B.1 and B.2 comprise pages 151-154 of *BAM*. The writing is fairly careful and fairly legible: not as neat as in A.3, much neater than in B.3. There is no heading above the first paragraph. I separate these into two documents here largely because of their later trajectories, even though they are run together here. The words within the curly brackets {these things} were written in the Theban script.

B.1. On Chants

Of old there were meny chants + / songs used especialy in the Dances. Meny of these have been forgotten by us here. but we know that they used cries of {IAU} / which seems muchly like the cries {EIO} or {EAUIE}[1] of the ancients. Much dependeth on the pronunciation if this be so. In my youth, when I heard {IAU} it seemed to be {AEIOU},

---

[1] Gardner may have intended "EUO" and "EUOEI" here, but it's hard to guess.

or rather, {AAA.EE.I.OOOO.UU}. This may be but the natural way to prolong it to make it fit for a call. but it suggesteth that these be possibly the {ENITIALS} of an invocation. as {AGLA} is said to be, + of sooth tis said that the whole {HEBREW ALPHABET} is said to be such. + for this reason is recited as a most powerfull charm, but at least this is certain, These cries during the dances do have profound effect, As I myself have seen.[2]

Other calls are IEHOUA and EHEIE; also Ho Ho Ho Ise Ise Ise.

IEO VEO VEO VEO VEOV OROV OV OVOVO may be a spell but is more likely to be a call. 'Tis like the EVOE EVOE of the Greeks and the "Heave ho!" of sailors. "Emen hetan" and "Ab hur, ab hus" seem calls; as "Horse and hattock, horse and go, horse and Pellatis, ho, ho, ho!"

"Thout, tout a tout tout, throughout and about" and "Rentum tormentum" are probably mispronounced attempts at a forgotten formula, though they may have been invented by some unfortunate being tortured, to evade telling the real formula.

Commentary on B.1

The first five entries in "Ye Bok of ye Art Magical" that I deal with here are all written from much the same viewpoint as *Witchcraft Today*. We find use of archaisizing language, a "present time" that seems to waver between the eighteenth and twentieth centuries, and a great concern with making it seem plausible that there could have been a "secret history" of witchcraft unknown to occultists, historians, and persecutors alike. As we will see, much of the material in these five sections was used in *Witchcraft Today* or in later documents in the Book of Shadows.

There is a certain amount of experimenting going on here, attempting to find just the right tone to use in *Witchcraft Today*. Consider

---

[2] This is all based on Graves' speculations about ancient mystical vowel sounds; see *The White Goddess*, particularly Chapter 16, pp. 286-7. This paragraph, from p. 151 of BAM, seems to be a precursor of the comments about chants in WT, p. 167. It was copied, and expanded, in "Text B," Gardner's second draft of the Book of Shadows (Farrars 1984, p. 92), from which I have taken the next three short paragraphs.

the opening lines: "Of old there were . . . Many of these have been forgotten by us here . . . In my youth, when I heard . . . These cries . . . have profound effect, as I myself have seen." Who is speaking here? Gardner? Apparently. But the implicit claim here to have been in the circle as a youth contradicts his published claim to have been initiated in 1939.

This paragraph was copied into Text B, where a second, similar paragraph, discussing various chants given by Murray, was added to it. Valiente[3] argues that this passage, since it cannot be true of Gardner, must be from Dorothy Clutterbuck's Book of Shadows. More likely, Gardner had simply not yet decided on all the details of what his public claims would be. More examples of writing from about 1952 in exactly the same tone as these documents also appear in Text B.

B.2. To Help the Sick

This is on pages 151-154 of *BAM*. I use square brackets here to flag missing or unclear words.

[1] Ever remember the promise of the Goddess, "For ecstacy is mine + joy on earth" so let there ever be joy in your heart. greet people with joy, be glad to see them. if times be hard, think, "It might have been worse." I at least [have] known the joys of the sabath. + I will know them again. Think of the grandour, beauty + Poelary of the rites. of the loved ones you meet through them. If you dwell on this inner joy; your health will be better. You must try to ban[ish] all fear. for ill realy touch you. it may hurt your body. but your Soul is beyond it all.

[2] And ever remember, that if you healp others it makes you forget your own woes. + if another be in pain, do what you may to distract his atten[tion] from it. Do not say "You have no pain" but, if you may administer the drugs which sooth as well as those that cure. but ever strive to make them believe they are ge[tting] better. install into them happy thoughts. If you can on[ly] get this into his inner mind so that it be always [true].

---

[3] Farrars 1984, p. 56.

[3] To this end it is not wrong to let people think that we of the Cult[4] have more power than we have. for the truth is, that if they beleive we have more power than we realy possess, we do realy possess these powers, inso much we can do good to them.

[4] You must try to find out about people. If you tell a slightly sick man, "You are looking better, you will soon be well," He will feel better, but if he is realy ill, or in pain, His Knowledge that he is in pain will cause him to doubt your words in future. but if you give him one of the [drugs] + then say, "The pain is growing less. Soon it will be gone" Because the [pain] goes, the next time you say, "The pain is going," he will beleive you + the pain will realy get less. but you must ever say so with conviction + this conviction must come from your beleiving it yourself. because you yourself know that if you can fix his mind so that he beleives you, it is true.

[5] Tis often better to look exactly between their eyes, looking as if your eyes pierced their heads, opening your eyes as wide as you may + never blink. This continued gazing oft causes the patient to grow sleepy. If they show signes of this, say "You are growing sleepy. You will sleep, you are tired. Sleep. Your eyes grow tired. Sleep." If they close their eyes, say "Your eyes close, you are tired, you cannot open your eyes." If they cannot, say "Your arms are tired, you cannot raise them." If they cannot, say "I am master of your mind. You must ever beleive what I tell you. When I look like this into your eyes you will sleep + be subject to my will" Then tell them they will sleep + wake up refreshed feeling better. Continue this with soothing + healing drugs, + try to infuse into them the feeling of ecstacy that you feel at the Sabbath. They cannot feel it in full, but you can command them to feel what is in your own mind, + try to concentrate on this ecstacy. If you may safely tell that you are of the Cult, your task may be easier. + it were well to command them to know it only with their sleeping mind, + forget it, or to be at least unable to tell anyone about it when

[4] Notice use of "Cult" here. Even in 1953 Gardner had not yet begun calling this religion "the Craft."

awake, a good way is to command than that if they ever are questioned about Witchcraft or Witches, to immediately fall asleep.[5]

[6] Ever remember if tempted to admit or boast of belonging to the Cult you be[6] endangering your brothers. for though now the fires of persecution may have died down but who knows when they be revived. Meny priests have knowledge of our secrets, + they well know that though much religious bigitery has calmed down, that meny people would wish to join our cult, + if the truth were known of its joys, the Churches would [lose] power, so if we take meny recruits, we may loose the fires of persecution against us again. So ever keep the secrets.[7]

[7] Think joy, think love, try to help others + bring joy into their lives. Children are naturally easier to influence than grown people. Ever strive to work through peoples existing beleifs, for instance more than half of the world beleive in Amulets. An ordinary stone is not an Amulet but if it hath an natural hole in it, it must be something unusual, so if the patient hath this beleif give him one. but first carry it next your skin for a few days, forcing your will into it, to cure pain, to feel safe, or against their particular fear, + this amulet may keep imposing your will, when you are absent. The masters of Talismans knew this fill well when they say they must be made in a Circle, to avoid distraction, by someone by someone who is mind on the object of the work.

[8] But keep your own mind happy. Remember the Words of the Goddess "I give unimaginable joys, on Earth certainty, not faith while in life + upon death, peace unuterable, Rest & Ecstacy, + the promise that you will return again.[8] In the Old days meny of us went to the flames

---

[5] Gardner seems to have in mind here a passage from the witch-trial records that he comments on in WT, p. 59; in it a prosecutor complains that some "witches" are able to fall asleep under torture. Gardner is proposing a knowledge of hypnotism to explain this phenomenon, and so to make plausible the "secret history" he has been concocting. Notice that this paragraph is a first draft of a passage in the Craft Laws.

[6] Here "belonging" was written, then scratched out.

[7] This paragraph is designed to make the "secret history," plausible and is a first draft of lines 133-147 in part I of "The Old Laws" and of lines 62-70 and 97-107 in part II of them. It was copied into "Text B" (Farrars 1984, p. 63).

[8] Here Gardner used the double quote to begin quoting from the same passage

laughing + singing, + so we may again. We may have joy in life + beauty, + peace + Death + the promise of return[9]

[9] The Bible speaks sooth, "A merry heart doeth good like a medicine but a broken spirit brieth the bones." But, you may not have a merry heart. perchance you were born under an evil star. I think that the effect of the stars are overestimated, but you cannot make a merry heart to order you say. But you can, in the Cult, there be secret Processes by which your will + immiganation may be influenced. This process also effects the body, & brings it to joy. Your body is happy, so your mind is happy You are well because you are happy, + you are happy because you are well.

[10] Prayer may be used with good result if the patient beleives it can & will work. Meny beleive it can, but do not beleive their God or saint will help. Prayers to the Goddess, especialy the Amathean Horn Prayer, as it causes stimulation to the body as well as to the mind.

Commentary on B.2.

Gardner apparently decided this document was not totally suitable for inclusion in the Book of Shadows, but it also is not a jotting down of ideas by free association. Rather, it is a careful weaving together of three different themes: altered states of consciousness (produced by chants, dancing, drugs, hypnotism, scourging, etc.); techniques for faith healing; and the need for dissimulation and secrecy. Try reading paragraphs [1], [6], [8] by themselves—this sequence is very close in tone and content to the "Preface" or "Warning" in B.5, which was later incorporated into the Craft Laws. Paragraph [6] was copied into Text B, but not the rest of this, which Gardner instead kept in reserve, raiding it for raw materials to be used in the Craft Laws. The mention of the Amalthean Horn prayer in [10] shows that scourging is, as always, uppermost in Gardner's mind.

Is there anything here that might be traditional? No, despite the attempt to claim traditional knowledge about chants, hypnotism, drugs, etc., there is nothing here that could be explained only as part of a pagan religious

---

of Crowley used in the Charge, and referred to also in paragraph [1] here.

[9] This is a first draft of lines 111-113 and 121-123 in Part I of "The Old Laws.".

tradition. Furthermore, the quotes from Crowley render it impossible for this all to be traditional. There is much more innuendo than information here, and the information could easily have come from books.

B.3. The Scourge and the Kiss.

This comprises p. 29 of *BAM*, and is so carelessly scrawled that it is very difficult to read. Documents B.3-5 seem to be first drafts of material Gardner then entered in "Text B" in about 1952.

[1] Invocation

Hail . . . from the Amathean horn
Pour forth thy store of Love. I lowly bend.
Before Thee! I envoke thee at the end.
When other Gods are fallen + put to scorn,
Thy foot is to my lips! My sighs inborn
Rise touch, Curl about thy Heart. Then spend
Pittifull Love, lovliest Pity descend
And bring me luck who am lonely + forlorn

This be powerfull in ill luck + for sickness. It must be said in a Circle, + you must be properly[10] prepared + well purified, both before + after saying, to bind the spell.

---

[2] Order + diciplin must be kept. A High Priest or Priestess may + should punish all faults to this end, + all of the Cult [must accept] such corrections willingly. Each fault should be corrected seperalty. The Priest or Priestess must be properly prepared + call the culprit to trial. They must be prepared as for initiation + kneel, told their fault + sentence pronounced. Punishment should be [the scourge], followed by an [illegible word] such as several [fivefold kisses] or somthing of this nature. The culprit must acknowledge the justice of the punishment by kissing hands and [scourge] on receiving sentence + again when thanking for punishment received.

---

[10] The next word written here was "purified," which was then scratched out.

3] The [scourgings] are 3, 7, 9 (thrice three), and 21 (thrice seven) 40 in all. The [fivefold kiss] is 5, but there [be] 8 {kissing points} viz., 2 {feet} 2 {knees, the womb} 2 {breasts + the mouth} 8 in all, + 5.8. are 40. So it be not mete to have less than 40, but more may be used if desired.[11]

[4] To make the anointing ointment, take some glased pans fill half full with grease or olive oil. Put in one sweet mint, majeram in another, ground thyme in a 3rd, + it you may have it, patcholi[12], dried leaves pounded. Place pans in hot water bath. Stir and cook for several hours, then pour into linen bags, and squeeze grease through into pans again, and fill up with fresh leaves. After doing this several times, the grease will be highly perfumed. Then mix all together + store in a well corked jar.

Anoint behind ears, throat, armpits, breasts + womb. Also, for all ceremonies where the {feet are kissed, they should also be anointed}.[13]

Commentary on B.3.

Like the preceding entry, this one has been constructed with more subtlety than is at first apparent, and was also rewritten into several other documents. Notice that paragraph [1] presents the charm used to accompany scourging as a means for working magic separately from initiation. The Farrars (1981, p. 41) say that it is a poem by Aleister Crowley, originally addressed to Tyche.[14] Gardner's chatty comments present the same sort of casual claim to historicity for the material, while disclaiming any specific knowledge of the details of that history, that we can see over and over again in *Witchcraft Today.*

---

[11] Notice that this paragraph appears to be a precursor of Document D.12; and that, combined with Document D.7, was copied into "Text B" (Farrars 1984, pp. 3, 52).

[12] Actually, "patchouli" is in parentheses, preceded by another word I cannot make out (Bob Matheisen says, "Maybe Qat?").

[13] Part [4] is quite similar to a passage in WT (p. 60) on making an anointing oil; it also was copied into "Text B" (Farrars 1984, p. 62).

[14] Farrars (1981, p. 41). Carl Watson, of Little River, South Carolina, was the first to write to me and identify this poem as being "La Fortune," on p. 120 of vol. III of the Yogi Publication Society edition of *The Works of Aleister Crowley.*

Paragraph [2], which Gardner appended to the Craft Laws in the 1960s, then deals with scourging as a means for enforcing discipline within the coven; it seems to be addressing a situation in which perhaps a dozen, rather than just two or three, people are meeting regularly as a coven. This, together with the carelessness of the handwriting, would point toward a date of around 1952 for this entry.

Schad-Somers, *Sadomasochism* (p. 39), says, "A mother who is uncomfortable with her own animalistic impulses... will persecute these same impulses in her own child, a process... [whose] goal is not teaching but *humiliation*. In the extreme, that form of persecution may entail that the child smiles after a severe punishment and—in one case I know of—that the child should first kiss the punishing parent and then kiss the very rod with which the beating has been administered."

Paragraph [3], rewritten into a passage in Chap. 10 of *Witchcraft Today*, and copied into Text B as an appendage to "The Eightfold Way",[15] deals with the number symbolism of the scourging, then with that of the fivefold kiss. "It is not meet . . . " means that Gardner needed at least forty strokes to become sexually aroused.

Paragraph [4], which underlies a passage toward the end of Chap. 4 of *Witchcraft Today*, and was also copied into Text B separately,[16] then discusses anointing because of its connection with the fivefold kiss.

That is, what we have here is not mere free association, but a careful attempt to build up a complex set of associations with scourging, kissing, and anointing, that is, to create a rich sacramental system focused on sexuality in general, and on scourging in particular.

B.4. The Priestess and the Sword

[This is a short note on page 278 of *BAM*. The writing is extremely careless.]

It is said, "When a woman takes the main part in worship of the Male God, she must be girt with a sword."

Note. This hath been explaind as meaning that a man should be High Priest representing the God, but if no one of sufficient rank + knowledge

---

[15] Farrars 1984, p. 52.

[16] Farrars 1984, p. 62.

be present, a woman armed as a man may take his place. The sheath should be worn in a belt. She should carry the sword drawn, but if she has to use her hands, she should sheath the sword. Any other woman in the circle while this worship is performed shall be sword in hand. Those outside the circle only have the athame. But alas, they cannot tell me what the rites were or in whose honour they were performed, possibly {Cerunnos} or {Hu} or {Appius}.[17]

Commentary on B.4.

Here "Ye Bok of ye Art Magical" is again being used as a notebook to work on a draft of a passage in *Witchcraft Today*, at the end of Chap. 3:

> *My great trouble in discovering what their beliefs were is that they have forgotten practically all about their god; all I can get is from the rites and prayers addressed to him. . . . there are certain rites where a man must by the leader, but if a man of requisite rank is not available, a chief priestess belts a sword on and is thought of as a man for the occasion. But although woman can on occasion take man's place, man can never take woman's place.*

We can observe not only similar wording, but the use of the third person plural, which Gardner uses throughout *Witchcraft Today* in order to sound like an outside observer, an anthropologist, commenting on the mores of a folk culture he is observing. We can certainly date this entry to the period when *Witchcraft Today* was being written. And why are quotation marks used in the first line? For the same reason that archaicizing language ("hath" and "it be" and suchlike) is used: it is an attempt to find a combination of technical tricks, viewpoint, tone, and attitude that will lend verisimilitude to the claims for a secret history of witchcraft.

B.5. The Warning

This document comprises the entry on p. 7 of *BAM*. As we will see, it is essentially the same as the version that was published in *Witchcraft Today*; yet there are some slight differences that are highly informative. Gardner's writing here is so slovenly that, without the published versions to guess

---

[17] I have no idea who is meant by "Appius." Bob Matheissen suggests "Apis."

from, I would find it extremely hard to read this entry. I introduce boxed numbers to number the lines on the page for future reference.

Keep this book in your own hand of
write. Let brothers + Sisters copy what they
will, but never let the book out of your hands,
+ never keep the writings of another. For if it be
found in their hand of write, they may well be
taken and tortured, each should guard his
own writings + destroy them whenever danger
threatens.

Learn as much as you may by heart,
+ when the danger is past, rewrite your book if
it be safe. For this reason, if any die, destroy their
book if they have not been able to, for, an it be
found, tis a clear proof against them, +
"Ye may not be a Witch alone," So all their
friends be in danger of the Question, so destroy
everything not necessary.
If you are taken[18] If your book be found
on you, tis clear proof against you alone, you may
be tortured. Keep all thought of the cult from
your mind. Say you have had bad dreams,
A Devil caused you to write this without your knowledge.

Think to yourself. I Know Nothing. I
Remember nothing I have forgotten All
Drive this into your mind.[19]

If the torture be to great to bear,
say, I will confess, I cannot bear this torment. What do you
want me to say? tell me + I will say it. If then they try + make you
talk of the brotherhood, do not, but if they try + make you speak

[18] The preceding four words have been inserted as an afterthought, since the second "if" is both capitalized and in the "drop straight down" position Gardner used to begin a new paragraph.

[19] The preceding is Gardner's underlining in the MS.

of impossibilities, such as flying through the air, consorting with the Devis, [slaying][20] Children, + eating mens flesh, to obton releif from torture, Say I had an evil dream. I was not myself. I was crased. Not all Magestrates are bad. if there be an excuse, they may show you mercy. if you have confessed aught, deny it afterwards. say you babled under the torture, you knew not what you did or said. If you be condemmed, fear not, the Brotherhood is powerfull. They may help you to escape if you are steadfast. if you betray aught, there is no hope for you, in this life, or that which is to co[me.] But, tis sure, that if steadfast you go to the pyre, drugs will rea[ch] you. you will feel naught, + you go but, "To Death + what lies beyond[,] The ecstacy of the Goddess. The same[21] with the working Tools Let them be but as ordinary things you have in your houses. The Pentacles shall be of wax that may be melted or broken at once. Have no names or signs on anything. Write them in ink when necessary, + wash it off at once when finished.

Commentary on B.5.

In introducing this passage in *Witchcraft Today* (p. 57), Gardner says, "In all witch writings, there is this warning, usually on the first page," and the

[20] Probably "Devil" is intended, but "Devis" is not impossible, and is what I see. I supply the final word from the version in WT. The word in the MS. is illegible, but it is too short to be "sacrificing"; Bob Matheisen suggests "slaying."

[21] What does "same" refer to? Grammatically, it must reach back to "destroy everything not necessary" in lines 15-16. Hence everything in lines 17 to 38 must have been added later--and only these lines have a close parallel in Document B.2.

passage follows. Now, this statement is certainly true of "Ye Bok of ye Art Magical"; the passage is on the first page after the list of contents. Hence we can be sure that he considered "Ye Bok of ye Art Magical" to be a "witch writing," that is, a Book of Shadows. Had he seen this passage in any other "witch writings?" There is no evidence that he had.

What this passage says is, "Copy this book—including this page—in your own handwriting, and here's why." That is, Gardner was thinking about having initiates write out their own copies of the Book of Shadows. But much in "Ye Bok of ye Art Magical" is unsuitable for a Book of Shadows; it would be simpler to copy only the suitable material into a new book. Gardner did just that about 1952. All of this "warning" (with Gardner's usual variations in wording) was also copied into "Text B",[22] but there it includes the last two sentences given in *Witchcraft Today*, which did not appear in "Ye Bok of ye Art Magical." Hence we can see that some of the content of Text B does postdate the writing of *Witchcraft Today*.

Have we any reason to think the content here traditional? Is it the sort of document that might have been written in a time of persecution? No, it is not. We have many examples of what people write to encourage their colleagues in the face of death, and this is nothing like them. Elliot Rose, in discussing this material in *Witchcraft Today*, begins his comments by acknowledging that Gardner

> *"recognizes that this cannot have genuinely referred to English conditions at any time; and I am bound to recognize that . . . it does indeed refer to the innocuous goddess-cult he describes. His view is that it is an uneducated translation from a continental source in the times of fierce persecution; and this is prima facie reasonable. However, he points out (and the text itself emphasizes) that witches do not keep old documents, but as a matter of policy copy what they require for their own use and destroy all dispensable relics. Thus, if he is right, we have to expect an extreme degree of textual corruption [as errors made by generations of copyists accumulate]; he does not claim to have seen manuscripts of any age . . . But I doubt if the text is genuine at all. It enjoins the frequent destruction of books, yet has itself survived after the tortures it speaks of have ceased to*

[22] Farrars 1984, pp. 50-51.

be feared, and in a country where they were never employed. . . . it still contains fancy archaisms that would have presumably dropped out if it had in fact been constantly recopied from memory: "ye" and "aught" and "'tis" and so forth. It makes . . . [a] feeble attempt at seventeenth-century grammar . . . and seems to disprove the accusations made against witches with a suspicious neatness. It seems designed to create an impression of injured innocence, and I suspect that someone has been supplying the cult in its modern form with retrospective historical evidence.

Rose is quite right about this. In fact, his last sentence is a wonderful example of a trained historical intuition at work.

Look at the third paragraph. What does "Same" refer to? It must refer back to "Destroy everything not necessary" in the first paragraph. That is, the text originally jumped from "everything not necessary" to "The same with the working tools." This earlier draft was thus concocted specifically to explain why no old witch books or tools exist; it was written as part of an overall strategy of making the "secret history" of witchcraft seem plausible. All the business about secrecy in the face of persecution was therefore inserted later, in order to create a plausible setting. That is, the reason for this entry is to "explain" why there is no evidence for the existence of a witch-cult so totally unlike what professional historians think might have existed. Such a problem is of no interest to persons facing persecution, but it is of great interest to persons who are inventing a new religion that they wish to claim is old. The fact is that for the last 250 years, anyone in England who could read and write was perfectly safe in owning any sort of weird literature or magical implements (although Doreen Valiente has pointed out to me that this was true only for the upper classes, not the working class); and given that safety, educated people would have stopped destroying old magical books by late in the eighteenth century. A book even 100 years old would seem antique enough to most current seekers after ancient wisdom. If Gardner had had something that old to offer, he would have said so. But he does not, because he has no such thing.

B.6. Of the Ordeal of the Art Magical

This passage, on pp. 71-73 of BAM, was one I could not copy in Toronto. Instead, the text here, which is a later rewriting by Gardner, is borrowed from the Farrars.

> "Learn of the spirit that goeth with burdens that have not honour, for 'tis the spirit that stoopeth the shoulders and not the weight. Armour is heavy, yet it is a proud burden and a man standeth upright in it. Limiting and constraining any of the senses serves to increase the concentration of another. Shutting the eyes aids the hearing. So the binding of the initiate's hands increases the mental perception, while the scourge increaseth the inner vision. So the initiate goeth through it proudly, like a princess, knowing it but serves to increase her glory."

But this can only be done by the aid of another intelligence and in a circle, to prevent the power thus generated being lost. Priests attempt to do the same with their scourgings and mortifications of the flesh. But lacking the aid of bonds and their attention being distracted by their scourging themselves and what little power they do produce being dissipated, as they do not usually work within a circle, it is little wonder that they oft fail. Monks and hermits do better, as they are apt to work in tiny cells and coves, which in some way act as circles. The Knights of the Temple, who used mutually to scourge each other in an octagon, did better still; but they apparently did not know the virtue of bonds and did evil, man to man.

But perhaps some did know? What of the Church's charge that they wore girdles or cords?

Commentary on B.6.

This material is more theologizing about scourging, attempting to justify its use in a magical context. As I have already said, there is certainly no mention of scourging in *The Greater Key of Solomon*, nor of the scourge as a magical tool. The tone and viewpoint are similar to those in various other entries here, in looking for ways to make the "secret history" plausible. Notice Gardner's standing assumption, which runs throughout the earliest entries, that the initiate will be a woman. Note also his homophobia, which was for a long time a source of political problems in the Craft movement in America. Aside from English bigotry in general, homophobia was particularly characteristic of flagellants, Gibson (p. 276) points out, the line of thought being something like, "Well, even if I am addicted to being beaten and humiliated by prostitutes, at *least* I'm not a faggot!"—as if homosexuality were somehow even worse.

Conclusions

The data provided by the Farrars show that several more documents were in the Book of Shadows by about 1953. These were: "Eightfold Path or Ways to the Center," and "To Gain the Sight," texts of which were included among the Weschcke documents, to be analyzed in Chapter 6.

What ends up being most interesting about *BAM* is how it evolved.

1. It began as a notebook on ceremonial magic, not intended to be read, but looking at how magic could be worked by a small group. During the 1930s and early 1940s, most magic was worked either by individuals, or by magical lodges descended from the HOGD; so a focus on small-group workings was itself an innovation.

2. With the entry of the initiation rituals in 1946-1949, it became a liturgical book, intended to be used in the rituals themselves.

3. Finally, about 1952, it became a notebook again, in which were recorded some experimental drafts of rituals and of passages that would appear in *Witchcraft Today*. These reveal a search for a stance that would lend plausibility to the claims that there was an earlier coven, that there was a pagan religion, that a pagan religion could have the characteristics described in *Witchcraft Today*.

Thus *BAM*, though not intended to be read, was written with an audience always in mind. But if it were a "witch's book," whether an individual's notebook or a group's liturgical manual, it would focus on the content of the religious tradition, not on manipulating audience reaction. This focus demonstrates that Gardner was thinking about the future growth of this new religious movement.

We have seen many sexual elements in the basic Gardnerian rituals—nakedness, Fivefold Kiss, scourging, anointings and kissing, Great Rite, Cakes and Wine—and we will see more in later rituals. Could all this have come from a non-Christian religion? Yes—but we cannot simply assume that such a religion existed in the 1930s, because that would be assuming the very thing we are trying to investigate. So far we know nothing about it except that it could have transmitted this sexual emphasis, which, by itself, is not enough reason for supposing that it existed. Furthermore, the transcendant evaluation of sexuality that we see in these rituals is radically different from what is known about ancient pagan religions; so we would still have to explain where this positive valuation of sex had come from.

Judging from the details of Gardner's rituals as they existed between 1945 and 1953, there were probably no more than half a dozen people active in the coven at any one time during this period. By 1953, Gardner had started a new coven in London, and the new religion that he and his friends had founded—for that is what they did—had evolved far from Murray's concepts. However, their system for working magic had not progressed much beyond the situation described in *High Magic's Aid*; there was still the uneasy amalgam of the male ceremonial magician and the female folk-magic witch.

Furthermore, there really wasn't very much in the Book of Shadows by 1953. Gardner was not prolific at creating rituals himself. Hence he was delighted to initiate a bright, hard-working young writer, who in 1953 began revising and augmenting the Book of Shadows, turning it into the type of liturgical manual still used by Gardnerians today. This writer was Doreen Valiente.

Chapter Six

Witchcraft Today

Here we will deal with Gardner's *Witchcraft Today*, which is easily available in paperback. I will quote from it four passages that I wish to analyze because they also appear in the Book of Shadows. Elliot Rose also focused on these passages as being significant for evaluating Gardner's historical claims, and I would like to review his comments, which have stood up well with time.

C.1. "The Myth of the Goddess"

Now G. had never loved, but she would solve all mysteries, even the mystery of Death, and so she journeyed to the nether lands. The guardians of the portals challenged her. "Strip off thy garments, lay aside thy jewels, for nought may ye bring with you into this our land." So she laid down her garments and her jewels and was bound as are all who enter the realms of Death, the mighty one.

Such was her beauty that Death himself knelt and kissed her feet, saying: "Blessed be thy feet that have brought thee in these ways. Abide with me, but let me place my cold hand on thy heart." And she replied: "I love thee not. Why doest thou cause all things that I love and take delight in to fade and die?" "Lady," relied Death, "'tis age and fate, against which I am helpless. Age causes all things to wither; but when men die at the end of time, I give them rest and peace and strength so that they may return. But you, you are lovely. Return not; abide with me." But she answered; "I love thee not." Then said Death: "As you receive not my hand on your heart, you must receive Death's scourge." "It is fate, better so," she said, and she knelt. Death scourged her and she cried: "I know the pangs of love." And Death said: "Blessed be," and gave her the fivefold kiss, saying "Thus only may you attain to joy and knowledge."

And he taught her all the mysteries, and they loved and were one; and he taught her all the magics. For there are three great events in the life of man—love, death and resurrection in the new body—and magic controls them all. To fulfil love you must return again at the same time and place as the loved ones, and you must remember and love her or him again. But to be reborn you must die and be ready for a new body; to die you must be born; without love you may not be born, and this is all the magic."

The concept of the goddess here as a goddess specifically of reincarnation has probably been borrowed from Theosophy rather than from any classical source (Gordon Melton points out to me). The Goddess of the Gardnerian movement is not pagan; rather, she has been created by investing the Blessed Virgin with some of the divine attributes of her son, and so arriving at a type of female monotheism. This new concept of the Goddess does lie, however, outside the boundaries of Christian theology, in a new or reclaimed spiritual territory. Genuine pagans, if they believe in deities rather than forces, certainly do not believe in a single universal personal deity.

This myth has obviously been created specifically to provide a theological justification for the binding and scourging as the central sacramental experience. It also does not sound like a religious myth: its "moral" is much too obvious, and the relationship it assumes between myth and ritual is much too simple.[1] Elliot Rose comments:

> *The passage might, of course, be exceedingly ancient; and the present writer might be the Queen of Sheba, but he is not... This Authorized Version was, obviously, produced by someone with literary ambitions. I rely on the thoroughly unmythlike character of this myth, and on the content itself... the narrative is exceedingly slight; almost the whole passage is taken up with the moral of it all, which in real myths (including those in the Bible) is precisely what lies behind and must not be confused with the actual story. Note how the personification of Death is... essential to... [the] story; this is a mark of sophistication, but it cannot be an accretion with the ages. But much more*

[1] I prefer not to get into the details of this topic here; for an excellent discussion, see Joseph Fontenrose's *Ritual Theory of Myth.*

important than this, the whole set of ideas reeks of twentieth-century literary fashion. What the "myth" boils down to, what the main characters are supposed to have done, is in a line of descent from D. H. Lawrence: the heroine achieves some thoroughly vague kind of spiritual insight, she Understands, as a result of sexual intercourse. The preliminary flagellation is inseparably linked with this process, though it is not clear how or why.

Is it conceivable that a story so unintelligible to most ages, and as a story so slight, could have been preserved through two millennia at the least of (presumably) oral transmission, and remain recognizably faithful to its original?

I find it hard to accept this myth as very ancient or in the least Celtic, or as a myth; but I am inclined to agree [that]... "it was coined to explain ideas and rituals already conceived, and to explain why the wiser, older, and more powerful god should give his power over magic to the goddess."[2] Perhaps it was. When? Not in ancient Babylon; the wiser, older, and more powerful god who gave powers to Ishtar was her father, Anu, and Alat, whom she visited in the underworld, was another goddess.[3]

Rose is correct in all this, except that he goes on to suppose that the myth was "coined" in the Victorian era. It is much simpler to suppose that this myth was devised in order to explain "ideas and rituals already conceived" in 1953. What needed explaining then? The use of flagellation, and the appearance of a goddess, since the pagan religion that Murray describes is not at all concerned with any goddess. We can see this pattern over and over again in Gardner's writings: he slyly admits the real facts in a manner that misdirects the reader's attention.

Let us think what the point of this "myth" is. It proposes the "suffering" of the goddess in her initiation into the mysteries of death as the model for the person being initiated into the mysteries of "the Art." That is, it establishes a type of sexual activity as a central "mystery" or "sacrament" of the religion. This concept is alien to the Ishtar cult; it might be modeled on the cultus of Demeter, in which the initiates imitated the actions and experienced of Demeter in her search for her stolen daughter. These included dancing around a sacred

---

[2] Notice how this contradicts the White Goddess myth.

[3] Rose, pp. 203-5.

well, sitting on the sacred stones where Demeter had sat, drinking the traditional "tea," and engaging in a torchlit search in the dark. However, despite the diatribes of the Church Fathers, the Eleusinia certainly did not include any overt sexual elements, since the classical Greeks were extremely prudish (or prudent) about sex; so the central point of this myth could not have come from there.

Rather, we must suppose that this "myth" is Gardner's own creation, although someone probably helped him get it into this final form, which is an order of magnitude better as literature than anything else Gardner ever wrote. It again uses misdirection very subtly, in this sense: suppose it were the story of a young god going before the Goddess of Death. Suddenly the scene would become recognizable as one straight out of the Victorian literature discussed by Ian Gibson.

C.2. The Charge

This document, which appears on p. 47 of *Witchcraft Today*, consists of two paragraphs of the "charge" that we looked at in Document A.3.

"Listen to the words of the Great Mother, who of old was also called among men Artemis, Astarte, Dione, Melusine, Aphrodite, and many other names. At mine altars the youth of Lacedaemon made due sacrifice. Once in the month, and better it be when the moon is full, meet in some secret place and adore me, who am queen of all the magics. . . . For I am a gracious goddess, I give joy on earth, certainty, not faith, while in life; and upon death, peace unutterable, rest and the ecstasy of the goddess. Nor do I demand aught in sacrifice."[4]

Commentary on Document C.2

Rose's observations about this document are as follows:

> *First, that string of names. Those ladies, or rather four of them (Dione is a name of Aphrodite) were worshipped, when they were worshipped seriously, as different people. At the utmost, I will allow that identification between Astarte and Aphrodite occurred in a syncretic age; it was not original, and*

---

[4] As was pointed out for Document A.3, this sentence is from Crowley's *Book of the Law* (Regardie, 1974, p. 82), no. 58.

Artemis and the siren Melusine cannot be dragged into it. Lumping them together and calling them the Great Mother is not possible in religion, but only in Comparative Religion. If you believe seriously in Aphrodite, you do not believe she is really Artemis; they may once in fact have been the same person in two aspects, but the worshipper who knows and accepts their separate legends will not believe it. (Myself, I doubt if they ever were the same; but I should be in a minority there today.) And did Isobel Gowdie of Auldearne know all this Classical Dictionary stuff? Would she have thought it important? Is it not plainly the product of an anthropologically minded age?

Then those youths... why specifically drag them in? Artemis has already been listed. The point must be the "due sacrifice." The reference, of course, is to ritual flagellation at the altar of Artemis Orthia... there are... others in Mr. Gardner's book, and some vague talk about "ordeals" and "frightening." The context in every case is initiation. All this is at least mildly interesting, because there is no hint of it in any earlier account of initiation ceremonies.[5]

He also points out that the "beatings" mentioned in *WCWE* are always to maintain discipline, and are unrelated to initiation.

Rose also perceives that the lumping together of goddesses here reflects the influence of Robert Graves, whose *The White Goddess* had appeared in 1948, and which became more and more central as providing a theology for the Craft during the 1950s.

This version of the Charge is still closer to the version in Document A.3 than to Valiente's later rewriting, because the quote from Crowley has been left alone here

C.3. The Yule Sabbat

This document appears on pp. 26 - 27 of *Witchcraft Today.*

I have seen one very interesting ceremony: the Cauldron of Regeneration and the Dance of the Wheel, or Yule, to cause the sun to be reborn, or summer to return. This in theory should be on December 22, but nowadays it is held on the nearest day . . . that is convenient for the

---

[5] Rose, pp. 206-7.

members. The ceremony starts in the usual way. The circle is cast and purified, the celebrants also being purified in the usual manner, and the ordinary business of the cult is done. Then the small ceremony is performed (sometimes called 'Drawing down the Moon') so that the High Priestess is regarded as the incarnation of the goddess.[6] The Cakes and Wine ceremony follows. Then a cauldron (or something to represent one) is placed in the middle of the circle, spirit is put in and ignited. Various leaves, etc., are cast in. Then the Priestess stands by it in the pentacle (goddess) position. The High Priest stands on the opposite side of the cauldron, leading the chant. The others stand round in a circle with torches. They are lighted at the burning cauldron and they dance round in the 'sunwise' direction, i.e. clockwise. The chant I heard was as follows, but others are sometimes used:

'Queen of the Moon, Queen of the Sun,
Queen of the Heavens, Queen of the Stars,
Queen of the Waters, Queen of the Earth
Bring to us the Child of Promise!

It is the great mother who giveth birth to him,
It is the Lord of Life who is born again.
Darkness and tears are set aside
When the Sun shall come up early.

Golden Sun of the Mountains,
Illumine the Land, Light up the World,
Illumine the Seas and the Rivers,
Sorrows be laid, Joy to the World.

Blessed be the Great Goddess,
Without beginning, without end,
Everlasting to eternity.
I.O.EVO.HE Blessed Be.'

They dance round furiously, crying:

---

[6] The procedures referred to here as "the usual way" have been partially described in Document A.1; we will see full descriptions of them in later documents.

I.O.EVO.HE

Blessed Be I.O.EVO.HE Blessed Be.'

Sometimes couples join hands and jump over the blazing cauldron, as I have seen for myself. When the fire had burnt itself out the Priestess led the usual dances. This was followed by a feast.

Commentary on Document C.3.

The Farrars report[7] that this ritual was "written by Doreen Valiente, with words suggested by a Christmas carol in Carmina Gadelica,[8] ...'It was the first chant or invocation I ever wrote for Gerald,' Doreen tells us—at Yule 1953, she thinks. He gave her the task of writing words for the evening ritual without warning, after lunch, deliberately throwing me in at the deep end to see what I would do.'" (This ritual must have been inserted into the manuscript of *Witchcraft Today*, which was published in 1954, at almost the last minute.)

Given this information, the ritual poses no problems for us. The concept of this dance is from Murray (*WCWE*, p. 13), who says, "To February 2, Candlemas Day, probably belongs the sun-charm of the burning wheel, formed by the whirling dancers, each carrying a blazing torch." To this Valiente added her own verse, based on that in the Carmina Gadelica. I believe her about all this because: (a) someone wrote the verse; (b) Gardner could not write verse at all; and (c) Valiente writes very competent verse.

Given that, we can see how very devious Gardner is being in what he says about this ritual: "I have seen," "I have heard," and so on. That is quite true—but he does not admit that this is a ritual he himself had commissioned. We therefore must be aware that this is probably the situation for everything he describes. Notice that this Sabbat is now held on the nearest day to December 22 that is convenient for the members, because so Gardner and Valiente and their coven decided. What is implied, but not said, is that it used to be held some other way—but there is no independent evidence that this sort of Sabbat ritual had ever been held for the winter solstice.

[7] Farrars, 1981, p. 148 n3.

[8] Carmichael, I, 133.

"Io Evohe" is based on the cry of the Bacchantes in Euripides' *The Bacchae.* Actually, I believe it is a multilingual pun based on "yod he vau he," the Tetragrammeton of the Kabala, since the Greek would otherwise transliterate more exactly as yo eh-oo-hoy. If the parting phrase of the Somersetshire witches, "A boy! Merry meet, merry part!" actually began with "Evohe!" (*WCWE*, p. 167), we must presume that their coven had been taken over by a renegade Elizabethan classicist, and that they are therefore not a trustworthy source for information about native English paganism.

C.4. The Warning

This document, which appears on pp. 57-59 of *Witchcraft Today*, is another version of Document B.5. I here italicize words that differ from the wording (or do not appear) in Document B.5.

In all the witch writings there is this warning, usually on the first page:

Keep a book in your own hand of write. Let brothers and sisters copy what they will but never let this book out of your hand, and never keep the writings of another, for if it be found in their hand of write they *will* be taken and tortured. Each should guard his own writings and destroy them whenever danger threatens. Learn as much as you may by heart and when danger is past rewrite your book.

For this reason if any die, destroy their book if they have not been able to *do so*, for *if* it be found, 'tis clear proof against them. 'Ye may not be a witch alone,' so all their friends be in danger of the *torture*, so destroy everything unnecessary. If your book be found on you, it is clear proof against you; you may be tortured.

Keep all thoughts of the cult from your mind. Say you had bad dreams, *that* a devil caused you to write this without your knowledge. Think to yourself, 'I know nothing; I remember nothing; I have forgotten all.' Drive this into your mind. If the torture be too great to bear, say: 'I will confess. I cannot bear this torment. What do you want me to say? Tell me and I will say it.' If they try *to* make you speak of impossibilities, such as flying through the air, consorting with the *Devil*, sacrificing children or eating man's flesh, say: 'I had evil *dreams*, I was not myself, I was crazed.'

Not all magistrates are bad. If there be an excuse they may show mercy. If you have confessed aught, deny it afterwards; say you babbled under the torture, you know not what you did or said. If you be condemned, fear not, the Brotherhood is powerful, they may help you to escape if you are steadfast. If you betray aught—THERE IS NO *HELP* FOR YOU IN THIS LIFE, OR IN THAT WHICH IS TO COME. If *you go steadfast* to the pyre, DRUGS WILL REACH YOU *and* you will feel naught, *but will* go to death and what lies beyond, the Ecstasy of the Goddess.

The same with the working tools. Let them be as ordinary things *that anyone may* have in their homes. *Let* the Pentacles be of wax that *they* may be melted or broken at once. *Have no sword unless your rank allows you one.* Have no names or signs on anything, write *the names and signs* on in ink *before consecrating them* and wash it off *immediately after. Never boast, never threaten, never say you wish ill to anyone. If any speak of the Craft, say: 'Speak not to me of such, it frightens me, 'tis evil luck to speak of it.'*

Commentary on Document C.4.

The italics here show how much rewriting was going on. Not much weight could be placed on the wording here, however, because it has passed under the eyes and pencil of a professional editor, who may have altered it significantly. We have already seen what Rose thinks of this material; I will save further discussion until we consider the Craft Laws.

A Final Comment on Witchcraft Today as a Whole

Rose's overall comment on *Witchcraft Today* is that:

> *on first sight of his work I was led to class him as a normal Murrayite by the circumstance that Miss Murray has supplied him with an introduction. I now realize that this was hasty; beyond accepting each other . . . as anthropologists in the same field, they disagree almost totally, though with true chivalry they affect not to notice this and hail one another as authorities—an unusual and edifying spectacle. The witch-cult described by Mr. Gardner as still existing is not that imagined by Miss Murray.*

Members of the Craft movement tend to notice the points of contact between Murray and Gardner, but not their areas of disagreement. The simple fact is that if the sort of religion described by Murray had survived somehow into the twentieth century, it would not in the least resemble what is described in *Witchcraft Today*.[9]

Rose's comments do, however, contain an especially remarkable insight: "much in Mr. Gardner's work suggests that the sect may have been reformed by a woman; a learned woman, after all, is nowadays a possibility." If he had not been misled into looking back to the 1920s and 1890s, he might have been alerted to look at the current Gardnerian scene more closely, and might then have guessed at the roles played by such women as Edith Woodford-Grimes, Dolores North, and Doreen Valiente.

Witchcraft Today is, in a real sense, a "charming" book. I think no one sensitive to the kinds of religious and theological issues it touches on could read it without thinking, "Well, maybe there would be something to be said for this kind of religion." The book zeroes in on all the areas in which modern Christianity in general, and the Roman Catholic church in particular, was weakest during the 1950s: need for small support groups rather than massive organization; need for broad, democratic participation, rather than hierarchic direction; need for full equality of men and women; need for theological concepts that deal with the femininity of the divine; need for direct practical help with personal problems, rather than impersonal moralizing of no practical use. Clearly, the Roman Catholic church is still not doing well on many of these issues[10], and as long as it does not, some disenchanted Catholics will find their way to the Craft—along with disenchanted Jews, Christian Scientists, Theosophists, and so forth.

What is most remarkable about *Witchcraft Today* is that this charming

---

[9] However, it might resemble the Los Angeles Russian immigrant coven that David Farren's wife was raised in; its focus was on working magic, and its concept of a deity was male.

[10] I'm not assuming that Protestant churches are doing any better, but as a birthright Papist, I simply don't know as much about Protestants, despite the valiant efforts by my professors at the GTU to raise my consciousness.

religion it describes so seductively DID NOT YET EXIST! As we will see from the analysis of the Weschcke documents in Chapters 7 and 8, in 1953 the "Craft" was still imaginary; it existed only in the minds of Gardner and a few others, as a projection of what they hoped to create in the future. And amazingly enough, within ten years this religion they had imagined was flourishing.

Chapter Seven

The Book of Shadows in 1957

In 1968 Charles Clark, with whom Carl L. Weschcke, President of Llewellyn Publications, had been corresponding for several years, casually mentioned in a letter, "I could offer you some copies of the late G.B. Gardner's rituals that he sent me for opinions from time to time, but they are not of any commercial value." Despite their probable lack of value, he did suggest that Carl might be interested in publishing them. Carl replied, yes, he would like to see them, and about a year later Clark managed to bundle them up and get them in the mail. When they arrived, Carl looked them over, decided (I gather) that they were rather messy versions of information that had already become available, and, except for publishing some cleaned-up extracts from them in various Llewellyn magazines, left them sitting in a file. I have explained in Chapter 1 how and why Isaac Bonewits came to send me copies of them and of some letters by Gardner.

When they arrived I could see that these were pages for a Gardnerian Book of Shadows. I was able to deduce immediately, by comparing them with Gardner's letters, that the materials were typed and/or handwritten by Gardner himself; the handwriting matched, and so did the two different typewriter fonts.

I was able to visit St. Paul in June 1974, at which time I autopsied the documents, and took detailed notes on their physical characteristics. Some of the documents could be roughly grouped together in terms of these characteristics; and I will explain this grouping as I come to the first document in each group during the analysis in this chapter.

During my visit, at one point I referred casually to the fact that the documents had been typed by Gardner himself. Carl, greatly surprised, stopped me in midsentence and asked how I knew that. Surprised in turn that he hadn't known, I explained that, although Gardner had not signed the documents, his authorship and typing could be established beyond the shadow of a doubt by the internal evidence and by comparison with the typed and handwritten letters from him that Carl also had. (I forget that most people just are not in the habit of playing literary detective with documents.)

Just to be sure, Carl later wrote Clark, who replied, "Yes, the MS. I sent you was Gardner's own; his corrections, etc., should prove it. I think I told you at the time how rare they were. Please treasure them." But in fact he had not mentioned that the documents were Gardner's "autograph" copies. If he had, Carl would surely have published them immediately--a copy editor would have cleaned up all the messy details that constitute the real historical evidence--and this book would never have been written.

I was asked at the time not to reveal Clark's name; so I called him Mr. Q in the first edition. Now that he has passed on and his role has become public knowledge, there is no further need for secrecy.

The documents are a motley assortment: some originals, but mostly carbon copies; typed variously on white bond, onionskin, and foolscap; of various sizes and conditions, some whole, some torn in half, some wrinkled from many foldings, some clean and never folded at all. Some have staple marks or holes punched in them, and had been fastened together in at least three different binders, no doubt being used in Books of Shadows; others show no sign of having seen such use. They were certainly not produced all at once, as a "fair copy" intended to be a single Book of Shadows. Instead, they look like, and are, miscellaneous drafts from various stages of the writing process, typed on whatever was handy.

That these documents were typed by Gardner can be demonstrated by means of the letters from Gardner in Carl Weschcke's files that Isaac had sent me copies of. The handwritten letter in Figure D.1 (p. 169) allows Gardner's handwriting on the documents to be identified. They were typed on two different typewriters. One had a very common typeface, Typeface I, in which the ratio of height to width for the Capital C is 4:3. The other, Typeface II, has tall, thin letters; the ratio of height to width for the capital C is 5:3. Carl Weschcke's letters from Gardner were typed on the same two typewriters. Figures D.2 (p. 170) and D.3 (p. 171) show a letter and a document in Typeface I; Figures D.4 (p. 172) and D.5 (P. 173) show the same for Typeface II. Notice in Figures D.2, D.4, and D.5 one of Gardner's peculiar typing habits: he usually, though not invariably, types a lowercase "ell" instead of a capital "eye." This habit also helps identify documents as being from his hand, as do his erratic spelling, punctuation, and grammar. There are also some first-person comments in the documents that only Gardner could have made; these I will point out as we come to them.

In transcribing these documents, I have used the following conventions.

1. Italics indicate words that are handwritten in the documents; unless I specify otherwise, such writing is Gardner's. Sometimes underlining has been typed in the original, and these cases I also note.

2. All parentheses are in the original document, but square brackets indicate my insertions or emendations (for example, where I spell out abbreviations and symbols).

3. I have tried hard to keep Gardner's punctuation as he typed it, but have indicated where presence or absence of punctuation could create a major shift of meaning.

4. I have also tried hard to keep Gardner's spelling, but have inserted occasional clarifications in square brackets.

5. All double quotation marks are in the originals, but I have inserted single quotation marks to flag passages that are quotations from other sources, insofar as I have been able to identify them.

6. A few items that are known to be in the Gardnerian Book of Shadows were not in the batch of documents that Clark sent to Carl Weschcke. However, the similar documents that Gardner gave to "Florannis" were later published in the pamphlet *Witch*, by "Rex Nemorensis," the pseudonym adopted by Charles Cardell, and do fill in these gaps. Indeed, with some of these documents, "Florannis" received the original of which Clark later received a carbon copy. Since I can compare some of the texts in *Witch* letter-for-letter with their copies

77 Malew St
Castletown
Isle of Man 6.8.57
England

Dear Mr Gordon Bry

In answer to your question in your letter of the 15. July

Actually I wanted to write about a witch & what she'd told me & she wouldn't let me tell anything about Witchcraft, but I said why not let me write giving to the World the Witches point of View. You are always persecuted & abused & never answer,

have a Tradition that all the Successful Sorcerers used to hire a Witch as a Sort of Medium, & in this way only did they get Results, Actually, I think Some Sort of Spiritualist Phenomena is induced, but I doubt the Spirits Power to do anything practical. In my book I tried to make this Clear. A Witch (a Trained Medium) is necessary & even then you only get good advice but the advice is Really good

Can't your Order, the Order of the Eagle give you advice on this Subject? I'm sorry I could help you more

Yours ffly

G. B. Gardner ☿

The Witches' Cottage,
77 Malew Street,
Castletown,
Isle of Man

TELEPHONE - CASTLETOWN 3248 Ext. 1

Dear Mr Weschcke

The darned trouble is, While 1 have no knowledge of the use of any Witches Cradle as Seabrook discribes, 1 can quite imagine somthing of the sort being made and used. But, while Seabrook discribes a somthing which looked horrible, lt would only be used very jently by any of the craft. The trouble is, 1 am not permitted to say what this is for.

But, 1 may say, 1 think the use of a cord wh had bound a corpse is only an old superstition, wh might have effect by suggestion. But, that presure applied to certain parts of the body does produce actual results, which 1 think are more than suggestion, but 1 cant be certain on this point.

1 do know , that for some people at least, This gives a feeling of rest and contentment,ammounting to actual mild pleasure, but whether this is only by suggestion or not, 1 am not sure. But, again for some people, lt is certainly a means of relaxing mind and body,and 1 think a real method of turning the attention inward.

1 know of legends of a "Magic Bridel" wh can turn peopleinto horses. 1 think they are just superstitions, wh may have come from the Church story, of Saints , etc, putting their girdle on a Dragon etc and taming them. Of course, under hypnosis, somone may have put a bridle on somone and told them they were a horse, and they believed it, because they were already familar with the legend.

1 dont know of any dealers in Magical equipment in London. tThere was lvor Mackey, of no 3 Thackery St. High St Kensington.London. who used to deal in magical equipment. 2nd hand, when he could get it. (He had a 2nd hand furniture store.) 1 take it, you mean what 1 mean by magical equipment not conjuring. 1 enclose a card wh may be of some use.1 think he is a good workman, but havent seen any specimins of his work. There is a man named Cardell, who advertized, he wd make you magical equipment, he wanted £137/10/- for a magic Bracelet, and he wd do no business by post. You had to pay him five pounds to speak to him, and,give him drawings of waht you wanted. People thought he was mad. and, no one was ever fool enough to pay £5/- to speak to him. or £137/10/for a £1/10/- bracelet.

In Aliester Crowleys time, there were two people who used to make things for Magicians. but the war seemed to sweep them away. Witches make their own Tools, also, theonly Magician who is worth anything. 1 told Bracelin about him and heis mentioned in his book. he makes all his own equipment. Anyhow, 1 look forward to seeing you sometime.over here.

Yours sincerely

G. B. Gardner

ALL ARE PURIFIED

Magus Concecrates Salt & Water ,

H Ps kneels at Altar, takes up Sword .says

"I conjure thee O Sword of Steel to serve me as a defence in all Magical OperationsGuard me at alltimes against mine enemies ,both visable & invisable, Grant thatI may obtain what I desire inall things wherin I may use thee ,wherefore do I bless Thee & Invoke thee in the Namse of ...&...

Gives Sword to Magus , who [kneeling] hands her vessel of Concecrated Water &Aspergulas, He Casts the Circle,Three circles. . She follows , Asperging Circle, & all present & finely herself. returns vessel etc to Magus, Who places them on Altar, or convinent place. [Hands her Sword] H.Ps walks slowly round Circle saying.

" I conjure Thee O Circle of Space,between the world of Men & that of the Dread Lords of the OUTER SPACES, That THOU be clensed Purified & strengthend to contain THAT POWER which we so ernestly desireto raise within thy bounds this night, Wherefore di I bless thee & intreet thee to aid me in the endevour in the names of ... &... [Hands Sword to Magus]

Magus then summons the Mighty Ones as usual.

H.Ps stands in front of Altar (Which may be pushed back for this)

H.Ps assumes Goddess Position (Arms Crossed,)

Magus Knealing in front of her,draws Pentical on her body with P headed Wand, Invokes, (Drawing down the Moon,)

"I Invoke and Beseach Thee ,O Mighty MOTHER ofall life and fertility . By seed and root, bystem and bud, by leaf and flower and fruit, By Life & Love do I invok Thee to decend into the body ofthy servent and H.Ps ..... (The Moon having been drawn down,I.E. Link established all Male Officers [Magus] give 5 S, All others bow.

~~[illegible] assembly form [illegible] north of Altar (Wh shd be [illegible] if [illegible] point of Swords & Athams in [illegible] of 13 candles [illegible]~~

H,Ps in Goddess Position says [Arms Crossed]

" I the Mother, Darksome and Divine,
Mine the Scourge and Mine the Kiss,
The Five Point Star of Love and Bliss;
Here I charge ye in this Sign, (Opens out Arms to Pentacle position,)
Bow before my Spirit Bright (All bow)
Aphridite Airanrod;
Lover of the Horned God,
Queen of Witchery & Night

The Witches'Mill
Castletown
Isle of Man 24.8.59.

My dear Mr Weschcke

What you quote is very intresting to me. Actually one of the Witch secrets is that restraint will produce powers. But I have taken oaths, and cant break them. But actually ,the witches I know havent anything exactly as discribed. As it does not hang from the Ceiling. When I read Seabrooks book I was puzzled, as he discribe it as as perverse a devise as twisted human ingenuity ever invented. I thought this meant it was a torture instrument. Witches have talked of it, and all were puzzled. The witch thing is beautifuly comfortable. I can see that if it was slung on chains it might be more ammsing.

Link", the "Witches Poppet" works all right. But the "Witch Law" is you may never use the "Power" to harm anyone.(Its not they are more ethical, Simply they have been through the persecution. when nine million people were tortured to death for witchcraft.) and they dont want another . As you cant work alone, and everything has to be talked over, as to whether it will harm anyone, before it may be done. And, headquarters are clair, voyant. if anyone did get up to anything. theyd all be down stamping on their necks at once. and."They gave you the power, and they can take it away." Thats what people are affraid of. Do tell me when your book will be out, as I am very intrested in this question.

Yours sincerely
G.B.Gardner
G.B. Gardner

P.S. In this Museum we have two "Witches Poppets" which worked. But, they were used in Blackmail cases. The people blackmailed had been to the police, and lawyers, and done all they could. Witches normaly wont interfear with people outside the Craft. but they liked these people. And they harmed noone. They simply prevented them harming others. In both cases the Poppet was bound round so the original could not move in the matter, and his lips pinned together so he could not speak in the matter. And they couldent.""" I am quite sure if the cord had been put round his neck and he was told to stop breathing, he would have. I also have Australian pointing bones. and Keris Magapahit. In all cases the victim does not know, what has been done. though he may guess, when things happen. Yours G.B.G.

FORMING THE CIRCLE, Must have a man and a woman.properly prepared.i.e naked.

Mark a circle nine feet across on the floor with chalk et The best way is to get a string.tie 2 loops.foun foot six in apart.put one loop over a nail ir somthing in the centre. put chalk in the other and run it round. If you cant mak marks on the floor. put furnature etc.round to form it. Have a table.to as an Alter.with all tools et-c on it. have a bowl of water, and some salt.

Place Athame on the bowl of water.say.

"I excorcise thee O creature of Water that thou cast out from Thee all the impurities and uncleannes of the Spirits of the World of Phantasm, in the name of """""" and """"" ". But ever mind that Water purifies the body, but the Z purifies the Soul."

Then place Athame on the Salt.say. "Blessings be upon this creature of Salt, let all malignity and hinderance be cast forth hensfrom, and let all good enter herin .Wherefore I bless thee that thou mayest aid me. In the name of """""" and """""" .

Then Trace Circle on the lines you have masked out. Starting at the East anr returning to the East.(Alewys go round the circle with your Right hand to the Altar, Never go Widershins.) BBBBBBBBBBB Then put the Salt into the water. and go round the circle again sprinkling it to purify it. Then go round again censing it.(Everyone in the circle must be sprinkled and Censed.) Then go to the East,Sword or Athame in hand, Draw an invoking Pentacle in the Air. Starting at the top. and going to the left hand Corner. say

"I summon ,and call thee up. Oh Ye Mighty ones of the East . to guard the Circle and witness our rites."then holding the point of Sword sor Athame upwards.do thesamet to the South.West and North and return to the Centre.to the south of the Altar.

Then each girl should bind her man.Hands behind back.and cable Tow to neck. he shd kneel at altar, and Z. when all men are thus "Purified" they purifie the girls in turn. No one may be in the circle without being thus purified. Then do whatever work wanted

When closing the Circle. The High Priestess, or whoever she tell to do it. saying." Hail, ye mighty ones of the East. I thank you for attending, and ere ye depart for your lovely reheims, We say. Hail and Farewell."

among the Weschcke documents, I know that Cardell published exact copies of the documents.

So much for issues about the text. Let me turn to some issues of historical and redaction criticism.

There was no way to know what in these 18 documents had come from an older tradition. However, I realized that I could identify most of the quotes or paraphrases of published sources, and set these aside; I could then ask whether what remained made sense as being from anything like the sort of native pagan tradition that Gardner claimed. As I carried out this procedure, I discovered some interesting facts.

First, some drafts were different versions of the same basic ritual, and sometimes incorporated revisions of other writings. I could therefore establish a relative internal chronology ("A is a revision of B; hence was written after B"). I also had absolute dates for the bits of ritual and verse that had been published in Gardner's books. I was thus able to establish that the 18 Weschcke documents were written between about 1954 and about 1960, and that most of them had probably been typed up about 1958 or 1959. This allowed me to see that many of the Book of Shadows rituals did not exist in 1954 (when *Witchcraft Today* was published), but instead were still being written.

Furthermore, where we can see that Gardner himself has inserted a new sentence into older material, whether his own or from known sources, this new sentence indicates Gardner's own theological concerns at the time he was revising the older document. This interpretive principle is the most important contribution to modern scholarship made by the discipline known as *redaction criticism.* In analyzing the Gospels, for example, where we see Luke rewriting Mark, inserting many more references to Jesus's praying than Mark had had, it is logical to conclude that Luke is especially interested in prayer. But one cannot conclude that Luke had more access than Mark did to older traditions about Jesus's praying; for one thing, to do so would violate Occam's Razor, since there is no independent evidence that any such traditions existed. Rather, redaction criticism supposes that the final authors of the Gospels were *authors*, not copyists, and that they simply wrote and rewrote according to their own best judgment—which is precisely what Luke says about himself in *Luke*

1:1-4. The parallel to Gardner is that when we see Gardner inserting new sentences about binding and scourging, we can conclude that he is especially interested in binding and scourging, not that he had access to any secret traditions about binding and scourging.

D.1. A Revision of the Casting Procedure

Documents D.1, D.5a, D.6, and D.13 were all typed on thin (about 12 lb.) white paper (watermarked "Kent White") in typeface I; D.6 and D.1 are blue carbons, the other two are black carbons. All four sheets were originally 8" x 10" (normal British letter size), but D.13 has been torn in half, and D.6 has been cut off at 8.625".

All four have two holes punched in them. On D.6, D.5a, and D.1 the variation in the placement of the holes along the left edge is more than half an inch, measuring from the top of the sheet; so these holes were punched after the documents were typed (prepunched holes would align exactly). Moreover, on D.5a, which is typed on both sides, the holes are punched along the torn edge, and have punched through one word on the front, two on the back. Documents D.3 and D.5 also have two holes punched along the left edge. Obviously, the holes were punched so that these seven (and perhaps other) documents could be held together in a ring or post binder. Furthermore, the back of Document D.5a shows pressure and rust marks from staples along the right edge; these match perfectly the staple and rust marks on the front left edge of Document D.8. On the front left edge of Document D.13 (that is, at right angles to the edge with the punched holes) there are pressure and rust marks from staples that do not match the marks on any other documents in this set. I deduce that after Documents D.6, D.5a, D.13, and D.1 had been in the ring or post binder, this binder was taken apart; and the pages in it were then placed in a clamp binder with other material, some of which was more recent than these four documents. Not all of this other material is included in this set of documents. That is, it appears that some of the documents here have been used in more than one Book of Shadows, probably that of Gardner himself and that of Clark.

ALL ARE PURIFIED

[1] Magus Concecrates Salt & Water ,

[2] H[igh] P[riestes]s kneels at Altar, takes up Sword. says

"I conjure thee O Sword of Steel to serve me as a defence in all Magical Operations Guard me at all times against mine enemies, both visable & invisable, Grant that I may obtain what I desire inall things wherin I may use Thee, Wherefore do I bless Thee & invoke Thee[1] in the names of... &... [2]

[3] Gives Sword to Magus , who kneeling hands her vessel of Conscrated Water[3] & Aspergulas, He Casts the Circle,Three circles .[4] She follows , Asperging Circle & all present & finely herself.[5] [She] returns vessel etc to Magus, Who places them on Altar, or convinent place. *& hands her Sword*.

[4] H[igh] P[riestes]s walks slowly round Circle, saying.

"I conjure Thee O Circle of Space, between the world of Men & that of the Dread Lords of the OUTER SPACES. That THOU be clensed Purified & strengthend to contain THAT POWER which we so ernestly desireto raise within thy bounds this night, `Wherefore di I bless thee & entreet thee to aid me in the endevour'[6] in the names of . . . & . . ."

---

[1] This formula bas been compounded from three formulas in GKS, pp. 101, 118, and 94. The whole concept of conjuring the tools comes from GKS as well.

[2] The current secret names of the God and Goddess appropriate for the level of initiation of those present would be inserted here. This formula has been rewritten from the form given by the Farrars (1984, p. 44) as having been used in 1954-1956. Hence this document seems to be a rewriting of "Text C," and to fall in 1955 or later.

[3] Here "Slat" had been typed, then crossed out, and "Consecrated Water" typed above it.

[4] Notice that in 1957 we see Gardner still using the triple circle of the ceremonial magicians.

[5] The general procedure for putting consecrated salt in consecrated water, and for sprinkling the circle, is given in GKS, pp. 96f and 107, as we saw for Document A.1.

[6] This formula is patterned after those in GKS, although only the part flagged by single quote marks is a close paraphrase of a line in GKS, p. 94. The specific

Hands sword to Magus.

[5] Magus then summons the Mighty Ones as usual.

[6] H[igh] P[riestes]s stands in front of Altar (Which may be pushed back).

H[igh] P[riestes]s assumes Goddess[7] possition (Arms Crossed,)

Magus knealing in front of her,draws Pentical on her body with P-headed[8] Wand, Invokes, (Drawing down the Moon,)

" l Invoke and Beseach Thee ,O mighty MOTHER ofall life and fertility. `By seed and root, bystem and bud, by leaf and flower nd fruit, By Life & Love -do I invoke Thee"[9] to decend into the body ofthy servent and H[igh] P[riestes]s ..... (The Moon having been drawn down,I.E. Link established *Magus* [&] all male officers give [fivefold kiss], All others bow.

~~**Assembly(?) form a semi circle at north of Altar, (Wh Shd be replaced if it has been moved,) H Ps in south, inserts point of Sword or Athame in decorated bundle of 13 candles ,saying**~~[10]

[7] H[igh] P[riestes]s in Goddess position says *Arms Crossed*[11]

"I the Mother, Darksome and Divine,
Mine the Scourge and Mine the Kiss,
The Five Point Star of Love and Bliss;
Here I charge ye in this Sign,
(Opens out Arms to pentacle position,)
Bow before my Spirite bright (All bow)
Aphridite Airanrod;

---

procedure given here for casting a circle to work in could come from GKS (e.g., pp. 14f, 964, 103) or from almost any grimoire.

[7] Here "God" was typed first, then "Goddess" typed above it, but "God" was not then scratched out. There is obviously some uncertainty here about the meaning of the arms-crossed position, although it is called the "God position" in WT, pp. 92f and 157f.

[8] The "P" here apparently stands for "phallus," according to Farrar 1971, p. 92.

[9] Quoted from CGM, p. 350.

[10] Typed over with m's. The reading is certain on all but the first word. This certainly would have been a curious procedure.

[11] More uncertainty about the arms-crossed position.

Lover of the Horned God,
Queen of Witchery & Night[12]

Commentary on D.1.

This innocent-looking document—a working draft from the process of writing what would become the standard Gardnerian procedure for beginning a Craft ritual—is the most important of all the documents I have seen, except for "Ye Bok of ye Art Magical" itself, for reconstructing the history of the Gardnerian movement.

This is certainly not a first draft; the consecration of salt and water in [1] and the summoning of the Mighty Ones in [5] are already "standard operating procedures." On the other hand, one does not type over two sentences with m's when copying or writing down an established procedure; that is what I have indicated by use of strikeout type. The sources of formula [2] are *The Greater Key of Solomon*, pp. 98, 101, 118; it has been rewritten from the form that Doreen Valiente says (in the Farrars 1984, p. 44) was used in 1954-1956; and that indicates a date for this document of sometime in or after 1957.

The censing in [3] agrees with the HOGD Neophyte ritual and with the procedures of *The Greater Key of Solomon*, pp. 96-97. The formula in [4] is patterned after those in *The Greater Key of Solomon*, although only the part flagged by single quotes is a close paraphrase of a line in *The Greater Key of Solomon*, p. 94.

Let see what becomes of the various elements here. The "Conjuration of the Sword" is soon dropped from the basic ritual (see E.3), but becomes part of the special procedure used for charging tools, in D.10. The "Conjuration of the Circle" in [4] and the formula for "Drawing Down the Moon" are still used in E.3, but have been slightly rewritten; the wording in E.3 is exactly that of the Alexandrian Book of Shadows (Farrar 1971, pp. 54, 64), and so the version here must be earlier.

There are handwritten corrections in [3] and [4], because Gardner, looking the manuscript over after it was typed, realized that he had asked the Priestess to walk around the circle with no tool in her hands; so he

---

[12] The next page, which would have continued this poem, was not among the Weschcke documents.

added the instructions that give her the sword. But this caused the circle to be cast first by the Magus in [3], then again by the Priestess in [4]. The casting procedure had to be greatly simplified to remove this redundancy, which still appears in D.6 and E.3, but has been eliminated in E.4.

Who is dominant here, the Magus or the Priestess? It is the Magus who consecrates salt and water, who casts the circle first and is followed around by the Priestess, who hands the Priestess the tools she is to use, who summons the Mighty Ones, and who calls down the Goddess onto the Priestess. That is, we are still in the universe of *High Magic's Aid*, in which the male magician must use the procedures of ceremonial magic to erect the magical circle before the female witch can work her folk magic in it. Yet there are also elements of change here: the uncertainty over whether the arms-crossed position should represent the Goddess or the God; the Magus' kneeling before her in [3] and [6]. These point forward to Gardnerian practice since the mid-1960s (see Farrar 1971, pp. 53-55, for example), in which the Priestess can work the entire ritual by herself. But reading the trend here backward, we can see that before 1957 the coven was presided over by a man, not a woman: and that is what I predicted from my hypothesis that the starting point for Gardner had been the data in Murray.

Let us, finally, consider dating. Doreen Valiente wrote the quatrain verse form of the Charge after a partial prose form had appeared in *Witchcraft Today*. Hence D.1 must date to 1954 or later—and, in fact, as we will see below, must be dated in late 1957—and D.6, D.10, E.2, E.3, and E.4, which all depend on D.1, must be later than 1957 (although some elements of the raw material in them date from the period 1948 to 1953). In other words, despite all the explicit and implicit claims made about rituals in *Witchcraft Today*, Gardner had still not established the basic working procedures of his "tradition," and was not yet clear about the relative importances of the Priestess and Priest within the coven, or about which of them should do what in a ritual, even in 1957. This is hardly the situation we would imagine if there had been a coven before 1939 that was organized well enough to hold rituals.

We can see from Tanya Luhrmann's description (pp. 223-4) of the procedure used by the London coven for casting the circle used in the late 1980s that it is still essentially that of "Ye Bok of ye Art Magical," although details have been altered in order to "paganize" it. Her description lists the following steps.

1. A circle is drawn with chalk and a string held down in the centre by the High Priestess's athame, just as in A.1 [1].

2. To begin the ritual, the circle is first cast with the athame in the air, retracing the circle, as in A.1 [2].

3. The salt is consecrated, as in A.1 [3].

4. The water is consecrated, as in A.1 [4].

5. The two are mixed, as in A.1 [5].

6. The circle is sprinkled, as in A.1 [6].

7. The quarters are invoked, combining the procedures of A.1 [9], [11], and [12].

8. Incense is presented to the quarters; this is substituted for the lighting of candles in A.1 [7].

9. A gate is opened, and the participants, who have been outside the circle so far, are now admitted; then the circle is retraced to close the gate. This agrees with the content of A.1 [8].

If you compare these steps with the sequence of events in D.1 here, or in D.6, E.3, and E.4, which all depend on D.1, you can see that they simply do not match; they all disagree with Luhrmann's description in far more ways than the procedure in "Ye Bok of ye Art Magical" does. In other words, Gardner's original coven was apparently still using the procedures specified in "Ye Bok of ye Art Magical" in the late 1980s, because Gardner did not write the procedures for casting the circle in D.1, D.6, E.3, and E.4 until after Doreen Valiente had stopped working with him in 1957, when he also left the original coven. These later procedures were included in the text of the Book of Shadows given to Gardner's initiates after 1957, and therefore appear in the Farrar's 1981 and 1984 books. In the latter books, although Doreen Valiente supplies commentary about what is in her Texts A, B, and C for everything else, she actually does not say anything about the procedure for casting the circle. As a result, it is not obvious that her book disagrees with the Book of Shadows as used by the great majority of Gardnerian Witches now; she confirmed in a letter that this is so, and that she did not write the

"Conjuration of the Circle" in E.3. What had happened is that, once she had stopped working with Gerald, he proceeded to rewrite her rituals and much else in the Book of Shadows, and it was this rewritten book that came into the hands of Monique Wilson and Patricia Crowther.

These conclusions also have major implications for the way in which the Craft conducts itself in America, since we can now see that rules about circles being "valid" only if cast by a Third-Degree High Priestess have no basis in Gardnerian practice in England before 1957, as Robert has been saying loudly for more than a decade.

O.2. The Prose Charge

THE CHARGE,[13] to be read while the initiate stands, properly prepared before the Circle.

[Magus]: Listen to the words of the Great mother,who was of old[14] also called among men, Artimis; Astarte; Dione; Melisine, Aphrodite. Cerridwen; Diana Arianrod; Bride; and by many other names.

[High Priestess]:

At mine Altars the youth of Lacedemon in Spata made due sacrifice. 'Whenever ye have need of anything, once in the month, and better it be when the moon is full. Then ye shall assemble in some secret place and adore the spirit of Me who am Queen of all Witcheries.

'There ye shall assemble,ye who are fain to learn all sorcery. yet who have not won its deepest secrets[15] To these will l teach things tha[t] are yet unknown.

'And ye shall be free from slavery,and as a sign that ye be realy free,ye shall be naked in your rites,and ye shall dance,sing, feast,make music,and love,all in my praise.'[16]

For mine is the ectasy of the Spirit,and mine is also joy on earth, For my Law is Love unto all beings.. Keep pure your highest[17] ldeals. strive

---

[13] "Charge" is used in precisely this way in Masonic rituals.

[14] An old document would not contain phrases like "of old."

[15] What is actually typed here is a 7/8 fraction.

[16] The preceding four sentences are a fairly exact quotation from Leland's *Aradia*, as I noted for A.5.

[17] Hear "heart" was typed, then "highest" typed over it.

ever towards it.Let naught stop you or turn you aside.

For mine is the secret which opens upon the door of youth;and mine is the cup of the Wine of Life: and the Cauldren of Cerridwen; which is the Holy Grail of Lmortality.

L am the Graceious Goddess who gives the gift of Joy unto the heart of Man.

Upon Earth l give the knowledge of the Spirit Eternal;and beyond death l give peace and fredom; and reunion with those who have gone before; Nor do l demand aught in sacrifice;[18] for behold. l am the Mother of all things; and my love is poured out upon earth.

[Magus]: Hear ye the words of the Star Goddess,She in the dust of whose feet are the hosts of Heaven; whose body encircleth the Universe.

[High Priestess]: "L who am the beauty of the green earth; and the White Moon amongst the Stars;an d the mystery of the Waters; and the disire of the heart of man;l call unto thy soul; arise and come unto me.

For l am the Soul of nature who giveth life to the Universe; 'From me all things proceed;and unto me, all things must return;'[19] Beloved of the Gods and men; thine inmost divine self shall be enfolded in the raptures of the infinite.

Let my worship be within the heart that rejoiceth;for behold; all acts of Love and Pleasure are my rituals;and therefore let there be Beauty and Strength; Power and compassion;Honour and Humility;Mirth and Reverance within you.

And thou who thinkest to seek me; Know that they seeking and yerning shall avail thee notl unless thou know the mystery, 'That[20] if that which thou seekest thou findest not within thee;Thou wilt never find it without thee.' For behold; l have been with thee from the begining, and l am that which is attained at the end of desire.

---

[18] This does contradict what has been said about those youths in Spata.

[19] The sentence seems to have been taken from the HOGD Neophyte ritual: "from him all things proceed, and unto him all things return" (Regardie, *Golden Dawn*, I, 37).

[20] Preceding three words were first typed as "my mystery, the," then changed.

Commentary on O.2

The last quote is from "Alipilli" on the title page of L. A. Cahagnet, *Magnetic Magic* (privately printed, 1898; 47 pages, paperbound), a book from Gardner's library that I looked at in Toronto. Here the contents of Document A.5 have been skillfully rewritten by Doreen Valiente to disguise the fact that the concepts in it are largely a pastiche drawn from Crowley's Gnostic Mass. On this, the Farrars comment, "Gardner drafted a first version [the one in A.5], very similar to the one we give here down to `all in my praise' . . . followed by some voluptuously worded extracts from Aleister Crowley. Doreen Valiente tells us she `felt that this was not really suitable for the Old Craft of the Wise . . . so I wrote a version of the Charge in verse, keeping the words from *Aradia*, because these are traditional.'[21] This verse version began 'Mother darksome and divine' . . . But most people seemed to prefer a prose Charge, so she wrote the final prose version . . . [which] still contains one or two Crowley phrases."[22]

O.3. Cakes and Wine[23]

High Priestess seated on Altar, God position.

High Priest kneeling. Kisses feet then knees. Bows with head below her knees, extends arms along her thighs, and adores.[24]

Fills cup and offers to High Priestess, who holding Athame between palms, places point in cup.

High Priest says: "As the Athame is the male, so the cup is the female, and conjoined they bring blessedness."

High Priestess lays Athame aside, and takes Cup and drinks, gives Cup to server, who puts a little in each glass. Meanwhile the High Priest

---

[21] This gives us an interesting insight into Doreen Valiente's assumptions: even though she knows this material has been lifted from Leland's *Aradia*, she can believe that it is traditional - that is, she believes there is an oral tradition behind it.

[22] Farrars 1981, p. 42 n8.

[23] This text is from *Witch*, by "Rex Nemorensis" (Charles Cardell), which was the first publication (in 1964) of any parts of the Gardnerian Book of Shadows. This ritual happened to not be among the Weschcke documents.

[24] This adoration has been added here from CGM, p. 351.

presents Pentacle with cakes to High Priestess, who blesses them with Athame. Takes Cake and eats, while the High Priest gives her the Cup again and kisses knees and adores.

All sit as Witches, and invite High Priestess to join them.[25]

Note. Of old it was usual for the server to say: "Oh Queen most secret, bless this food unto our bodies, bestowing health, wealth, strength, joy and peace, and that fulfillment of love that is perpetual happiness." When serving cakes, this is usually omitted nowadays. It is difficult to get a good server.[26]

Commentary on D.3

The actions here, and the words in the fifth paragraph, come from Crowley's "Gnostic Mass" in *Magick in Theory and Practice*, pp. 351, 356f, 359f. All my comments about B.5 still apply here. I believe this is one of the most important times in the working of any coven. This sort of communal eating, drinking, and conversing is intended to be sacramental—and therefore it is so. Another version of this ritual is given by Farrar 1971, pp. 18-19.

D.4. The Sabbat Rituals

Most of Document D.4 was typed in Typeface II on letter-size white bond paper watermarked "Rossendale Bond." However, sheets 6 and 7 of its eight sheets are watermarked "Aviemore" and are legal size, sheet 7 being torn off at the bottom, sheet 6 merely folded up. The eight sheets of Document D.4 are originals, typed on one side only (except for sheet 8), and almost entirely in capital letters, which I see no reason to reproduce. The sheets were never fastened together or folded in any way, although the righthand corners show a little dogearing; they may have been in a Book of Shadows, but they did not get hard use. All of Gardner's handwritten notes on them are in pencil.

---

[25] In plain English, everyone sits in a circle crosslegged, eats, drinks, and talks business.

[26] For one thing, very few in this younger generation can say the line with a straight face. The Farrars (1981, p. 47 n 15, identify it as being adapted from CGM, p. 359). Again, this is a first-person comment by Gardner.

Sun in Aquarius[27]

Feb Eve. Feast of Torches. St Brides Eve. Candlemas Feb 1st

After usual opning all are doubly purified.

Dance round outside circle. H[igh] P[riestes]s with sword girded on and srawn.P wand[28] in left hand. Enter circle. H[igh] P[riest] God position. H[igh] P[riestes]s gives [Fivefold Kiss].Lnvokea.

"Dread Lord of death & resurection. `life and the giver of life.' `Lord within ourselves,whose name is Mystery of Mysteries.'

'encourage our hearts, Let the light chrystalize in our blood, fulfilling of ud resurecton,' for 'there is no part of us that is not of the gods.'[29]

Descend we pray thee upon this,thy servant and Priest.....

Alll should be purified in sacrifice before him. He then purifies the H[igh] P[riestes]s with his own hands . and others if he will.

Cakes and wine.

Great Rite .Lf possible.in token or real.

Games and dance as the people will.

Spring equinox March 22nd

The symbol of the wheel should be placed on the altar.Upright, decked with flowers.Flanked with burning candles. The cauldren ,containing spirit is in the east. H[igh] P[riest] in west? H[igh] P[riestes]s in east with P wand or pine cone tipped [wand] .or broomstick,or riding pole, broom upwards.

H[igh] P[riestes]s lights cauldren saying.

"We kindle fire this day!
Ln the presence of the Holy Ones:

---

[27] All italic (or underlining) here represents Gardner's handwriting. However, I'm not flagging his handwritten editing of the headings for the Sabbats.

[28] Judging from Farrar 1971, p. 92, this means "phallic wand" throughout.

[29] This invocation has been put together from bits and pieces of Crowley (CGM, pp. 351-1, 360). Crowley wrote "fulfilling us of resurrection"; Gardner managed to reverse the two short words. That this reversal appears in Farrar 1971, p. 93, proves that Sanders' version depends on this document, not directly on Crowley--that is, Sanders' BoS is based on Gardner's, and not vice versa.

Without malice,without jelousey,without envy.
Without fear of aught beneath the sun.
But the High Gods.
Thee we invoke: O light of life:
Be thou a bright flame before us:
Be thou a guiding star above us:
Be thou a smooth path beneath us;
Kindle thou in our hearts within,
A flame of love for our neighbour,
To our foes,to our friends,to our kindred all:
To all men on this broard Earth.
O merciful son of Cerridwen
From the lowest thing that liveth
To the name that is highest of all."

H[igh] P[riestes]s draw [pentacle] upon H[igh] P[riest] with wand.[kiss] gives it to him. He does likewise½ They lead the dance round the circle all couples leaping burning fire. The last couple as the fire goes out should be well purified?3 times.

And each should give [Fivefold Kiss] to all of opposite sex.

Cakes and wine.

If the people will, the cauldren dance can be done again,many times. Or other games can be played.

Sun in Taurus May Eve Eve of May 1st

Lf possible ride poles,brooms etc. H[igh] P[riestes]s leading,quick dance step.

Singing

" O, do not tell the priests of our arts.
For they would call it sin,
For we will be in the woods all night,
A conjuring summer in.

And we bring you good news by word of mouth
For women,cattle,and corn.

The sun is coming up from the south,
With oak and ash, and corn."[30]

(Meeting dance if possible.) Form [circle] as usual,purify.
H[igh] P[riest] lnvokes, draws down moon.

"L lnvoke thee and call upon thee,
O mighty Mother of us all,
bringer of all fruitfulness,'By seed and root.
by stem and bud,by leaf and flower and fruit,
by life and love ,do we invoke thee.'
to descend upon the body of the servent and Priestess here.[31] [Fivefold Kiss]

All should be purified in sacrifice before her, and she should purify H[igh] P[riest] and some others with her own hands.

Cakes and wine. Games.
Great Rite if possible, ln token or truley.

May [Sun in Taurus] Bull
Lammas August [Sun in Leo] Lion
Halloween [Sun in Scorpio] Eagle
Candlemas [Aquarius] Man

The Summer Solstice Midsummer June 22nd

Form [circle]. Lnvoke , Purify. Cauldren is placed before altar.Filled with water, wreathedd with summer flowers. The people, men & woman alternatly,stand round [circle]. H[igh] P[riestes]s stands in north,before cauldren, holding wand,(Wh slould be P.or tipped with a pine cone.(anciently the thyrsus)[32] or a riding pole.or a broomstick. H[igh] P[riestes]s holding this raised invokes the sun. "Great One of Heaven, Power of the Sun, we invoke thee in thine ancient names.

---

[30] This is a bit of Kipling, of course. The last word should be "thorn"; Farrar (1971, p. 96) corrects it.

[31] Quote from CGM, p. 350. The phrase "the servant" is elsewhere "thy servant."

[32] And obviously this is a comment by a modern enthusiast for the classics.

Michael. Balin .Arthur . Lough. Herne. Come again ,as of old into this thy land. Lift up thy shining spear of light to protect us. Put to flight the powers of darkness, give us fair woodlands and green fields,blossoming orchards, and ripnening corn . Bring us to stand upon thy hill of vission, and show us the path to the lovely realms of the gods.

H[igh] P[riestes]s draws invoking pentacle on H[igh] P[riest] with wand. Who comes forward sunwise and takes wand with [kiss]. H[igh] P[riest] plungeswand into cauldren and holds it upright saying, " The spear to the cauldren, the lance to the Grail , spirit to flesh, man to woman , sun to earth."

He salutes H[igh] P[riestes]s over cauldren,then rejoinespeople. Still bearing wand. H[igh] P[riestes]s takes aspergillus,stands by cauldren. Says . "Dance ye about the cauldren of Cerridwen the Goddess,and be ye blessed with the touch of this conseccrated water,even as the sun, the lord of light arriveth in his streangth in the sign of the waters of life."[33]

The people dance sunways about the alter and cauldren led by H[igh] P[riest] bearing wand, H[igh] P[riestes]s sprinkles them lightly as they pass her.

Ritual of cakes and wine.

Any other dances,rites or games as the P[riestes]s & people wish.

Lammas

Sun in Leo *August Eve* Eve of Aug. 1st

Lf possible ride poles,Broomsticks, etc, Meeting Dance if Possible. Form [circle]. Purify.

H[igh] P[riestes]s [drawing of pentacle].[34]

H[igh] P[riest] lnvokes her.

"O mighty Mother of us all. Mother of all fruitfulness.

give us fruit and grain.flocks and herds and children, to

---

[33] The Farrars (1981, p. 101n3) state that the material from "Great One of Heaven" down to "Waters of Life" was written by Doreen Valiente.

[34] This presumably means, "High Priestess stands in pentacle position."

> the tribe (or Craft[35]) that we be mighty, by thy rosey love,do thou descend upon thy servent and Priestess.... here

[Fivefold Kiss].

Cakes and wine, Candle game. Seated, the men form a circle, passing a lighted candle from hand to hand,"dieosal". The women form circle outside,trying to blow it out ?over their shoulders, Whovers hand it is [in] when it is blown out is 3 times purified wy whoever blew it out. Giving [fivefold Kiss] in return. This game may go on as long as the people like.

Cakes and wine, and any other games you like.

Autumn equinox Sept. 22nd

The altar shouldd be decorated with symbols of autum.pine cones, oak sprigs,acorns, or ears of corn. And should have fire or burning lncense on it as usual. After usual purification the people stand round, man and woman alternatly. H[igh] P[riest] at west of altar in God position. H[igh] P[riestes]s stands at east of altar,facing him ,and reads the incantation.

> "Farewell O Sun, ever returning light. The hidden god, who ever yet remains½ He separts to the land of youth, through the gates of death, to dwell enthroned, the judge of gods and man.

The horned leader of the hosts of air. Yet, even as stand unseen about the circle ? the forms of the Mighty Lords of the Outer Spaces. So dwelleth he,'the lord within ourselves.'[36] So dwelleth he, within the secret seed. The seed of new reaped grain,the seed of flesh. Hidden in the earth,the marvellous seed of the stars. 'Ln him is life, and life is the light of men.'[37] that which was never boen,and *never dies. Therefore ,the*

---

[35] Gardner is uncertain which word to use: clearly "Craft" has just started being used as a technical term; so this was typed about 1958-59.

[36] Quote from CGM, p. 352. The Farrars (1981, p. 119n2) say this was written by Doreen Valiente. If so, she has here not rewritten the direct quotes from Crowley, which would seem odd. Hence this may actually be by Gardner.

[37] Gardner or Doreen Valiente has copied this from CGM, p. 352, not realizing

Wica weep not, but rejoice."

The H[igh] P[riestes]s goes to the H[igh] P[riest] with S. He lays aside A & $. & S.[38] The H[igh] P[riestes]s hands him her wand,which should be P, or a branch tipped wit[h] a pine_cone.Or a riding pole, or a broomstick. (anciently the thyrsus.) They lead the dance,she with a systrum or rattle,he with wand. The people falling in behind them.Dancing 3 times round the altae½ Then the candle game is played.

Cakes and wine.

Great Rite lf possible.

Dances and games.

Sun in Scorpio November Eve Hallowe'en Eve of Nov. 1st

Walk or slow dance. H[igh] P[riest] leading H[igh] P[riestes]s,both carrying P wand or broom.people with torches or candles. Witch chant or song.[39]

Foem [circle] Purify. H[igh] P[riest][40] God position. H[igh] P[riestes]s invokes with Athame. " Dread Lord of the shadows, god of `life and the giver of life. Yet is the knowledge of thee the knowledge of death.'[41] Open wide L pray thee,thy gates through whlch all must pass.

Let our dear ones who have gone before,return this night to make merry with us.

And when our time comes, as it must.

O thou the comforter, the consoler, the giver of peace and rest, we will enter thy realms gladly and unafraid. For we know that when rested

---

it is from the New Testament

[38] This could be interpreted in several ways: the High Priest lays aside the three things he is holding, that is, athame, scourge, and sword (but how could be hold all three?); he lays aside his athame, scourges the Priestess or is scourged by her, and is kissed or gives a kiss.

[39] There are differing opinions on what song is intended here. The Farrars (1981, p. 133n2) state that the following speech is by Gardner, but do not explain how they know this; presumably Doreen Valiente told them so.

[40] A symbol is drawn here, a large X with a small circle above it, which I take to be a stick-figure rendition of the skull and crossbones.

[41] Quote from CGM, p. 351.

and refreshed among our dear ones, we shall be born again by thy grace, and the grace of the Great Mother, let it be in the same place and the same time as our beloved ones?,and may we meet and know, and love them again.

Descend we pray thee upon thy servent and Priest .??....... [Fivefold Kiss]. (Lt is good to purify a few girls as sacrifice)

Cakes and wine

Great Rite if pssible.

The Winter Solsise Dec 22

Form [circle] in usual manner.invoking the Mighty Ones.

The Caulderon of Cerridwen is placed in the circle at the south wreathed with holly,Ivy, & mistletoe,with fire lighted within it. There should be no other light except for the candels on the altar and about the circle.

After all are purified, the Moon should be drawn down. Then,the H[igh] P[riestes]s stands behind the cauldren[42] symbolising the rebirth of the sun. The people, man and woman alternatly,stand round the [circle]. The H[igh] P[riest] stands facing the H[igh] P[riestes]s,with a bundle of torches,or candles, & the book of words of the incantation,one of the officers stands beside him with a lighted candle,so that he may have light to read by.

The people begin to slowly move round the circle sunwise.As each passess him the H[igh] P[riest] lights his candle or torch.From the fire in the cauldren,which may be simply a candle .Till all have lighted candles or torches. Then the people dance round slowly as he reads the incantation.

(A real fire must now be kindled in the cauldren.)

"Queen of the Moon,Queen of the Sun.
Queen of the Heavens,Queen of the Stars.
Queen of the Waters,Queen of the Earth.
Who ordained to us the child of promise:

---

[42] Here "altar" was typed first; it was blacked out, and "cauldren" typed, followed by a space, probably for a pentacle symbol, since the Priestess here stands in pentacle position (see WT, p. 26).

Lt is the Great Mother who gives birth to him,
He is the Lord of Life who is born again,
Darkness and tears are set behind,
And the star of guidence comes up early.

Golden sun of hill and mountain
Illumine the land,illumine the world
Illumine the seas,illumine the rivers,
Grief be laid,and joy be raised.

Blessed be the Great Mother
Without begining,without ending,
To everlasting,to eternity,
IO. Evoh, Blessed be."[43]

The Dance commences slowley ,in rythm with the chant.[44] all taking up the call. L.O. Blessed be. The Pristess joines dance & leads them with a quicker rythm. The cauldren with burning fire is pushed so that the dancers leap or step over it,ln couples. Whichever couple is passing it as it goes out,should be well purified, 3 times,each. and may pay any ammusing forfit as the H[igh] P[riestes]s may ordain. Somtimes the cauldre[n] ls relighted several times,for this purpose.

Commentary on D.4

These rituals have been published before: in Farrar (1971, Chapter 7), which provides a detailed commentary on them; in *GLS*, who gives a somewhat later version of them, but also censors the sexual elements a great deal; and by the Farrars (1981). There have also been general descriptions, as in Johns and Glass.

Of these eight rituals, those for February Eve, the spring equinox, May Eve, the autumn equinox, and Hallowe'en contain nothing traditionally pagan except for the notion of leaping over the bonfire, here turned

---

[43] There are many differences in wording between this version of the verse and that in WT; that Gardner has felt free to rewrite it again shows that it is not traditional.

[44] The dance must commence very slowly, since this chant has no discernible rhythm at all.

into a gamelike charm. In the summer solstice ritual, the only traditional element is the blessing by the cauldron, which derives in concept from the type of fertility magic once worked at this time of the year for the growth of the crops.

Obviously, if Gardner had known any traditional rituals for the Sabbats, he would have used them, instead of piecing these rituals together from bits of folklore, quotes from Crowley, and parts of the workings intended to be used at almost any meeting. The focus here remains on sexuality as sacramental.

The Farrars (1981, p. 78n2) state that the verse in the Spring Equinox ritual was adapted by Doreen Valiente from two verses in Carmichael's *Carmina Gadelica*, vol. I, on pages 231 and 49; this was the work she had also used as a source for her Yule ritual. Notice that this ritual does not follow the pattern that Gardner used for the four earlier Sabbats, of many scourgings, followed by the Great Rite. Similarly, the Summer Solstice ritual does not follow Gardner's pattern; the Farrars (1981, p. 101n3) state that the material in it from "Great One of Heaven" down to "Waters of Life" was written by Doreen Valiente.

The quote in the autumn equinox ritual is from Crowley's "Gnostic Mass" in *Magick in Theory and Practice*, p. 352. It seems very odd that Valiente would have used this quote, given her normal strategy of getting rid of Crowley; so perhaps Gardner wrote that particular Sabbat ritual. It also is closer to the pattern of the four earlier Sabbats by Gardner, since it calls for the Great Rite.

The winter solstice ritual here has also been throughly rewritten from the text that appeared in *Witchcraft Today*. Gardner has done some of this revising, since it is likely he who would add the detail that the couple who are leaping over the cauldron when it goes out are to be "purified" with 120 strokes each.

D.5a. Eightfold Path or Ways to the Centre.

[See inital commentary on Document D.2]

1. Meditation or Concentration, This in practice means forming a Mental,immage of what is desired,& forcing yourself to see that it is fulfilled, with the fierce belief and knowlege that it can & will be fulfilled,

& that you will go on willing till you force it to be fulfilled. Called for short. "Intent".

2. Trance, projection of the Astral,

3. Rites , Chants,Spells , Runes , Charms ,etc

4. Insense , Drugs, Wine ,etc, whatever is used to release the Spirit. (Note,One must be very careful about this, Insense is usually harmless, but you must be carefull, if it has bad after effects, reduce the ammont used, or the duration of the time it is inhaled, Drugs are very dangerous, if taken to excess, but it must be remembered that there are drugs that are absulutly harmless, though people talk of them with bated breath, but Hemp is especially dangerous, because it unlocks theinner eye swiftly & easily, so one is tempted to use it more & more,if it is used at all, it must be with the strictest precautions, to see that theperson who uses it has no controll over the supply, this should be doled out by some responasable person, & the supply strictly limited,

5. The Dance, & kindred practices.

6. Blood controll, (the Cords) Breath Control, & kindred ctices.[45]

7. [Scourge].

8. The great Rite.[46]

1[9] These are all the ways, you may combine many of them into the one experi[ment][47], The more the better. The most important is "Intention" you must know that you can & will suceed, it is esential in every opperation.

2[10] Preperation. (You *must* be properly prepered according to *the rules of the Art.*Otherwise you will *never suceed.*

3[11] The Circle must be properly formed & purified. ~~Likewise all~~

---

[45] All this is described more fully in later documents.

[46] Entry 8 is followed by a line partway across the page, and the next five entries are typed with their beginnings aligned under the first eight numbers. The numbers for these five entries are typed in the margin, as if by afterthought. The numbers 1 to 5 align with the entries, but the numbers 9 to 13 are above the line. They were added as yet another afterthought, probably because Gardner found that having two sets of things numbered 1 to 5 confused his comments.

[47] This word runs off the page, but just enough of the "m" is visible to show that it was not "experience."

~~opperators.~~[48]

4[12] You all must be properly purified, several times if necessary, & this Purification should be repeeted several times during therite.

5[13] You must have properly Consecrated tools.[49]

These five esentials, & Eight Paths or Ways, cannot all be combined in one rite,Meditation & Dancing do not combine well. but Forming the mental image & the dance may be wellcombined, with Chants , Spells etc,combined with [scourging] & No 6. followed by [50] No 8. form a splendid combination.[51] Meditation, following [scourging]. Combined with Nos3 & 4 & 5 Are also very Good. For short cuts .Concentration. Nos 5,6 ,7 & 8, are excelent. Nos 9, 10 LL[52] 12 ,& 13 are esential in all experiments.

Commentary on D.5a.

Did Gardner learn these techniques from an older coven? It is clear from his long note after paragraph 4 that he was personally not familiar with the use of drugs as part of a magical training process—whereas this is one of the few things we could expect of almost any sort of native shamanism—and so was not trained in such use by an earlier coven; instead, he has learned the concept from reading. It also follows that

---

[48] Typed, then crossed out, because a circle is "purified" quite differently from a human being. That is, after typing these words, Gardner realized that a separate rule was needed for people. Hence we can see here that Gardner was making these rules up as he went along, as is also indicated by the long, "thinking out loud" parenthesis after entry 4, and by the fact that these five "essentials" were not numbered until after they had been typed.

[49] The concept comes from GKS, e.g. (p.98), "In order to properly carry out the greatest... Operations of the Art, various instruments are necessary." Notice "operations," another term that Gardner uses. All the underlining in these "five essentials" is typed.

[50] A three-letter word was typed here, then typed over with m's; I cannot make out what it was.

[51] The grammar and punctuation here are impossible to untangle.

[52] Gardner's typed two capital ells here; so the typing is his. There is no handwriting on this document to identify it.

his organizing of these methods into an "Eightfold Path" was his own idea, not part of what he might have learned from an earlier coven. Only the first two or three of these eight "ways" make sense as part of the techniques of an HOGD-type of magical lodge; Gardner could have gotten the rest of them from Thelemic sources. The use of a Buddhist term here points toward the simplest, most probable conclusion: that Gardner had learned about all these "mind-altering" techniques by reading about Tantric systems, but almost certainly at second hand, via Randolph, whose *Eulis* was in his library, or Crowley (see Melton, "*The Origins of Modern Sex Magick*," 1985). His listing of binding and scourging among these magical techniques is his own contribution; and notice that #12 emphasizes the use of several scourgings during every working. Notice that his recommended sequences of 3, 7, 6, 8, and 5, 6, 7, 8, both reproduce the typical sexual pattern for a flagellant.

Rules 10 to 13 seem to be a rewriting of passages in *The Greater Key of Solomon*, p. 14: "If thou wishest to succeed, it is necessary to make the following Experiments . . . with the requisite solemnities and ceremonies... which can in no way be brought to perfection without the Circle; and in order to accomplish this perfectly it is necessary to take note of all the preparations which the Master of the Art and his Disciples must undertake before constructing the circle." Gardner's use of "experiment" is good evidence that he had this passage before him. Also, his use of "Art" throughout these documents derives from *The Greater Key of Solomon*; "Craft" came to be used only in the late 1950s. The concept in Rule 13 comes from *The Greater Key of Solomon*, e.g. (p.98), "In order to properly carry out the greatest... Operations of the Art, various instruments are necessary." Notice "operations," another term that Gardner uses.

The page in Text B titled "The Ways of Making Magic" is a rewriting of this material, which therefore must date to 1953 or before.

D.5b. The Eightfold Path or Ways

Documents D.5b and D.7 are in Typeface I, very dark carbons, on letter-size blue foolscap watermarked "Wemco." The typing on the two documents is quite similar: singlespaced, but with an extra line between paragraphs or entries. The documents are quite neat, with far fewer errors in spelling, punctuation, and grammar than is typical in the other documents, and with almost no corrections made in them. They appear to be "fair copies," written out specifically to be used in a Book of Shadows, and were probably typed, not by Gardner, but by Doreen Valiente.

Document D.7 consists of four sheets, which were stapled together (with two staples) at the top. Pressure marks from other staples are visible on the rear top edge of the last sheet; these match the staple marks in Document D.8. Other pressure marks from staples are visible along the right rear edge of the last sheet; these do not match the marks in any other document here. The corners and bottom edges of the sheets (especially the first one) are dogeared and worn; this document has been used in more than one Book of Shadows. All four sheets had been folded together in half at one time, in thirds at another; and the first two sheets had been folded in thirds differently at yet another time. Hence I can deduce that these pages had been mailed at least three times: first from Valiente to Gardner; second from Gardner to Clark; and third from Clark to Carl Weschcke.

1. Meditation or concentration, actually by the firm knowledge that you can & will suceed - forming a clear picture
in your mind or your requirements.
2. Trance states, Clairvoyance, Projection of the Astaral
etc.
3. Drugs, Wine, Inscense.
4. Dance, Performing Rites with a purpose.
5. Chants, Spells etc.
6. Blood control (Cord etc.), Breath control.
7. $[courge]
8. The Great Rite

N.B.

The great thing is to combine as many of these paths into the one operation. No 1 must be in all - for if you have no clear picture of what you wish and no certainty you will not suceed - 'tis useless. No 2 can be combined with this easily. Nos 3, 4, & 5 are all good preliminaries - also 6

& 7; but No 3 is dangerous and therefore if possible should be avoided, except for insence, which is harmless if too much is not used.

The best combination is Nos 1, 4, 5 & 7, for small purposes - with No 8 if great force is necessary. Also a combination of 1, 6 & 7 is good if more can not be done - this if properly performed leads to No 2.

Commentary on D.5b

This is a revision of Document D.5a, which it must postdate. However, since this document, like Document D.7, was probably typed by Doreen Valiente, it would fall somewhere in the period 1954 to 1957. The "five essentials" (entries 9-13 in Document D.5a) are missing here; perhaps they were on the next page of the Book of Shadows this sheet came from. However, the "N.B." here consists of the material in D.5a.9 combined with that in the last paragraph of commentary in Document D.5a. The long parenthesis about the dangers of drugs in D.5a.4 has here been reduced to a single clause. We will see that Document D.14[2] amounts to a rewriting of the concepts in the note to D.5a.4 and in D.5a.9-13. For this reason, I would expect the "essentials" of Document D.5a to be dissociated entirely from the "Eightfold Path" in most later versions of the Book of Shadows.

Notice that Gardner has here rearranged the contents of paths 3, 4, and 5—since he feels free to rearrange this material, we may suppose he devised the arrangement of it in Document D.5a. We saw no strong reasons to consider anything in Document D.5a to be derived from an older coven rather than from books; we have even less reason to consider this rewriting of Document D.5a to be traditional in any way.

D.6. The First-Degree Initiation

Document D.6 has been typed doublespaced (and almost entirely in capital letters, which I see no reason to reproduce), and had been folded roughly in half at some time. This is the second page—as a "2" just before the first line shows—of a copy of the first-degree initiation. The rest of the pages were not included in this set of documents, but we can see that this ritual must have been virtually identical with the one printed by Cardell in *Witch*.

Draw Circle with Magic Sword or Athame.

Sprinkle with Exorcised Water.

Go round Circle with Magic Sword or Athame, Saying, "I conjure thee, O Circle of Power, that thou beest as a Boundary and a Protection to contain the magic power which I will raise within thy bounds. So do I bless thee, in the names of Aradia and Cernunnos."

Go round, saying at East, South, West, and North, "I summon, stir, and call thee up, ye Mighty Ones of the East (South, West, North), to witness the rites and to guard the circle."

Magus draws down Moon on High Priestess.

Read Charge, then say, "O thou who standest on the threshold between the pleasant world of men and the dread domains of the lords of the outer spaces, hast thou the courage to make the assay?" (Place point of the Magic Sword or Athame to Postulant's heart.) "For I say verily it were better to rush on my blade and perish than to make the attempt with fear in thy heart."

Postulant: "I have two perfect words: perfect love, and perfect trust."

Say, "All who have are doubly welcome."

Entering position: "I give you a third to pass you through this dread door." Gives it [kiss].

Lead Postulant sunwise to south of altar, and say, "O thou who hast declared intent to become one of us, hear then that which thou must know to do. Single is the race of men and of Gods; from a single source we both draw breath, but a difference of power in everything keeps us apart, for we are as nothing, but the Gods stay forever. Yet we can, in greatness of minds, be like the Gods, though we know not to what goal by day or in the night Fate has written that we shall run. Beyond all seas and Earth's last boundaries, beyond the Spring of night and the Heavens' vast expanse, there lies a majesty which is the domain of the Gods. Thou who would pass through the Gates of Night and Day to that sweet place, which is between the worlds of men and the domains of the Lords of the outer spaces, know that unless there is truth in thy heart, thy every effort is doomed to failure. HEAR THEN THE LAW: that thou lovest all things in nature; that thou shalt suffer no person to be harmed by thy hands or in thy mind; that thou walkest humbly in the ways of men and the ways of the Gods. Also it is the law that contentment thou shalt learn, through suffering, and from long years and from nobility of mind and of purpose, FOR THE WISE NEVER GROW OLD. Their minds are nourished by living in the daylight of the Gods, and if among the vulgar some discoveries should arise concerning some maxims of thy belief in the Gods, so do thou, for the most part, keep silent. For there is a great risk that thou mayest straightway vomit up that which thou hast not digested, and when someone shall say to thee, "Thou knowest naught," and it bites thee not, then knowest thou that thou hast begun the work. And as sheep do not bring their food to the shepherd to show how much they have eaten, but digesting inwardly their provender, bear outwardly wool and milk, even so, do not thou display the maxims to the vulgar, but rather the works that flow when they are digested. Now there is the ordeal."[53]

Tie cord around Postulant's right ankle, leaving ends free; say, "Feet neither bound nor free."

Leading postulant, proclaim at four quarters, "Take heed, ye Lords of the Watchtowers of the East (South, West, North), that (name) is properly prepared to be made a priestess and a witch."

Three times round the Circle with Dance step and chant.

Place Postulant in East; say, "Kneel."

Postulant kneels.

Strike eleven knells on bell; say, "Rise. In other religions the postulant kneels while the priest towers above him, but in the Art Magical we are taught to be humble, and so we kneel to welcome them, and we say:

> "Blessed be the feet that have brought you in these ways
> [kiss];
> "Blessed be the knees that shall kneel at the sacred altar
> [kiss];
> "Blessed be thy womb (or organ of generation), without
> which we would not be
> [kiss];

---

[53] This speech was added after 1960, but there isn't any other convenient place to insert in the structure of the BoS.

"Blessed be thy breasts, erected in beauty and in strength [kiss];
"Blessed be thy lips, which shall utter the sacred names [kiss].[54]
" Before ye are sworn.art willing to pass the ordeal & be purified?"
(P[ostulant] I am.)

(Take measure.) [height (tie knot); around head (tie knot); around heart (tie knot); around hips (tie knot). Prick postulant's thumb; catch blood on measure. Place measure on altar.]

Secure. [Have postulant kneel, tie postulant's feet together, and secure cable tow to altar.] Three strokes on bell.

[Scourge] 3, 7, 9, 21.

~~Art always ready to help, protect, + defend thy name~~

Say. "Ye have bravely passed the test.

Art ready to swear that thou willt always be true to the Art?[55]

(P[ostulant] I am.)

"Art always ready to help ? protect .& defend thy brothers & sisters of the Art?."

(P[ostulant] I am.)

" Then say after me. "1 .N or M. in the presence of the Mighty Ones. doof my own will & accord.most solomnly sweare that I will ever keep secret.& never reveal the secrets of the Art.except it be to a proper person.properly prepared.within ~~such~~ a circle such as I am now in.

All this I swear by my hopes of a future life.mindfull that my measure has been taken.and may my weapons turn against me if I break this my solomn oath."[56]

[Loosen cords from ankles and from altar, and remove blindfold;]

---

[54] Here begins the transcript of the second page of the First-Degree ritual that is among the Weschcke documents.

[55] Note use of "Art" rather than "Craft."

[56] The oath given here is shorter (and probably earlier) than the one in HMA.

assist to rise.

I hereby sign thee with the tripple sign [the point-down triangle formed by touching the genitals, the right breast, the left breast, and the genitals again.]

I consecrate thee with oil.

I consecrate thee with wine.

I consecrate thee with my lips, Priest (Priestess) and Witch."

Remove Cords [kiss].

"I now present to you the working tools(weapons)[57]

First the magic sword. With this, as with the athame.**y**thou canst form all magic circles. dominate. subdue.& punish all rebellious spirits & deamons. & even persuade angels & good spirits. With this in your hand .you are ruler of the circle." ($)[58]

"Next I present to you the athame. This is the true witches weapon. & has all the powers of the magic sword." ($)[59]

"Next I present the white-handled knife. Its use is to form all instruments used in the Art. It can only be used in a magic circle." [kiss]

"Next I present the wand. Its use is to call up and control certain angels and genie to whom it would not be meet to use the sword or athame." [kiss]

"Next I present the pentacle. This is for the purpose of calling up the appropriate spirits." [kiss]

"Next I present the censer of incense. This is used to encourage and welcome good spirits, and to banish evil spirits." [kiss]

"Next I present the scourge. This is a sign of power and domination. It is also used to cause purification and enlightenment, for it is written, `To learn you must suffer and be purified.' [kiss] Art willing to suffer

---

[57] This parenthetical "weapons" is a gloss, added because Gardner expected the terminology to be unfamiliar to the reader. We can date the retyping of the document to 1959-1960, when Gardner was sending documents to Clark.

[58] What appears at the ends of these lines is the scourging symbol, as typed, although we know from the parallel documents that this is usually the S for "kiss."

[59] This is where the second page of the First-Degree ritual among the Weschcke documents ends; so here I revert to the Farrars.

to learn?"

Postulant: "I am."

"Next and lastly I present the cords. They are of use to bind the sigils of the art, also the material basis. Also they are necessary in the oath." [kiss]

"I now salute you in the names of Aradia and Cernunnos, Newly made Priestess and Witch."

Lead round and proclaim to four quarters, "Hear, ye Mighty Ones, (name) has been consecrated a priestess of the Goddess."

Now present new Witch to coven members. All should kiss and hug new Witch as welcome into membership.

To close circle proclaim to four quarters, "Ye Mighty Ones of the East (South, West, North), I thank you for attending and, ere ye depart for your lovely realms, I say hail and farewell."

Commentary on D.6

Observe that the procedure for casting the circle at the beginning of this version of the initiation has been influenced by the revised procedure in D.1. That is, Gardner had rewritten some of the first-degree initiation before he gave the script of it to Olive Green in 1958 or 1959.

D.7. The Second-Degree Initiation

See the commentary introducing D.5.

2nd Degree[60]

Form Circle in usual manner, invoking the Mighty Ones at the Four Quarters. The Initiate should be properly prepared and bound with the Cords. *All are Purified. including Initiate*[61]

[60] This title, and the sentence at the end of the first paragraph, are in Gardner's handwriting. He must have added them before mailing this document to Clark in 1959 or 1960. Notice that he has thus only recently--AFTER this ritual had been typed by Doreen Valiente--added the requirement that all must be scourged at the beginning of the ritual. Note that "properly prepared" in Gardner's vocabulary means only "skyclad," not "scourged."

[61] This is in Gardner's handwriting. All other underlining in this document is

Circle once, proclaiming at the Four Quarters :- "Hear Ye Mighty Ones ??? (N), a duly consecrated P[riestess] and W[itch], is now properly prepared to be made a High Priest and Magus (High Priestess and W[itch] Q[ueen])."[62]

Circle three times, with dance step and chant.[63]

Initiate then kneels before the Altar and is secured with the Cords.

Priestess or Magus:-

"To attain to this sublime Degree it is necessary to suffer and be purified. Art willing to suffer to learn?"

Initiate:-

"I am."

Priestess or Magus:

"I purify thee to take this great Oath rightly".[64]

Strike three strokes upon the bell. [Scourge] 3, 7, 9, 21.

"I now give thee a new name :- ?????? [kiss]

Repeat thy new name after me, saying :- 'I ?????? swear, upon my mother's womb and by mine honour among men and my brothers and sisters of the Art, that I will never reveal to any at all any of the secrets of the Art, except it be to a worthy person, properly prepared, in the centre of a Magic Circle such as I am now in. This I swear by my hopes of salvation, [65] my past lives and my hopes of future ones to come and I devote myself and my measure to utter destruction if I break this my solemn Oath'.

Kneel. Place L[eft] H[and] under I[nitiate]'s K[nee] and R[ight] H[and]

---

typed.

[62] The beginning of the ritual here differs little from the version in HMA (pp. 301-303). "Magus" is used only in the earlier documents, and is evidence that the content being typed here is early.

[63] This is a new development. Farrar (1971, p. 85) says the chant used here is the "Witches Rune" (see D.9), but this is not certain.

[64] A scourge symbol is hand-drawn above and to the right of this line.

[65] This obviously Christian term is still in Farrar 1971.

on H[ead][66], thus forming Magic Link, saying :-
"I will all my power into thee."
WILL.
Loose, assist to rise.
<u>Consecrate:-</u>
"I consecrate thee with oil,
I consecrate thee with wine,
I consecrate thee with my lips,
High Priest and Magus (High Priestess and W[itch] Q[ueen])."[67]
Loose remaining Cords. [kiss]
"You will now use the Working Tools in turn,
First the M[agic] S[word] (Form Circle) [Kiss]
Second the Athame. (Form Circle) [Kiss]
Third the W[hite]-H[andled] K[nife] (use) [Kiss]
Fourth the Wand. (Wave to 4 Quarters) [Kiss]
Fifth the Pentacle. (Show to 4 Quarters) [Kiss]
Sixth the Censer. (Circle, cense) [Kiss]
Seventh the Cords. (Use) [Kiss]
Eighth the [scourge] :- 'For learn, in w[itchcraf]t you must ever give as you receive, but ever triple. So where I gave thee 3 return 9, where I gave 7 return 21, where I gave 9 return 27, where I gave 21 return 63'.
(Use, 9, 21, 27, 63. i.e. 120 in all [kiss])
"Thou hast obeyed the law. But mark well, when thou receivest good, so equally art bound to return good threefold".

The Priestess or Magus is then loosed from the cords and says :- 'Having learned thus far you must know why the Wica are called the Hidden Children of the Goddess'.

Then the Legend of the Goddess is either read or acted out [68]. If

---

[66] There's no reason for Gardner to be secretive about this bit of ritual, since it had been published in HMA; so at least part of this ritual is being typed from a draft dating back to 1946 or 1947.

[67] Here HMA has "Wizard," not "Magus." Why be secretive about this procedure, which was published in full in HMA? Again it would make sense if the content here goes back to a draft before HMA.

[68] The enactment of the myth does not appear in BAM or HMA, but the idea of including it goes back to 1953, since WT (p. 44) says it "forms the central

it is possible to act it out, the new Initiate may take one of the parts. One of the Coven should act as Narrator and another as Guardian of the Portal. The Priestess, or another woman, may act the part of the Goddess,and the Magus, or another man, may act the part of the God. The Priestess - or whoever is taking the part of the Goddess - takes off her necklace and lays it on the Altar. Then she goes outside the circle and is dressed in a veil and jewellery. The Magus - or whoever is taking the part of the God - is invested with a horned crown and girds on a sword, which he draws and stands in the God position with sword and [scourge], by the altar.

Narrator:-

"In ancient times our Lord the Horned One was, as he still is, the Consoler, the Comforter; but men knew him as the Dread Lord of Shadows - lonely, stern, and hard. But our Lady the Goddess[69] would solve all mysteries, even the mystery of Death - and so she journeyed to the Nether Lands. The Guardians of the Portals challenged her :-

(The Priestess - or whoever is taking the part of the Goddess - advances to the side of the Circle. Whoever is taking the part of the Guardian of the Portal challenges her with the Sword or Athame).

Narrator:-

'Strip off thy garments, lay aside thy jewels, for nought may ye bring with ye into this our land'.[70] So she laid down her garments and her jewels and was bound, as are all who enter the realms of Death the Mighty One".

(The Priestess takes off the veil and the jewellery and lays them down

---

part of one of their rituals." The "legend" first appeared in print in WT, p. 45.

[69] In WT (p.45), the preceding words are merely "Now G. had never loved, but she"; given the revised wording, her cry under the scourging makes no sense. The version here also appears in Farrar 1971, p. 87. These new words reveal a revision of the "myth" after the publication of WT, which is absolute proof that this new version of the ritual was written after 1954.

[70] This line is adapted from the seven times repeated challenge of Ishtar in the legend of her descent into the underworld. The single quotes here are in the original document: Doreen, who is typing it, understands the literary convention; Gardner did not.

outside the Circle. The Guardian of the Portal binds her with the Cords and brings her inside the Circle).

Narrator :-

Such was her beauty that Death himself knelt and laid his sword and crown at her feet,[71] and kissed her feet.

(The Magus - or whoever is playing the part of the God - comes forward and lays the Horned Crown and the Sword at the Priestess's feet and kisses her feet)

Narrator :-

Saying - 'Blessed be thy feet that have brought thee in these ways. Abide with me, but let me place my cold hand on thy heart'. And she replied - 'I love thee not. Why dost thou cause all things that I love and take delight in to fade and die ?' 'Lady', replied Death, "tis Age and Fate, against which I am helpless. Age causes all things to wither; but when men die at the end of time, I give them rest and peace and strength, so that they may return. But you - you are lovely; return not - abide with me.' But she answered - 'I love thee not'. Then said Death - 'An you receive not my hand on your heart, you must receive Death's scourge'.

(The Magus rises and takes up the Scourge from the Altar.)

Narrator:-

'It is fate, better so', she said, and she knelt.

(The Priestess kneels before the altar, and the Magus uses the [scourge] 3, 7, 9, 21).

Narrator:-

"And Death scourged her tenderly, and she cried - `I feel the pangs of love'. And Death raised her, and said - `Blessed be', and he gave her the Fivefold Kiss, saying - `Thus only may you attain to joy and knowledge"'.

(The Magus raises the Priestess, gives her the [Fivefold Kiss] and unties the Cords)

Narrator:-

"And he taught her all the Mysteries and gave her the necklace[,] which

---

[71] The preceding nine words, which are not in WT, but are in Farrar 1971, are more rewriting to adapt the "myth" to the ritual.

is the Circle of Rebirth".[72]

(The Magus takes the Priestess's necklace from the Altar and replaces it about her neck. The Priestess takes up the Sword and the Horned Crown from the floor, where the Magus placed them, and gives them back to him. Then he stands as before by the Altar, in the position of the God, and she stands by his side in the pentacle position, as Goddess).

Narrator:-

"And they loved and were one; and he taught her all the Magics. For there are three great events in the life of man - love, death, and resurrection in a new body - and magic controls them all. To fulfill love you must return at the same time and place as the loved one, and you must remember and love them again. But to be reborn you must die and be ready for a new body; to die you must be born; without love you may not be born - and these be all the magics".

-

The Priestess or Magus then replaces the Sword, Crown, Scourge etc., upon the Altar and taking the new Initiate by the hand and holding the Athame in the other, passes once round the Circle, proclaiming at the Four Quarters:-

"Hear, Ye Mighty Ones, ... hath been duly consecrated High Priest and Magus (or High Priestess and W[itch] Q[ueen]).

Commentary on D.7

The content of this document probably dates to 1953 or earlier, since it uses terms like Magus and Art that disappear soon after 1953. On the other hand, there are differences in wording that postdate *Witchcraft Today*, and that are given by Farrar 1971, who invariably gives later versions of wordings; and the typing, spelling, and punctuation are much better than in other documents. The simplest explanation is that the content here goes back to that in Document A.3, but this cleaned-up version

[72] The preceding eleven words are not in WT, but do stand in Farrar's BoS, since he gives the accompanying instruction (1971, p. 88); more rewriting to adapt myth to ritual. The comma is needed here, because all necklaces (see WT, p. 189), not just a certain necklace, stand for the Circle of Rebirth.

was typed by Doreen about 1956.

Aside from the hands to head and feet device borrowed from *WCWE*, p. 78, the only aspect of this ritual that might conceivably be traditional is the "myth" of the Goddess's descent, but we have already looked at that in the discussion of *Witchcraft Today*.

We have all the documents needed to show how this ritual was written. The pre-1949 second-degree ritual in "Ye Bok of ye Art Magical" does not contain the myth about the descent of the Goddess. The myth first appears in print in 1954 in *Witchcraft Today*, and its language had to be tinkered with in order to fit it into the second-degree ritual.

Notice also that the changes here are in line with Gardner's own agenda. An instruction has been added at the beginning requiring all to be scourged. The "Myth of the Goddess" has also obviously been added; not only is it a theologizing of the scourging, but when acted out it includes another scourging.

D.8. The Third-Degree Initiation

Document D.8 is a carbon on letter-sized yellow foolscap in Typeface I. The verses of the poem are singles-paced; all else is in one-and-a-half spacing. The document consists of two sheets. The first sheet has two sets of staple marks along the top edge: the lower set matches one set of marks on Document D.13; the upper set matches the one set of marks on the second sheet. There is a fold line on both sheets just below the top edge. There are also five staple marks, along the left edge of the back of the second sheet, which match the staple marks in Document D.1 and D.2; Document D.8 was therefore facing backward, as is also indicated by the fact that there are notes on the left margin of the first sheet. Clearly Document D.8 had been in two different binders, one clamping shut at the top, the other along the side; so it had apparently been used in two different Book of Shadows. We now have evidence for three different Books of Shadows: one in a ring or post binder, one clamped at the top, one clamped along the edge.

3rd Degree[73]

H[igh] p[riest] gives 5S [Fivefold Kiss]. "I beg purification at thy hands." [Scourge]

Warlocks[74] H[igh] P[riestes]s.Circle ,Proclaims. to 4 quarters,

"Take heed ye Mighty Ones, The Lady ——— H[igh] p[riestes]s & Witch Queen is properly prepared to celebrate the Great Rite," [Scourge].

H[igh Priest][75] kisses feet. "Ere l dare proceed with this sublime degree, l must again beg purifacation at thy hands." [Scourge]

Note: if H[igh] p[riestes]s has not preformed thisrite before, say. "Here I reveal to you a great mystery."[76]

"Assist me to build
As the Mighty One willed,
An Altar of praise,
From begining of days,
Thus doth it lie,
Twixt the points of the sky,
For thus it was placed
When the Goddess embrased
The Horned One, Her Lord,
Who taught her the word,

---

[73] Here "3rd" was typed, then "3rd degree" added in Gardner's handwriting.

[74] Here the term "warlock" is intended to mean "bind." The OED (pp. 3688, 3693) gives this as an obsolete and rare meaning, probably from association with "warrok" (also spelled "warrick"), which does have this meaning, has survived as a technical term for a type of winch in English shipyards, and is also used by Gardnerians.

[75] The MS. gives only "H"; the Farrars 1984, p. 35, confirm that the High Priestess scourges the High Priest here.

[76] In the left-hand margin, extending from the second line of the MS. down to the seventh line of the verse, is written, "Kneel and place couch in position so as to face north." This is not in Gardner's handwriting. It is not clear how much of what follows is said only when the Priestess has not performed the ritual before.

[Priestess lies down in such a way that her vagina is approximately at he centre of the circle]

Which quickened the womb,
And conqured the Tomb.

Be thus as of yore,
The Shrine we adore, [kiss]
The feast without fail,
The life-giving Grail, [kiss].
Befor it upreare,
The Miraculous Spear,
And invoke[77] in this sign
The Goddsee divine.

Invoke[78]: Thou who at noon of night doth reign,
Queen of the starry realm above,
'Not unto Thee may we atain
Unless Thine Image be of Love.[79]
[kiss].

By moon-rays silver shaft of power,
By green leaf breaking from the bud,
By seed that springeth into flower,
By life that courseth in the blood.

By rushing wind and leaping flame,
By flowing water and green earth,
Pour to us the wine of our desire,
From out Thy Cauldren of Rebirth.
[kiss].

Here may we see in vision clear,
The Secret Strange unvailed at leangth,

---

[77] Here "adore" was typed, then typed over with dashes, and "invoke" typed above.

[78] Typed underlining.

[79] This is a quote from CGM, p. 350, as was discussed for A.4.

The wonderous Twin-Pillars rear,
Errect in Beauty and in Strength.[80]
Altar of Mysteries manifold,
The Sacred Circles, central point,
Thus do l sign thee as of old,
With kisses of my lips anoint.[81]

(Eightfold Kiss: 3 points, Lips, 2 Breasts and back to lips, & 5 points[82], with oil, wine, & kisses)

Open for me the Secret Way,
The pathway of intelligence,
Between the Gates of Night and Day,
Beyond the bounds of time and sence[83]

Behold the Mystery aright,
The Five True Points of Fellowship,
Here where the Lance and Grail unite,
And feet and knees and breast and
lips."

(Exchange Names.)

3 points L. 2 Bs and back to lips.
5 points[84]

Commentary on D.8

This versified version of the third-degree ritual is given almost verbatim by "Rex Nemorensis"; so it must date from before August 1959. However, it must be later than the version in "Ye Bok of ye Art Magical", whose prose is here being versified. I had deduced by 1981

---

[80] Here the second page of this document begins.

[81] Here a pentacle surmounted by a point-up triangle is drawn.

[82] These are shown by a drawing to be: genitals, left foot, right knee, left knee, right foot, and back to genitals.

[83] This is a versifying of a passage in CGM, p. 352.

[84] The handwriting here is not Gardner's; so the sketch is probably not by him either.

that Doreen Valiente had written this verse ritual about 1954; so I see no reason to doubt the statements to that effect by the Farrars (1981, p. 92 n3). Notice that a second scourging of the High Priest has been added at the beginning; this would, of course, better enable Gardner to carry out the Great Rite.

The invocation given by Farrar 1971 is quite different from that in Document D.8. It consists of an extract from Document A.4, and so incorporates a long quote from Crowley's Gnostic Mass, as Farrar correctly points out. It then finishes up with the last three stanzas of the verse version here. The Farrars (1981, p. 52n3) state that "From 'altar of mysteries manifold' to the end of the invocation was written by Doreen Valiente, who also composed a fully rhyming version." Hence Farrar (1971) gives the version intermediate between those in Documents A.4 and D.8.

It would appear that Farrar's 1971 version of this ritual was arrived at by someone who, faced with only what had been typed here, did some tinkering and guessing, and so sometimes guessed wrong. That is, Sanders did not have the information represented by the handwritten notes and sketch here. What do these mean?

We have seen that the first-degree ritual[85] includes an anointing in the form of a point-down triangle, which is therefore used by Gardnerians as a symbol for the first-degree witch. Similarly, the second-degree ritual[86] includes an anointing in the form of an inverted pentacle, which is used similarly as a symbol for the second-degree witch. Now, it is well-known that the triangle over the pentacle—the symbol here drawn to the right of the word "anoint"—is the symbol for the third-degree witch. So we can interpret the notes and sketch as follows. The first line means, "The three points are the lips, the two breasts, and back to the lips." The five points that make up the pentacle are the genitals, the knees, and the feet, as numbered in the sketch. And presumably this anointing is carried out thrice, with oil, wine, and kisses, as it is for the other two degrees.[87]

But Farrar 1971 mentions nothing about anointing in this ritual. Why

---

[85] See Document A.2, and Farrar 1971, p. 16.

[86] See HMA, p. 303, or Farrar 1971, p. 86.

[87] This is now confirmed by the Farrars 1984, pp. 37-8.

not? First, because nothing like these notes and sketch appeared in Sanders' copy of the Book of Shadows. Second, and most importantly, because Sanders had not received the "oral tradition" that explained how to work this ritual. That is, to put it bluntly, Alex Sanders had not received the Gardnerian third-degree initiation. Does this mean that Alexandrian initiations are invalid? No, not at all, but the reasons why delve into a sphere of theology not relevant to my goals here.

Finally, is there anything traditional here? No, not at all. We saw nothing traditional in Document A.4, and a rewriting of that must be even less traditional.

D.9. The Witches' Chant or Rune

This is an original, in Typeface I, on a sheet of white letter-size paper with no watermark; it is typed singlespaced, with an extra line between stanzas. Two holes are punched on the lefthand edge, and have been torn through to the edge; the right-hand edge is badly worn and dogeared. Obviously, this sheet had been used in the same Book of Shadows as Documents D.1, D.3, D.5a, D.5b, D.6, and D.13, and had not been used in any other.

Save for the last two lines, this is virtually identical with the versions of this song published by Farrar (1971, p.12) and by Holzer (p. 17), who says it is "The Witches Rune, which Alex Sanders has revived and rerecorded from old sources"—which was simply a barefaced lie. Doreen Valiente stated in *Witchcraft for Tomorrow* (p. 21) that she and Gardner had written it about 1954 or 1955, and this document was probably typed by her.

Darksome night and Shining Moon,
East, then South, then West, then North,
Harken to the Witches Rune:
Here come I to call thee forth.

Earth and Water, Air and Fire,
Wand and Pentacle and Sword,
Work ye unto my desire,
Harken ye unto my word.

Cords and Censer, Scourge and knife,
Powers of the Witches Blade,
Waken all ye into life,
Come ye as the Charm is made:

Queen of Heaven, Queen of Hell,
Horned Hunter of the Night,
Lend your power unto the Spell,
Work my will by Magic Rite.

If chant is used to reinforce a work already begun, end with this:

By all the power of land and sea
By all the might of moon and sun,
What is my will- "So mote it be,"
What I do say- "It shall be done."

Witch gives the last two lines as "As I do will, so might it be, Chant the Spell and Be it Done."

O.10. Consecrating Tools

Consecrating the Sword or the Athame

(Note. if possible lay any ney weapon touching an already consecrated one.. Sword to sword . Athame to Athame etc. The [scourge] l send you is thus consecrated .)[88]

[1] Prepare Circle and purify .all tools must be consecrated by a man and a woman. both as naked as drawn swords.[89]

[2a] Place sword. or Athame on altar. Touching with already consecrated weapon say. "L conjure thee O Sword (Or Athame) or Steel, that thou serve me for a strength and a defence in all Magical opperations, against all mine enemies , visable and invisable. ln the names of """""""" and """""""". l conjure thee anew by the Holy Name """""" and """""", that

[88] Notice that this is a first-person comment by Gardner to Clark. Apparently he found the carbon of this document at hand, added some notes to it, and typed up some other documents to accompany it.

[89] The phrase "naked as the drawn sword" is also used in HMA (p. 159) in a context concerning the charging of a sword.

thou servest me for a protection in all adversities, So Aid me."[90]Sprinkle and Cense. say. "l conjure thee O Sword of Steel, by the Great Gods and the Gentle Goddesses, by the virtue of the Heavens, of the Stars, of the Spirits who preside over them.`that thou mayest recieve such virtues that l mayest obtain the end that l desire in all things wherin l shall use thee,' by the power of """""""""" and """""""""

Consecrating the Wand or any other tool

[2b] """""""""" and """""""""" `Deign to bless and to consecrate this Wand, that it may obtain necessary virtue' through thee for all acts of love and Beauty. sprinkle and cense. """""""""" and """""""""" Bless this instrimunt prepared in thine honour."(Ln the case of the [scourge] and Cords, add "That it may only serve for a good use and end,"and to thy Glory."[91]

[3] All instruments when consecrated should be presented to their User by giving the [point-down triangle] sign.salute(if they are oorking in the 1st degree or the sign of the higher degree if they are working that.)[92]

[4] Then it should be placed between the breasts, and the two workers should embrace.it being held in place by their bodies. The New Owner should use it imediatly. i.e. Cast. (Trace)[93] Circle with Sword or Athame. Wave wand to 4 quarters. cur somthing with white handled knife. etc. Cords and [scourge] should be used at once. (This is one of the jokes of the Craft. you are always finding that someone must be purified.)[94]The tool should

---

[90] The formula is adapted from GKS.

[91] The phrase indicated by single quotes is from GKS, p. 101.

[92] Presumably Gardner means that the presenter uses each instrument to trace the inverted triangle, pentacle, or triangle/pentacle combination, depending on which degree of initiation the new owner has received. This concept of signs and salutes associated with degrees of initiation is straight out of the HOGD system.

[93] Gardner is defining the term "cast" for the reader.

[94] Only Gardner would have made this first-person comment. Notice that here "Craft" is used in its current sense as a name for the religion, whereas WT routinely uses "cult" wherever "Craft" would now be used. This entire document is a revision of the 1954-6 form given by the Farrars (1984, p. 47), which still talks of "Art Magic" and "Magus" - that is, this is a later draft than

be kept in as close connection as possible to the naked body for at least a month, i.e., kept under pillow, etc. When not in use, all tools and weapons should be put away in a secret place; and it is good that this should be near your sleeping place, and that you handle them each night before retiring. Do not allow anyone to touch or handle any of your tools until they are thoroughly impregnated with your aura; say, six months or as near as possible. But a couple working together may own the same tools, which will be impregnated with the aura of both.

Commentary on D. 10

The phrases indicated by quote marks are from *The Greater Key of Solomon*, pp. 98, 101, 118. Despite the headings, paragraphs [3] and [4] apply to the consecration of the sword or athame as well as to that of the wand; so paragraphs [2a] and [2b] are alternatives within the same procedure. Only two details in this document might conceivably be connected with some sort of pagan magical religious traditions. The first is the idea of touching a new magical tool with an old "charged" tool, in order to transfer some of the "charge" to the new tool. But this is a standard sort of magical procedure, quite in keeping with Frazer's laws of magic, and hence far more likely to have been learned from books than from a previous coven. The second is the male-female embrace, to "charge" the tool with sexual energy; it is another example of the Craft's radical sacramentalizing of sexuality. The use of the cords and scourge at the end has been added in this draft.

D.11. Of Spells[95]

Of spells, the exact words matter little if the intent be clear and you raise the true power, and sufficient therof.

Always in rhyme they are, there is something queer about rhyme. I have tried, and the same seem to lose their power if you miss the rhyme. Also in rhyme, the words seem to say themselves. You do not have to

---

the one Gardner gave to Patricia Crowther.

[95] This is from *Witch*, by "Rex Nemorensis" (Charles Cardell). This little passage is a rewriting of "Of Chants and Spells," and hence is also related to a passage in WT, p. 167.

pause and think: "What comes next?" Doing this takes away much of your intent.

D.12. The Scourge and the Kiss[96]

It is not meet to make offerings [scourgings] of less than two score[97] to the Goddess, for here be a mystery. The fortunate numbers be: 3, and 5. For three added to two (the Perfect Couple) be five. And three and five be eight; eight and five be thirteen; thirteen and eight be twenty-one.[98]

Also, fortunate numbers be: 3, 7, 8, and 21. Which total be 40, or two score. So a lesser number would not be perfect prayer.

If more are required make it a perfect number as four score or six score.

In the 5.S. [Fivefold Kiss] be called 5., but there are 8 kisses, for there be: 2 [feet] & 2 [knees] & [genitals] & 2 [breasts] & [the lips].[99]

And 5 times 8 be two score. For each man and woman hath ten fingers and ten toes, so each totals a score. And a perfect couple be two score.

Also there be Eight Elemental Weapons.

D.13. The Amalthean Horn.

The Spell

(Feet. Knees & Wrists should be tightly bound to retard blood.) S[courge] 40 or more,to make skin tingle. then say, invoking Goddess.

Hail .... From the Amathean horn,

---

[96] This is from Cardell's *Witch*. It is a revision of material seen earlier, e.g., paragraph [3] of B.3, and *WT*, pp. 134-5. It continues the focus on sexuality as sacramental, and provides some of the concepts that allow all these ritual procedures to function as a system for working magic.

[97] Perhaps the scourge symbol belongs here rather than where it appears.

[98] What Gardner is describing here is the Fibonacci series, discovered in the fourteenth century by the Italian mathematician Nicholas Bonaccio. It is important for certain phenomena in demographics, and it converges in the limit to the "golden ratio" used in classic architecture. It has nothing whatsoever to do with magic, but it might be useful in Trivial Pursuit.

[99] Blank spaces have been left on the page in the pamphlet; I fill them in by comparison with B.3.

Pour forth thy store of love; I lowley bend,
Before Thee; I adore Thee at the end,
When other Gods are fallen & put to skorn,
Thy foot is to my lips; my sighs inborn,
Rise ,touch, curl about Thy heart; then spend,
Pittifull love, lovliest pity descend,
And bring me luck, who amlonely and forlorn.

~~Scourge Again~~[100] Ask the Goddess to help you to obtain your desires, Then S[courge] again to bind the spell.

Before starting you must make a very clear picture in your mind of what you wish,make yourself see the wish obtained,be sure in your own mind exactly what it is & how it is to be fulfilled. This spell is the one that was taught to me long ago & I have found it works, but I don't think there is any special virtue in these words,[101] any others can be subsitued provided they ask the goddesses (or gods) help,[102] & say clearly what you wish & you form the clear mental immage,& if it dosent work at first keep[103] on trying till it w[orks]. Your helper , who wields the S[courge] must know what you wish, & also form thememental immage .& at first at anyrate,it will beb be better for you to work the spell. then forethegirl to take your place & work it also, you S[courge] her,dont try anything dificult at first, & do it at lea[st] once a week till it works, you have to ge[t] inti sympathy with [each] other, before anything happens, & regular working helps this,

This repeats the verse from Document B.3[1], with an expanded explanation of its use for magic, probably typed about 1959. A verse

[100] Typed over with ems, probably because Gardner decided to add the instruction about "ask the Goddess" before the final scourging. This is clear evidence that he is here author, not copyist.

[101] This is clearly a first-person comment by Gardner to Clark. It indicates how subtly Gardner could manage to make claims of traditionality about material--such as this poem by Crowley - that cannot possibly be traditional.

[102] Possible readings: goddesses' (or gods') help; goddesses (or gods) for help; goddess's (or god's) help, which is the most likely.

[103] Verso begins here.

by Crowley cannot, of course, be part of a pagan tradition. The procedure described here combines paths 6 and 7 in Document D.5a. The document as a whole appears to be an early draft of Document D.14, especially of D.14[4]. The tone here is chatty, that of a letter to a friend; whereas Document D.14 is formal and flowery, intended for the Book of Shadows.

D.14. To Gain the Sight

[1] This cometh to different people in diverse ways, tis seldom it cometh naturaly, but it can be induced in many ways.

Deep and prolonged medatation may do it but only if you be a natural,& usually prolonged fasting was also necessary.

Of old. Monks and Nuns obtained vissions by long vigils, combined with fasting,flagalation till the blood came ,& other mortifications of the flesh ,& so undoubtedly had vissions. ln the East it i s tried with various tortures, at the same time sitting in crampped postures, which retard theflow of blood ,and these torments,long & continued, give good results. But, in theArt,[104] we are taught an easier way to intensify the imiganition, at the same time controling theblood supply, & this may best be done by using the Ritual.

[2] lncense is also good to propitiate the Spirits,but also to indse relaxation & to help to build up the atmosphere which is necessary to sugestability. (For our human eyes are [so] blind to what realy is, that it is oftennecessary to suggest that it is there , before we may see it.) As we may point out to another somthing at a distance before they may see it themselves.

Gum mastic.Arematic Rush Roots, Cinamon Bark, Musk, Juniper, Sandlewood, & Ambergris, in combination areall good. but Patchouli is best of all, And if you may have Hemp, tis better still. but be very careful of this.[105]

[3] The Circle being formed all properly prepared, and the Rites done,

---

[104] Notice use of "art" rather than "Craft." The preceding sentence is a direct reference to Tantric yoga.

[105] Compare with D.14[4].

and all purified.

The aspirant should Warlock & take his tutor round the Circle, Saluting the Mighty Ones. & invoke them to aid the opperation.[106]Then both dance round till giddy, invokig, or using Chants, [scourge][107]. Then the Tutor should Warlock very tightly, but not so to cause discomfort, but enouth to retard the blood slightly. Again they should danceround, chanting, Then [Scourge] . with light ,steady, monotonous ,slow strokes. lt is ver good that the pupil may see them coming. (This may be arranged from position. or if a big mirror is available, this can be used with excelent effect.) As this has the effect of passes[108] & helps greatly to stimulate theimiganition, and it isimportant that they be not hard, the object being not to do more than draw the blood to that part and so away from the brain. This with the tight warlocking, which should beWarricked.[109] slows down the circulation of the blood, and thepasses soon induce a drowsynes and a stupor.the tutor should watch for this, as soon as the Asperant sleeps, the [scourging] should cease.

The Tutor should also watch that the pupil become not cold, And if they struggle. or become distressed [they] should be at once awakned. (Note, if it cannot be arranged [for] the Pupil to see., the wand may be used, for a time, then return to [scourging].)

[4] Do not be discouraged if no results come after two or three attempts. lt will come, when both arein the right state. When you get someresult, then results will come more quickly. S oon someof theritual may be shortned, but never neglect to invoke the Goddess, & the Mighty Ones. or to form the Circle & do everythng rightly. And , for good and clear results, it is ever bette r to dp too much ritual than too little.

[5] lt hath been found that thi s pracice doth often cause a fondness between Aspirant and Tutor, & tis a cause of better results if this be

---

[106] Notice this use of "operation" from the GKS vocabulary.

[107] Probably there should be a full stop before the $ symbol. That is, the sequence here would be: first dance; then scourge; then "warlock" tightly and dance again; then scourge again.

[108] Typed underlining.

[109] The distinction between "warlocking" and "warricking" is not one known to the OED. Rather, we have here technical terminology peculiar to the Gardnerian tradition.

so. If for any reason it is undiserable that there be any gret fondness between Aspirant and Tutor this may be easily avoided by both parties from theonset firmly resolving in their minds that if any doth ensew[110] it shall be that of brother and sister or parent and child. And it is for this reason that a man may only be taught by a woman & a woman by a man. And that Man & Man . and Woman & Woman should never attempt these practices together. And may all the Curses of the Mighty Ones be on any who makethe attempt.[111]

[6] Remember, the Circle , properly constructed is ever necessary to prevent the Power released [from] being dissapated, it is also a barrier against any disturbances of mischivious forces. For to obtain good results you must be free from all disturbances. Remembr [that] darkness, points of light gleaming amid the surounding dark, Lncense , and thesteady passes by a white arm,are not stage effects. They are the mechanical implements which start the sugustions, which later unlocks the knowledge that it is possible to obtain[112] the divine ecastacy,& so atain knowledge ang communion with the Divine Goddess. When once youhave attained this, Ritual is not needed,as you may atain the state of ectasy at will, but till then, or if you having atained this yourself, wish to bring a campanion to this state of Joy. Ritual is best.

Commentary on D.14.

There are two rough drafts of this document in Gardner's notebooks in Toronto; these date from somewhere in the early 1950s. Likewise, since a rewriting of this document is included in "Text B" (see the Farrars 1984, p. 58) we can date it to 1953 or later. Let us look at how it is constructed.

First, notice from the language, especially the verb tenses in [1], that this is strictly a modern document, despite the use of archaicizing

---

[110] Presumably "ensue" is meant.

[111] The content of this paragraph is referred to on pp. 78, 85, and 86 of WT, and therefore goes back to 1953 or earlier. The paragraph itself has been included in late versions of the Craft Laws; see the Appendix in Johns, or laws ##157-161 in GLS.

[112] Preceding seven words were repeated by dittography.

verbiage. Second, notice that [2] rewrites the ideas in the long note to no. 4 in D.5a; [3] explains in detail the procedure used with the Amalthean Horn prayer described in 3.10; [4], and all but the first two sentences of [6], expand the ideas in the chatty commentary appended to the Amalthean Horn verse; and the third sentence in [4], and the first two sentences of [6], expand the ideas in items 9 to 13 in "The Eightfold Way." Consider, finally, the formal tone and rather flowery language of the whole. Obviously, what we have here is a rewriting of earlier notes, jottings, and comments—some of which we happen to have—into a formal document suitable for inclusion in a Book of Shadows.

Now consider paragraph [5]. Its content is referred to several times in *Witchcraft Today*, which also helps to date it. Notice that it formalizes what is implicit in the commentary on the Amalthean Horn prayer, that a man and a "girl" should work together, just as the surrounding paragraphs, [4] and [6], formalize other matters touched on in that commentary. Since we even have early drafts of it in the notebooks, we can be quite certain that this document was written all in one piece, and does not show any evidence of including quotations from earlier, traditional documents. That is, we have here a paragraph, [5], later claimed to be part of Craft Law, in its original context, and analysis of the document gives us no reason to suppose this paragraph is being quoted from any other source.

The procedures described in this document, and all the comments about them—except for those in [5]—seem perfectly sensible as part of a basic shamanistic technique. But we need not suppose that Gardner had such information from any source other than books. Rather, we have here yet another example of his theologizing about scourging.

Final Comments on the Book of Shadows in 1957

There were apparently a few other paragraphs in the Book of Shadows in 1957 that do not appear in any materials available to me, except in the Farrar's 1984 book. These include:

- the paragraph on their pp. 53-54 entitled "Power";
- the paragraph on their pp. 54-55 entitled "Properly Prepared";
- the paragraph on their p. 55 entitled "The Meeting Dance

(although it is summarized in *Witchcraft Today*, Chap. 13);
- the paragraph on their pp. 56-57 entitled "The Cone of Power";
- the paragraph on their p. 59 entitled "To Leave the Body";
- the paragraph on their p. 61 entitled "The Working Tools"
- the paragraphs on their pp. 62-63 entitled "Making Tools" various instructions.

I have no doubt that these paragraphs are from Gardner himself, and that they therefore belong in any complete Gardnerian Book of Shadows. But since I have nothing scholarly to add concerning the text of these paragraphs, and since they do not affect my historical argument, I do not think it would be fair for me to give them here. I may already have stolen far more of the Farrars' thunder than I would have liked. So let me compensate for that by recommending that you buy their excellent 1981 and 1984 books, if you haven't already, and copy these passages into your own Book of Shadows, IF you find the passages useful, interesting, or relevant to your own concerns.

Chapter Eight

The Book of Shadows in 1961

"I refuse to invent missing documents."
Georges Dumezil, Camillus, p. 170.

We have already seen in Chapters 1 and 3 what the Craft Laws are in general, where the later forms of them were published, and what my general conclusions about them are. Here we will look specifically at the documents which, as far as I know, constitute the oldest draft of them, and will analyze them into their sources. We will begin with the two-part draft of the Craft Laws included among the Weschcke documents, look at the laws that were tagged onto this early draft in the published forms, and then look again at the document that, I am convinced, inspired the creation of the Craft Laws as a unified document.

These two documents are carbons, in Typeface II, on lightweight white 8" by 13" (British legal size) paper. Document D.1 is typed double-spaced on five sheets, one side only; the typing ends about four inches down on the fifth sheet. Document D.2, in contrast, is typed single-spaced on both sides of a single sheet, and the typing ends about nine inches down from the top. Since we can see where the typing ended, we can be sure that no continuing sheets are missing, and that Documents D.1 and D.2 were indeed typed as separate documents. They were, however, fastened together, with five staples along the left edge, and they have identical fold marks along the left edge, along the bottom (where the excess three inches were folded up), and in the middle, from being folded in half backward at one time, in thirds forward at another. The right corners are dogeared; clearly these documents had seen service in a Book of Shadows.

I have, of course, reproduced these documents as exactly as possible. I am numbering the lines as originally typed by means of the numbers in square brackets at the beginning of every fifth line. I have also introduced the capital letters in square brackets, to label the literary units into which these texts can be analysed.

D.1. The Old Laws, Part 1.

The old LAWS[1]

[A] The Law was made and Ardane[2] of old.

The law was made for the Wica ,to advise and help in their troubles.

The Wica should give due worship to the Gods & obey their will

which they Ardane, for it was made for the good of the Wica.As rhe

[5] Wicas worship is good for the Gods.

For the Gods love the Wica,as a man loveth a woman,by

mastering her. So the Wica should love the Gods. by being mastered by them. And it is necessary that the Circle ,which is the Temp e of the Gods,should be truely cast and purified,that it

[10] may be a fit place for the Gods to enter. And the Wica should

---

1 In Gardner's handwriting, in black ink. The reason why these are called the OLD laws, and why the phrases "of old" and "the old law" are repeated so many times throughout these two documents, is that these laws are new, and need this sort of pseudepigraphic validation (compare John 21:24). Notice that this sort of persuasion is directed at the members, not outsiders. These documents were not originally intended for public consumption.

2 This "ardane" is probably not an archaicizing of "ordained" (which was never spelled thus), but Gardner's misspelling of "aredan," which the OED (p. 110) says is a participle form of "arede," a Saxon word meaning "to determine by counsel, to decree, to declare by supernatural counsel, to prophesy, to divine, to make known," with recorded uses dating from the ninth to the seventeenth centuries. It is an archaic word introduced into this document in order to make it look old. The comments in MW, pp. 74-75, about unusual words used in the Craft reflect this search for archaic words, since we know MW and the "Craft Laws" were being written at the same time. Doreen Valiente wrote to me that Gardner gave her a copy of the list of unusual words he had gleaned from the OED when he gave her the replacement copy of "The Old Laws."

be properly prepared and purified ,to enter into the presence of the Gods.[3] With love and worship in their hearts they shall raise power from their bodies to give power to the Gods, as has been tought us of old.

[15] For in this way only may man have communion with the Gods, for the Gods cannot help man without the help of men.[4]

---

[3] Notice that this sentence and the preceding one each begin with the "and" typical of manuscript glosses. They follow the sequence of items 11 and 12 in "The Eightfold Path," and have been inserted here in order to make these "laws" agree with the ritual prescriptions in that document. They seem based on WT, p. 18: "When drawn the circle is carefully purified, as also are all who celebrate the rites. Witches attach great importance to this, for within the circle is the gods' domain." Note that being bound and scourged has thus been made part of the Craft Laws.

[4] Section [A] has been woven together from the following materials:

HMA, p. 83:"`We witches have our gods also, and they are good, at least to us, but they are not all-powerful, and so they need our aid. They desire fertility for man, beast, and crops, but they need our help to bring it about, and by our dances and other means they get that help."

(WT, p. 145, says, "The faith of the cult is summed up in a witch's book I possess which states that . . . " and then this passage from HMA is paraphrased. As before, we find that the only "witch books" Gardner has are what he has written himself--and that is what I find is true of these Craft Laws.)

MW, p. 26: "They think that the God and the Goddess assist them in making their magic, as they assist the God and the Goddess in their turn by raising power for them by their dances and by other methods."

WT, p. 28:"The Witches' Circle . . . is to keep in the power which they believe they can raise from their bodies."

MW, p. 136: "The Gods are not all-powerful, they need the aid of men and women. If sufficient nerve power is raised by the worshippers the Gods will become all-powerful. . . . the `Sacred Marriage' was not merely for the satisfaction of those who took part; their powers were dedicated to . . . giving great power to the Gods, . . . bringing the Gods into communion with their worshippers."

Again we have sexuality conceived as sacramental. Notice also that line 2 is redundant; that the sense runs on quite well from the end of line 5 to the sentence that begins in line 12; that the sentence which runs from the beginning of line 6 into line 8 could easily follow line 2; and that the concept in line 16 is duplicated in lines E.2.30-31.

[B] And the High Priestess shall rule her Coven as representative of the Goddess,and the High Priest shall support her as the representative of the God. And the High Priestess shall chose whom she [20] will, if he have sufficient rank., to be her High Priest.

For. the God himself,kissed her[5] feet in the 5 fold salute, laying his power at the feet of the Goddess. because of her youth & beauty,

her sweetn ss kindness,her wisdom & Justice, her humility & generosity, So he resigned his lordship to her, But the Priestess should

[25] ever mind that all power comes from him.[6] It is only lent when it is used wisely and justly. And the greatest virtue of a High Prieste[ss] is that she recognises that youth is necessary to the representative of the Goddess, so that she will retire gracefully infavour of a younger woman, Should the Coven so decide in Council. For the true

[30] High Priestess realsies that gracefully surendering pride of place is one of the greatest of virtues, and that thereby she will return to that pride of place in another life, with greater power beauty.[7]

---

[5] Who does "her" refer to? Grammatically, to the High Priestess, but clearly the content refers to the Goddess. If we remove everything after "Goddess" in line 18, and all of lines 19-20, the pronoun reference makes sense; so we can see that this discussion of the High Priest here was added to earlier material, as is also indicated by the telltale initial "ands."

[6] The second half of the sentence restates the obvious, in order to change the subject. Notice that "The High Priestess shall rule . . . resigned his Lordship to her" reads like a preamble to the material that begins on line 54. Notice also that lines 1-16 (without the two sentences discussed in note 4) would lead quite naturally into lines 33-53. Apparently lines 17-32 were inserted into the document after lines 1-16 and 33-53 were already written.

[7] Section [B] has been compounded out of the following materials. First, we have the references to the "Myth of the Goddess" (WT, pp. 45-46) that has been incorporated into the Second-Degree initiation.

Lines 17-20 are based on WT, p. 154: "Now the god is represented by the high priest (if there is one) and . . . `He is whoever the high priestess appoints to take this position.' In practice she always appoints her husband if he has sufficient rank; but she may appoint anyone who is eligible."

Lines 21-32 are based on MW, pp. 128-9: "Among the virtues she must have is the realisation that youth is among the requisites necessary for the representative of the Goddess, and that she must be ready to retire gracefully in favour of

[C] ln the days when Witchdom extended far,we were free and
worshipd in Alther[8] Greatest Tempels. But, in these unhappy times
we must hold our sacred mysteries in secret.
So it be[9] Ardane , that none but the Wica may see our mysteries.[10]
for our enimies are many , And torture looseth the tongues of many.
lt be ardane that each Coven shall not know where the next Coven
bide, or who its members are. save the Priest and Priestess.
That there shall be no communication between them..save by the Messenger of the Gods. or the Summoner. Only if it be safe, may the Covens meet, in some safe place. For the great festavals. And while there ,none shall say whence thay come, or give their true names.
To the end that if any are tortured, in theiragoney, they can
not tell if they know not. So it be Ardane that no one may tell any not of the Craft who be of the Wica. nor give any names,or where they Byde, or in any way tell anything which can betray any to our foes. Nor

---

a younger woman in time. She will then become one of the Elders, whose decisions are powerful in council. But as the Old God told the Goddess, `Age and Fate wither all things, and against them I am helpless. But when men die and come to me I give them rest and peace so that they may return.' [Again from the myth, WT, p. 45.] So a true Priestess realises that gracefully surrendering pride of place now is one of the greatest virtues, and she will return to that pride of place the next time, in another incarnation, with greater power and beauty." Doreen Valiente wrote to me that she had felt this section to be sexist upon her first reading of "The Old Laws" in 1959, which was why her coven burned "The Old Laws" in their cauldron.

8 "Alther" is the archaic genitive plural of "all," and was used in the sixteenth century as a prefix to form the absolute superlative; the OED (p. 57) gives examples from the eleventh to the sixteenth centuries, including one from Shakespeare. The assertion here is not "we worshipped in each and every one of the greatest temples," but rather "we worshipped in the greatest of all temples"; that is, "our temples were the best."

9 Notice: not "be it," but "it be." That is, not "let it be ordained," but "it has been decreed." Another correct usage of an archaic construction.

10 Here "secret" was typed first and scratched out, then "mysteries" was typed above it; apparently mere rewriting.

may they tell where the Covenstead be. or where is the Covendom.

or where be the meetings. or that there have been meetings. And if any break these laws, even under torture, The Curse of the Goddess[11] shall be upon them.so they never be reborn on earth, And may they remain where they belong, in the Hell of the Christians.

[D] Let each High Priestess govern her Coven with Justice and

love.with the help of the advice of the elders. Always heading the advice of the Messenger of the Gods. If he cometh. She will heed all complaints of brothers,And strive to settle all differances among them. But it must be recognized that there be people who will ever strive to force others to do as they will.

They are not necesseraly evil. & they often do have good ideas.

andt such ideas should be talked over in council. And if they will not agree with their brothers, or if they say,I will not work under this High Priestess,[12] It hath always been the old law, to be convenient for the bretherin, and to void disputes,[13] Any of the Third may claim to found a new Coven because they live over a league from the Covenstead,or that they are about to do so. Anyone living within the Covendom withsing to form a new Coven,to avoid strife,shall tell the Elders of his intention And on the instant void his dwelling and remove to the new Covendom. Members of the old Coven may join

the New one when it be formed, but if they do, must utterly void the old Coven. The Elders of the New and the Old Covens should meet in peace and brotherly love ,to decide the new bounderies.

Those of the Craft who dwell outside both Covendoms may join

either indifferent, but not both. Though all may, if the Elders

agree, meet for the Great Festavals , if it be truely in peace and brotherly love. But splitting the coven oft means strife. So for

this reason these laws were made of old. And may the curse of the GODDESS be on any who disreguard them. So be it Ardane.

---

[11] This phrase was first used in WT, p. 86: "the curse of the goddess may be on any who break this law."

[12] This really is a non sequitur, caused by sheer bad writing.

[13] The sense could be intended to run on here.

[E] <If you would> keep a book<, let it be> in your own hand of write,[14]

let brothers and sisters copy what they will,but never let the book out of your hands, and never keep the writings of another,for if it be found in their hand of write, they <well may> be taken and <Engined>.[15]

Each should guard his own writings & destroy it whenever danger threatens. Learn as much as you may by heart, & when danger is past, rewirit your book <an> it be safe.[16] For this reason, if any die,destroy their book if they have not been able to. For <an> it be found, tis clear proof against them, <And, our oppressors well know>,[17] "Ye may not be a witch alone" So all their <kin &>[18] friends be in danger of torture. So ever destroy anything not necessary.

If your book be found on you. tis clear proof against you <alone>.You may be <engined>. Keep all thoughts of the <Craft>[19] from your

---

[14] This expands the wording in the Warning in BAM, "Keep a book in your own hand or write," in order to create a better transition here. This document was typed after 1953, and incorporates expansions of earlier materials. Sections [E] and [G] here are, of course, based entirely on the Warning. Throughout sections E and G I use angle brackets to flag words added to or altered from the earlier text.

[15] The OED (p. 867) says that "engine" as a verb can mean "to put on the rack; to torture"; that is, "to put on an engine of torture." However, "tortured" was the word used at this place in B.7; so here the more archaic word has been purposely introduced into a later draft (even though the earlier one had been published!) in order to make it look older. Observe that you simply do not need to make a genuinely old document sound old.

[16] Here the archaic "an" has been substituted for "if."

[17] The preceding four words were not in the Warning; they have been added to "explain" the "quotation" that follows (if it is actually a quotation, I don't know what it could be from).

[18] "Kin and" has been added here to improve the appearance of historical verisimilitude.

[19] In line 91, "engined" has been substituted for the "tortured" used in the earlier versions; where "cult" was used earlier, it has been replaced by "Craft," which began to be used as a name for the religion only rather late in the 1950s.

mind. Say you had bad dreams, a devil caused you to write it without your knowledge. Think to yourself. l know nothing. l remeber nothing. l have forgotten everything. Drive this into your mind.

lf the torture be to great to bear. Say, l will confess. l cannot bear this <torture>,[20] What do you want me to say? l will say it. if they try to make you speak of the brotherhood, Do NOT. But if they try to make you speak of imposabilaties such as flying through the air, Consorting with the <Christian>[21] Devil, or sacrificing children, or eating mens flesh.

To obtain relief from torture. say. l had an evil dream,l was 4 not myself. l was crased.

Not all Magestrates are bad, if there be an excuse they may show mercy. lf you have confessed aught, deny it afterwards, syy you babbled under torture. You knew not what you said. lf you are condemed, fear not. The Brotherhood is powerfull. They may help you to escape,if you stand steadfast.

But if you betray aught. There is no <hope>[22] for you, ln this life, or in that which is to come.

<Be sure.> lf steadfast you go to the pyre, <Dwale>[23] will reach you, you will feel naught . You go but to Death and what lies beyond. The Ecstacy of the Goddess.

[F] Tis probable that before you are Engined,Dwale will reach you.

Always remember that Christians fear much that any die under

---

[20] In the earlier versions, this "torture" was "torment"; it is probably an error here.

[21] The word "Christian" was not in the earlier versions; it has been added here as a theological clarification.

[22] Was "help" in the earlier versions.

[23] "Dwale" is defined by the OED as being either nightshade or a soporific drink made therefrom; the examples run from the tenth to the nineteenth centuries. Here is another archaic word, introduced where Gardner earlier had "drugs." Gardner mentions it specifically in MW (p. 74) as a word peculiar to the Craft; the business of finding archaic words was under way in 1957 to 1958. Notice also that lines 111-113 are a rewriting of paragraph [9] of B.2.

torture.

At the first sign of swoon,they cause it to be stopped, and blame the tormenters, for that reason, the tormenters themselves are apt to feign to torment, but do not, so it is best not to die at first.

If Dwale reaches you, tis a sign that you have a friend somwhere.

[120] you may be helped to escape, so dispair not. If the worst comes , and you go to the Pyre. wait till the flames *and smoke*[24] spring up, bend your head over,& breath in with long brewths, you choke & die swiftly & wake in the arms of the Goddess.[25]

[G] <To void discovery, Let> the working tools

[125] be[26] as ordinary things that any may have in their houses. Let the Pentacles be of wax, so they may be broken at once. Have no sword unless your rank allows you one.[27] Have no names or signs on anything.

Write the names and signes on them in ink before consecrating them and wash it off immediatly after.[28] <Do not Bigrave[29] them.

[130] lest they cause discovery. Let the colour of the hilts tell which is which.>[30]

---

[24] Inserted between the lines in Gardner's handwriting.

[25] The material in lines 114-123 does not appear in the earlier versions, or in Johns or GLS. It seems to be concerned with using "dwale" several more times, and is apparently a rewriting of paragraphs [5] and [9] of B.2. It also depends on *WT*, p. 151: "In the old days many witches went to the flames laughing and singing; they had a joy of life and of beauty, and the Peace of Death with the promise of return, so they braved the fires, for they believed that they were going to a better world, and they died happy."

[26] Here the earlier versions read, "The same with the working tools. Let them be."

[27] The sentence about the sword was not in BAM, but was added in WT, to improve the historical verisimilitude.

[28] The material in lines 124-129 has been heavily rewritten from what was here in WT, in order to create a better transition within this larger document; again, this is not how a person treats genuinely traditional writings.

[29] "Bigrave": another purposely introduced archaic term; here WT has "engrave."

[30] Lines 124-131 assume the use of tools of the Key of Solomon type - but this is kabalistic magic, and has nothing to do with pagan traditions.

[H] <Ever remember, ye are the Hidden Children of the Gods. So never do anything to disgrace them.>[31]

Never boast, Never threaten, Never say you would wish Ill to anyone. If <you or> any <,not in the Circle,>[32] speak of the Craft,

[135] say, "Speak not to me of such, it frightens me. tis evil luck to speak of it" For this reason . The Christians have spies everywhere These speak as if they were well affected,as if they would come to Meetings,saying "My mother used to go, to worship the Old Ones.

I would that I could go myself." To these ever deny all knowledge.[33]

[140] But, to others ever say, tis foolish, men talk of witches flying through the air,to do so, they must be light as thistle down. and. Men say that wirches all be bleared eyed old crones, so what pleasure can there be in witch meetings ? such as folk talk on? Say, Many wise men now say there be no such creatures. Ever

[145] make it a jest, and in some future time, perhaps the persecution will die. and we may worship safely again. let us all pray for that happy day.[34]

---

[31] Everything in lines 129 (from "Do not") to 132 is new material inserted after 1953 into the text as given in WT; and "Hidden Children of the Gods" is a reference to the second-degree ritual. The content here seems related to a passage from MW (p. 150; see below), which was written after Ned had become High Priest of the second coven.

[32] The preceding four words are not in WT; they have been taken from the oaths of initiation.

[33] Lady Epona points out that this is precisely what Charles Cardell had claimed; that is, this paragraph is a response to Cardell, and so it was probably inserted into the Craft Laws after the run-in with the Cardells and Olive Green in 1959. This is an indication that Gardner did not promulgate the Craft Laws as a document for the Book of Shadows until about 1960. This passage also depends on B.2 [5]: "Ever remember if tempted to admit or boast of belonging to the cult you be endangering your brothers, for though now the fires of persecution may have died down <but> who knows when they be revived? . . . if we take many recruits, we may loose the fires of persecution against us again. So ever keep the secrets." Here combined with concepts in Rules 2, 5, and 8.

[34] Lines 145-147 are a "prediction after the fact," and so allow an "earliest possible date" to be assigned to this document. The document wishes us to think of the late eighteenth century; in fact, what it actually refers to is the repeal of

[I] May the blessings of the Goddess and the God be on all who keep thei-r Ardane.[35]

D.2. The Old Laws, Part II

[J] If the Craft hath any Appenage[36] let all brothers guard it,and help to keep it clear and good for the Craft,& let all justly guard all monies of t e Craft. But if some brothers truely wrought it , Tis right that they have t eir pay,an it be just. And this be not taking money for the use of the Art. but for good and honest work. And even the Christians say " A labourer is worthey of his hire." But if any brothers work willingly for the good of the craft without pay, tis but to their greater honour. So it be Ardane.

[K] If there be any disputes or quarrels among the bretheren The High Priestess shall straight Convene the Elders & enquire into the matter, and they shall hear both sides. first alone. then together.

And they shall decide justly, not favouring the one side or the other Ever recognising that there be people who can never agree to work under others. but at the same time there be some people who cannot rule justly. To those who ever must be chief,there is one answer, Void the Coven & seek another, or, make a Coven of your own, taking with you those who will to go, To those who cannot rule justly. The answer be. those who cannot bear your rule will leave you, For none may come to meetings with those with whom they are at variance. So an either cannot agree. get hence.For the Craft must

---

the last witchcraft law in 1951. Section [H] is woven together out of material from HMA, p. 214; WT, pp. 151-2; B.2 [5]; the Warning; and MW, p. 150.

[35] This closing exhortation for the document could not have stood alone. I think the first draft that Gerald sent to Doreen and the rest in 1959 ended here.

[36] According to the OED (p. 95), this French word came into English in the late sixteenth century. It is used here in its precise and original sense of "land possessed to provide one with the means of subsistences." Not only is this an archaic word being used precisely, but the first sentence has been written specifically to use it. "Coven" would make more sense than "Craft" here; what is being discussed is the affairs of a small group, not of a large religious movement. Lines 4-9 make little sense unless you have already read lines 70-76 in the first document; section [J] should have been inserted there.

ever survive. So it be Ardane.

[L] ln the olden days when we had power,we could use our Arts against any who illtreated any of the Brotherhood. But in these Evil Times, we may not do so, For our enimies have devised a burning pit of everlasting fire, into which they say their God casteth all the people who worship him, except it be the very few who are released by their priestes spells and Masses.and this be chiefly by giving money and rich gifts torecieve his favour, for their Alther[37] Greatest God is ever in need of Money.

But as our Gods need our aid to make fertility for men and crops.[38] So the God of the Christians is ever in need of mans help to search out and destroy us. Theyir priests tell them that any who get our help or our cures are damned to the Hell forever,so men be mad for the terror of it,. But they make men believe that they may scape this hell if they give victims to the tormenters. So for this reason. All be forever spying, thinking an l can but catch one of the Wica l will scape this fiery pit. But we have our hidels, and men searching long and not finding say,"there be none, or lf they be, they be in a far country."[39]

But, when one of our oppressors die. or ,even be sick,ever is the cry"This be Witches Malice." and the hunt is up again. and though they slay ten of their people , to one of ours, still .they care not, they have

---

[37] See earlier note on "alther." The meaning here is "Greatest God of all," and is intended to be sarcastic.

[38] Section [L] to this point seems concocted from HMA, p. 83: "`In the Christian belief you have a good God . . . all-powerful, and who greatly desires worshippers . . . yet you . . . must give money or other rich gifts before you can hope to receive favor. . .[Here occurs the passage quoted earlier] . . . your god so loved the world he made that he devised a burning purgatory of everlasting fires, into which he casteth all the peoples he had created for many thousands of years, except a few of a chosen race. Then, it seems, he changed his mind, and casteth all that chosen race into this fiery pit, all save a few who embraced a new faith which he had made!'" Gardner quotes the beginning of this passage in WT, p. 165, as something told to him!

[39] This passage has clearly been created to link the preceding passage with the following one. It would have no point if it stood in isolation.

many thousands, while we are few indeed.

So it is Ardane, that none shall use the Art in any way to do ill to any. how evermuch they have injured us. And for long we have obe yed this law. "Harm none" and nowtimes, many believe we exist not.[40]

So it be Ardane that this law shall still continue to help us in our plight. "No one,however great an injury or unjustace they recieve, may use the Art in any to do ill or harm any."[41]

But , they may, after great consulations with all, use the Art to prevent or restrain Christians from harming us and others. but only to let or constrain them and never to punish.

To this end. Men say, "Such an one is a mighty searcher our and persecutor of Old Women whom he deemeth to be Witchse. and none hath done him Skith[42]. so this be proof they cannot, or more truely, that there be none." For all know full well,that so many folk have died because somone had a grudge against them, or were persecuted because they had money or goods to sieze. or because they had none to bribe the searchers. And many have died because they were scolding old women. So much so, that men nowsay that only Old Women are witches. And this be to our advantage, and turns suspicion away from us. In England tis now many a year since a witch hath died the death.[43] but any misuse of t e power might raise the Persecution again. So never break this law, however much you are tempted. and never consent to its being

---

[40] Assuming the dot after "law" is intended to be a comma, this sentence claims to have been written long after the end of the persecution. We can certainly believe that.

[41] The quotation marks seem to be used merely for emphasis; this nonliterary usage has surely been introduced by Gardner.

[42] Here "Skait" was typed first, then typed through with dashes, and "Skith" typed after it. Both are Saxon terms for "harm," and survive in modern usage only in the term "unscathed." Here again we see Gardner poking about for old words.

[43] This is another admission that the writing is taking place long after the end of the persecutions.

broken, If you know it is being broken in the least, you must
work strongly against it, And any High Priestess or High Priest
who consentes to it must be immediatly deposed. For tis the blood
[69] of the Bretherin they endanger.Do good, an it be safe , and only if it be safe. for any talk may endanger us.[44] [M] And strictly keep to the Old Law, never accept money for the use of the Art, for money ever smeares the taker. Tis Corcerers and Conjurers and Priests of Christ who ever accept money for the use of their Arts. and they sell Dwale
[74] and evil love spells and pardons to let men scape from their sins.

Be not as these. "Be not as these."[45] If you accept not money,you will

---

[44] Lines 40-70 are based on MW, p. 150: "if witches could kill their enemies so easily, why was there not a notable number of deaths among their `Oppressors'? . . . I think that when first attacked they hit back, but the actual `initiated witches' as distinct from the `Congregation' were few. . . . It is a tradition among witches, that thousands of people were tortured and burnt for every one witch . . . The witches met and decided, `We can't fight against this terror[;] every time we strike, so many thousands were massacred, the only way any of us can survive, is to go underground, never hurt any, however much they have wronged you, then in time we will be forgotten.' They did so, and with a bit of skilful propaganda, made witchcraft a figure of fun, an old woman with a black cat, flying on a broomstick, and so, slowly, they were forgotten, all laws against them having been repealed, as soon as it was known how harmless they were." What is going on here is not an attempt to explain historical evidence, but an attempt to create a plausible explanation of why there is no historical evidence, from the fifteenth to seventeenth centuries, of the existence of any such sort of religion as Gardner is postulating. Paragraph [6] of B.2 has been worked in here also. Lines 64-70 again work in the passage from MW, p. 127. Doreen Valiente, in the Farrars 1984, p. 63, gives a line that stands in her Text B: "All are brothers and sisters, for this reason, that even the High Priestess must submit to the scourge."

[45] This second "Be not as these" is underlined and has had the quotation marks added by hand. Apparently Gardner thought it worth emphasizing--no doubt because the Cardells were charging money to teach the Gardner/Valiente material. Notice the use of "dwale" in line 73. Here note two passages in MW: pp. 25-6,: "there is a strong witch tradition that they may never take money for practising their art; that is, they may not work for hire"; and p. 205: "Witchcraft .

be free of temptation to use the Arf for evil causes. [N]All~~You~~[46] may use the Art for your own advantage, or for the advantage of the Craft , only if you be sure you harm none. But ever let the Coven debate the matter at length, only if all are satisfied that none may be harmed

[80] may the Art be used. lf it is not possible to achieve your ends one way without harming any, pervhance the aim may be achieved by acting in a different way, so as to harm none[47]. May the Curse of the Goddess be on any who breach this law. So it be ardane.

[O] Tis adjudged lawful an anyone need a house or land,an none will

[85] sell. to incline the owners mind to be willing to sell,provided it harmeth him not in any way, & that the full worth is paid , without

haggling. Never bargain or cheepen anything which you buy by the Art.[48]

So it be Ardane.

[P] lt is the Old Law and the most important of all Laws,

[90] That no one may do or say anything which will endanger any of the Craft,or bring them in contact with the law of the land. or the Law

---

. . is a religion . . . and no genuine practitioner will perform its rites for pay."

[46] There is no space between the period and the A. Here "You" was typed first, then typed through with dashes, and "All" was typed before it, being squeezed into the space between the sentences. However, the "your" in line 77 was not then changed to agree.

[47] Section [N] is based on MW, p. 127: "They believe a certain law to be important, `You must not use magic for anything which will cause harm to anyone, and if, to prevent a greater wrong being done, you must discommode someone, you must do it only in a way which will abate the harm' This involves every magical action being discussed first, to see that it can do no damage, and this induces a habit of mind to consider well the results of one's actions, especially upon others."

[48] This is a gemara based on the preceding laws against harmfulness, for which the parallels are ample. As is typical of gemara, it cites an applicable precedent, a magical one, on line 87, which is apparently based on Crowley, *Magick*, p. 64: "buy whatever may be necessary without haggling." Note that the point here is ethical: if you use magic to persuade a man to sell, then you cannot also beat down his price, because that would be taking unfair advantage of him.

of the Church or any of our persecutors. ln any disputes between the bretheren, no one may invoke any laws but those of the Craft.

or any Tribunal but that of the Priestess and the Priest and the

[95] Elders. And mat the Curse of the Goddess be on any who so do.[49]

So it be Ardane.

[Q] lt is not forbiden to say as Christian do. "There be Witchcraft

in the Land" Because out oppressors of old[50] made it Heresy not to believe in Witchcraft, & so a crime to deny it. which thereby put

[100] you under suspicion. But ever say l know not of it here, perchance they may be , but afar off. l know not where. but ever speak so you cause others to doubt they be as they are Always speak of them as old Crones, consorting with the Devil and riding through the air.

But ever say,but how may men ride through the air an they be not

[105] as light as Thistle Down? But the Curse of the Goddess be on any who cast any suspicion on any of the Brotherhood.orspeaks of any real meeting place. or where any bide. So it be Ardane.[51]

[R] Let the Craft keep Books with the names of all Herbs

[109] which are good for man.and all cures, that all may learn. But keep

another book with all the Banes & Apies.[52] & let only the elders and trustworthy people have this knowledge. So it be Ardane.

[S] And may the Blessings of the Gods be on all who keep these

Laws and the Curses of both God and Goddess be on all who break

---

[49] Based on Rules 2 and 6, and on HMA, p. 214: "In the old days all knew where the Sabbath was to be held, and who would attend it, so when a few were taken and tortured, it was easy to find out all who went to the meetings, their leaders and priests, and often even who represented the God Himself. . . . only officers must know who are the leaders of the covens, and especially, who is our God."

[50] Again, "of old" reveals that the time of writing is after the time of persecution; so lines 97-100 are discussing a past situation. But then lines 100-107 attempt to speak as if persecution were a present danger.

[51] Sections [P] and [Q] are another rewriting of the passages already used from MW, pp. 127 and 150.

[52] "Banes" is an archaic word for poisons, but "apies" baffles me.

them So it be Ardane.

Gardner apparently felt that the first draft, sent to Doreen and the others in 1957, was not long enough; so he worked on expanding it during 1958 and 1959, by writing sections J to S. This addition duplicates the first draft in both content and structure; but the overall effect is very much like that of traditional documents. Four more sections were also added during Gardner's last few years, canonizing the early paragraphs that I pointed out in discussing C.3 [2] and C.14.

The following two sections were added after 1960.[53]

[T]138. Remember the art is the secret of the gods and only may be used in earnest and never for show [or pride] or vainglory.

139. Magicians and Christians may taunt us saying, "You have no power. [Show us your power.] Do magic before our eyes. Then only will we believe." Seeking to cause us to betray [our] (the) art before them.

140. Heed them not. for the art is holy and may only be used in need. And the curse of the gods be on any who break this law. [So be it ardane.]

[U]141. It ever be the way with women and with men also that they ever seek new love.

142. Nor should we reprove them for this.

143. But it may be found [to the disadvantage of] (a disadvantage to) the craft.

144. [And] (As) so many a time it has happened that a High Priest or High Priestess impelled by love, hath departed with their love, that is, they have left the Coven.

145. Now if [a] (the) High Priestess wishes to resign, [they] (she) may do so in full Coven.

146. And this resignation is valid.

147. But if they should run off without resigning, who may know if they may not return [in] (within) a few months?

---

[53] The following are given as part of the Craft Laws by both Johns and GLS. My convention here is to present as text only the words that Johns and GLS agree on; words in square brackets are only in Johns, and those in parentheses are only in GLS.

148. So the Law is, if a High Priestess leaves her Coven, [but returns within the space of a year and a day, she shall be]_taken back and all [shall] be as before.

149. Meanwhile, if she has a deputy, that deputy shall act as High Priestess for as long as the High Priestess is away.

150. If she returns not at the end of a year and a day, then shall the coven elect a new High Priestess.

151. Unless there [be] (is) a good reason to the contrary.[54]

152. The person who has done the work [shall] (should) reap the benefit of the reward, maiden and deputy of the High Priestess[55]

There is no need to continue following Johns and *GLS* here, since the material they number 153-155 is simply paragraph [5] of Document C.14; #156 in GLS says, "And may all the Curses of the Mighty Ones be on any who makes such an attempt"; and ##157-162 in *GLS* (156-161 in Johns) are merely paragraph [2] of Document C.3. Here we can see passages being wrenched from their original context and tagged onto the body of the "Craft Laws"; as we have now seen, the entire document was constructed in this way.

Notice that we have seen archaic words purposely being sought out and substituted for the ordinary terms used in the two earlier drafts of "The Warning." This is a tactic of "creative history," not of ordinary history. We have also seen that significant rewriting, and additional writing, of these "traditional laws" was going on well after 1953. This is not how traditional writings are dealt with by persons who are genuinely concerned about their traditionality. If I may quote Lewis Carroll:

> *"'That's not a regular rule: you invented it just now.'*
> *"'It's the oldest rule in the book,' said the King.*
> *"'Then it ought to be Number One,' said Alice."*

---

[54] The numbering has made it ambiguous whether this clause belongs to the preceding sentence or to the following one.

[55] This discussion of the role of the Maiden as an assistant Priestess seems to be based on WCWE, pp. 189-190. One can only speculate about what sort of political fight actually inspired the writing of this section.

Proposed Rules for the Craft.*

In the Ripley's correspondence file is a letter from Jack Bracelin to Gardner (it is signed only with a J, but is much concerned with business affairs at their nudist club), dated July 8, 1957. Its fourth paragraph begins, "No doubt that by now you have had Ameth's letter enclosing copy of Ned's proposals for the Craft. I do not in view of Ameth's added comments think there is much point in going into it any further, as you will see her comments make the whole thing unworkable. I note that there is a lot of comments on your behaviour." This seems to refer to an undated, unsigned document in the file, titled "Proposed Rules for the Craft," which we looked at in Chapter 2, but need to look at again here.

Proposed Rules for the Craft.

1. No member of the Craft will initiate any person unless that person has been interview by at least two Elders and accepted as suitable.

2. No affairs of the Craft will be discussed by members in the presence of uninitiated persons, or in places where conversation is likely to be overheard.

3. No copies of any papers relating to the Craft will be made or retained without the Elders' permission. Such papers as are permissible will be kept in a secure place.

4. As it is essential for the successful working of ritual by a group that here should be unity of purpose and an harmonious psychic atmosphere, members who create dissension and discord within the Craft will be asked to resign. Should they fail or refuse to do so they will be informed in writing by the Elders that they have been expelled.

5. No member of the Craft will give any information or interview about the Craft to any journalist or writer, or cause any such information to be published in any way, without the approval of the Elders, nor will any of the Elders do so without the approval of the rest of the Elders.

6. If any member of the Craft feels that he or she has reason to complain of the conduct of any other member in matters affecting the Craft, or of any misdemeanour towards any member whilst on Craft

premises, he or she will bring the said complaint to the notice of the elders as soon as possible. The Elders, after considering all available evidence, will, if they find the complaint justified, take appropriate action.

7. No member will be present at any meeting where the working is that of a higher Grade than he or she has attained, except by invitation of the Elders. These invitations will only be extended on very rare occasions where special circumstances exist.

8. No member will disclose the name and address or telephone number of any other member to any person whatsoever, without the said other member's previous permission.

9. Members will meet upon the traditional occasions, or as near to them as possible, and such meetings will be arranged by the Elders, or such Officers as the Elders authorise to do so. If the Elders be not present at such meetings, they will receive a report of them. Members may arrange other meetings for their private working if they so desire, but if more than two members be present at such a meeting the elders will receive a report of it. This report will take the form of a short letter to the Elders giving place and date of the meeting, names of members attending, and details of ceremonies carried out. Where convenient, verbal reports will be accepted.

10. Members will endeavour to acquaint themselves with the traditions of the Craft, and will not introduce innovations into the workings without the Elders' approval. Nor will the Elders give approval to any important innovation without first asking the approval of the rest of the Craft.

11. In the event of any member resigning from the Craft, he or she will honourably observe the Oath of Secrecy taken at initiation, and will also return to the Elders any written matter relating to the Craft which may be in his or her possession.

12. All members will receive a copy of these rules, and all new members will be given a copy of these rules upon initiation. New members, prior to initiation, will read these rules and declare upon their honour that they will abide by them in letter and in spirit. This declaration will be made to the Elders in writing, and signed.

13. It will be understood by all members that these rules are equally binding upon all Grades of the Craft, including the Elders, and that

serious and/or persistent breach of these rules will be grounds for expulsion.

Let's see what relationships we can notice between these "proposed rules" and the "Craft Laws."

1. Rules 1, 3, 10-12 seem to have no parallels in Documents E.1 and E.2.

2. Rules 2, 5, and 8, like E.1.46-50, E.1.134-139, E.2.89-95, and E.2.105-7, are concerned with secrecy.

3. Rules 4 and 6 could obviously be a first draft of E.1.54-71, E.2.9-21, and E.2.89-95.

4. Rule 7 shares a general concern with E.1.36.

5. Rule 9, like E.1.38-42 and E.1.71-78, is concerned with the Elders' authority to oversee all meetings.

6. Rule 13, like E.2.65-69, is concerned with the concept that the laws are equally binding on all members of whatever grade.

Now, if the "Craft Laws" had been in existence in July 1957, at least half these rules would not have been needed. And if these unnecessary rules were intended as paraphrases of the "Craft Laws," why do they not mention the "Craft Laws"? Wouldn't the most likely explanation be that the "Craft Laws" were not there to be mentioned? Bracelin would hardly have called these rules "unworkable" if they could claim to be in any way based on Craft tradition. Hence we must conclude that these "Proposed rules" occasioned the writing of the "Craft Laws" as a single document, sometime after mid-1957.

Let us notice that these 13 rules are concerned strictly with the authority of the Elders, that is, the third-degree initiates. Notice also that the term "Craft" must actually mean "coven" (in rules 4, 6, 10, and by implication, 9), just as we found in E.2.1-7 and E.2.108; that is, it is the affairs of a single coven that are being dealt with here. Fred Lamond told me that the original coven, in which Gardner was High Priest and Doreen Valiente was High Priestess, divided in two in February 1957, with Doreen taking Ned to be her High Priest. This was amicable growth, not a schism, since the correspondence file in Toronto shows that Gardner, Doreen, and the others, despite personal frictions, continued working closely together on the Craft during the five years 1957-1962. But in 1957 there was, for the first time, not a single small group, which could run by unwritten rules, but an organization, the "Craft," with at least two covens, which therefore needed written rules that all could agree on. Obviously, there were not so many members in all that the group consultations required by rules 5 and 10 would have been clumsy to carry out.

Equally obviously, these rules must have arisen out of the sort of "constitutional crisis" that any organization must go through. Fred told me that after the division into two covens, his coven, in which Gardner remained High Priest, elected to use circle dancing, rather than scourging, as its major technique for raising power, and that Gardner soon wandered off in search of others more to his taste. It was after this that the run-in with Florannis and the Cardells occurred, and I cannot help suspecting that some of the "proposed rules" may be concerned with this sort of problem. At the least, we can suppose that some (if not all) of the things forbidden by these new rules had been happening; else why have a rule against them? That is, we can suppose that Gardner had in fact been: initiating newcomers without having them screened; talking to the uninitiated, including reporters, about Craft business; passing out copies of the rituals; fighting with others in the circle; giving out personal information; holding secret or unauthorized rituals; introducing innovations without discussing them; refusing to abide by group decisions; and so on.

In these circumstances, the Elders felt they had to insist on their authority to maintain order in the organization. But in Documents E.1 and E.2 an uneasy compromise between the authority of the Elders and that of the High Priestess is revealed by the many rough seams and grammatical disagreements. If we suppose that the "Proposed Rules" arose out of a real situation, then we can suspect that they were rewritten into the "Craft Laws" by a process that (1) balanced the authority of the High Priestess against that of the Elders, and (2) created a document in the sort of flowery language that Gardner considered appropriate for the Book of Shadows. Here we have an hypothesis about how the "Craft Laws" were written. Since all the available evidence about the "Craft Laws" has now been developed, we can test this hypothesis in the course of pulling this evidence together to see what it indicates.

Table E.1 lists all the correspondences between "Craft Laws" and passages in Gardner's published and unpublished writings, as identified in the notes to Documents E.1 and E.2, along with the correspondences to the "Proposed Rules"; we thus find that we have accounted for all but 37 of the 263 lines in Documents E.1 and E.2, that is for 85 percent of the "Craft Laws" as they stood in those documents. Now, for any one passage, we could not be sure whether the "Craft Law" is based on the parallel passage or vice versa. But looking at the situation as a whole, it seems highly probable that the "Craft Laws" are a rewriting of the earlier passages, and highly unlikely that the reverse could be true, since these passages in their earlier contexts are NOT said or implied to be taken from any sort of traditional, authoritative document (except those from MW, which was being written at the same time as the "Craft Laws").

E1

Lines		Internal		External	
		Exact	Conceptual	Exact	Conceptual
E1	1-7				
	8-12				B.1[11-12]
	8-10				WT, p.28
	13-16		E.2:31-32		HMA, p.83
	17-20				MW, P.140
	21-32			MW, pp 128-129	
	21-24				WT,p.45
	35-50		E.2:89-107		HMA, p.214
	33-37	E.2:22-24			
	36				Rule 7
	38-42				Rule 9
	39, 44-45			WT,pp 151-152	

Lines		Internal		External	
		Exact	Conceptual	Exact	Conceptual
	46-53	E.2:90-95, 105-107			Rules 4 and 6
	51				WT, p.86
	54-71	E.2:9-21			Rules 4 and 6
	71-78				Rule 9
	79-113			Doc B.5	
	111-113				Doc B.2[9]
	114-118				Doc B.2[5]
	119-120				Doc B.3
	121-123				Doc B.2[9]
	124-129a			Doc. B5	
	129b-130		E:69-70		
	131-136				MW, p.150 Doc B.2[9]
	133-147			The Warning[56]	
	134-139				Rules 2,5,8
	140-147			E.2:89-107	HMA, p.214
	140-144	E.2:101-105			
	148-149				
E2	1-8				
	9-21	E.1:54-74		Rules 4 and 6	
	22-24a	E.1:33-37			HMA, p.214
	24b-31				HMA, p.83
	31-32a		E.1:13-16		HMA, p.83
	32b-37				

Lines		Internal		External	
		Exact	Conceptual	Exact	Conceptual
	38-70				MW, p.150
	38-39	E.2:53-56			
	40-41	E.2:63-64			
	44-52		E.2:77-82		MW,p.127
	44-45	E.2:48-49			
	48-49	E.2:44-45			
	505-2	E.2:78-80			
	53-56	E.2:38-39			
	62-70				Doc. B.2[5]
	63-64	E.2:404-1			
	65-69				Rule 13
	69-70a		E.1:131-136		
	70b-76				MW, 25f, 152.205
	77-82		E.2:44-52		MW, 127 & 150
	78-80		E.2:50-52		
	83-86				
	87				Crowley, p.64
	88				
	89-107		E.1:33-53		HMA, p.214 p.140 - 147
	89-95	E.1:46-53			Rules 2,5,8
	92-95			Rule 6	
	97-107				Doc B.2[5]
	101-105	E.1:140-144			

What about those other 37 lines? Could they be traditional? Let's look at them.[56]

[56] ie The version of the warning which appeared in *WT*

E.1.1-7. We found no precise parallel to these, but they are a preamble, saying essentially, "The following laws were ardane by the gods." They could not exist in isolation, and were probably written last.

E.1.129-130. These are lines expanding the material that appeared in *WT*, to create a bridge to Section [H]; they could not have stood alone.

E.1.149. This closing exhortation for the document could not have stood alone.

E.2.1-8. This is a late gemara[57] that happened to get attached to the front, rather than the rear, of this second batch of laws. Since it is dependent on E.2.70-76, for which there are ample parallels, it cannot be traditional in this form.

E.2.32-37. This passage has clearly been created to link the preceding passage (based on HMA, p. 83) with the following one (based on *MW*, p. 150). It would have no point if it stood in isolation.

E.2.83-88. This is a gemara based on the preceding laws against harmfulness, for which the parallels are ample. As is typical of gemara, it cites an applicable precedent, a magical one, on line 87.

E.2.108-11. Another gemara aginst harmfulness, also dependent on various preceding passages for its point.

E.2.112-4. The closing exhortation, which could not have existed in isolation.

Obviously, then, these 37 lines are merely part of the literary structure of Documents E.1 and E.2 as we have them, not independent pieces of tradition, nor anything like a cohesive document in themselves. This analysis therefore strengthens my hypothesis about how the "Craft Laws" were written.

At this point, some readers might object that the argument presented so far is not conclusive: Gardner could have known many of these traditions all along, as "oral tradition" learned from an earlier coven, but need not have referred to them as "laws" in *High Magic's Aid* or *Witchcraft Today*; furthermore, if it is not certain that any one of these "Craft Laws" depends on an apparent parallel, then dependence is no

[57] The Gemara is the commentary upon the older central text - the Mishnah - in the Talmud (if you already knew this, why did you read this footnote?).

more certain for all of the "Craft Laws" taken together. I have to grant all that. I have often noticed that when a scholar resorts to claiming something is obvious, you had better count your change. Let me see if I can do better.

We have noticed (1) that the "Proposed Rules" are concerned strictly with asserting the authority of the "Elders" over the "Craft," and (2) that in them "Craft" seems to mean only a single coven (or a group not much larger than a single coven). If the "Proposed Rules" were the starting point for the construction of Documents E.1 and E.2, then these two internal characteristics may still be visible in the "Craft Laws"; and if they are, then we can be sure the "Craft Laws" are based on the "Proposed Rules." To decide whether these characteristics are still visible in the "Craft Laws," we will need to answer two questions.

1. If we replace the term "Craft" with "coven" in Documents E.1 and E.2, do the passages in question still make as much sense?

2. In Documents E.1 and E.2, did passages that discuss authority in the Craft or in a coven originally emphasize the authority of the Elders, of the Priestess, of the Priest, of all of them, or what?

The answer to the first question is fairly easy. We have already noted that in E.2.1-7 and E.2.108, "Craft" must mean "coven," because the current meaning, of the religious movement as a whole, makes no sense. You can inspect the other passages (E.1.47, E.1.73, E.1.91, E.1.134, E.2.20, E.2.77, E.2.91-93), and see that the meaning "coven" makes good sense, usually more sense than the alternative. It cannot be argued that, since "coven" also appears in most of these contexts, "Craft" must mean something different, because we have the same combination of terms in E.2.143-144, where it is obvious that "Craft" must mean "coven." (To be fair, I think this peculiar situation arose because, although "Craft" was intended to mean "the religion as a whole" in these documents, it was hard to keep that in mind when dealing with the problems of only a small group.)

Now, in order to deal with the second question, we need to analyze the way in which the various key terms are used in Documents E.1-E.2. This analysis is shown in Table E.2, which shows what terms appear in each of the Sections, which are the obvious literary units within the documents.

Table E.2. Word Usage In Documents E.1 And E.2.[58]

Unit	Priest	Priestess	Elders	Craft	Coven	Art	Gods	Goddess
A(E.1:1-16)							X	
B(17-32)	X	X			X			X
C(33-53)	X	X		X	X		X	X
D(54-78)		X	X	X	X		X	X
E(79-113)				X				X
F(114-123)								X
G(124-131)								
H(131-147)				X			X	
I(148-149)							X	X
J(E.2:1-8)				X		X		
K(9-21)		X	X	X	X			
L(22-70)	X	X				X	X	
M(71-76)						X		
N(77-83)				X	X	X		X
O(84-88)							X	
P(89-96)	X	X	X	X				X
Q(97-107)							X	
R(108-111)			X	X				
S(112-114)						X	X	
T(138-40)						X	X	
U(141-152)	X	X		X	X			
V(153-156)						X		
W(157-162)	X	X		X				

[58] I have included the final units that were added after 1960 for comparative purposes. I analyzed the use of several other words as well (Witch, brethren, God, council), but found no pattern to their use. "Circle" and "Wica" occur only in units with the term "Gods."

First, let's look at how the term "Priest" is used. It never appears by itself, but only in combination with "Priestess" (in E.1.18-20, E.1.39, E.2.67, E.2.94, U.144, and W.158). Furthermore, only the Priestess is mentioned in E.1.54, E.1.63, and E.2.10. It is clear that the Priest has been added in all these places as an afterthought; the passages were not originally written with him in mind. This example makes it easier to see what is happening in the passages where the Priestess is mentioned. They are as follows.

E.1.17-32; Section [B]. This passage was originally written with the Priestess in mind, and is a rewriting of *MW*, pp. 128-9. Significantly, one sentence in this *MW* passage ("She will then become one of the Elders, whose decision is powerful in council") has been left out. Why? We also saw that this passage was inserted late in the writing process, since it breaks the more natural transition from E.1.16 to E.1.33. Why? Probably because someone wanted a passage emphasizing the authority of the Priestess to appear before the following sections, which emphasize that of the Elders. Notice also that neither "Elders" nor "Craft" appears in this Section, and that it gives the coven as a whole, not just the Elders, the right to elect or depose a High Priestess.

E.1.33-53; Section [C]. Here "Priest and Priestess" are mentioned only in line 39, but the mention is clearly an afterthought: it is clumsy, ambiguous, and contrary to the intent of the rest of the passage.

E.1.54-78; Section [D]. In lines 54-57 the Priestess is said to govern on her own authority, with only advice from the Elders. But in lines 66-78, only the Elders are mentioned as having any authority. Notice that insertion of the clause about the Priestess in lines 62-63 has created an apparent *non sequitur*, which disappears if the clause is eliminated. Notice that the point of Rule 6 is that the Elders should settle disputes between the members. Clearly this Section originally began "The Elders shall rule the coven [or Craft] with justice and love, always heeding . . . They will heed . . ." and so on; the beginning was rewritten in order to work in the Priestess.

E.2.9-21; Section [K]. This is also directly dependent on Rules 4 and 6. Lines E.2.17-18, "To those who cannot rule justly, the answer be, those who cannot bear your rule will leave you," obviously concern a group rule, not rule by a single person. Although the Priestess is mentioned at the beginning of the Section, the Elders have the authority in the rest of it; so here too we must suspect that line 10 was rewritten to work the Priestess in.

E.2.67. Here the phrase "High Priest or High Priestess" is introduced to emphasize that they can be deposed for breaking the rules—precisely the provision of Rule 13. But it is not clear whether the Elders or the coven as a whole do this deposing.

E.2.89-96; Section [P]. This section results logically from combining Rules 2 and 6. Obviously the passage could, and probably did, originally refer only to the Elders. Perhaps the members wanted the "laws" which this tribunal would enforce to be written down; this would have been another reason for creating Documents E.1 and E.2.

E.2.141-52. Here, as in E.1.17-32, the entire passage is concerned with the Priestess, the Elders are not mentioned, and the coven as a whole has the right to elect the new Priestess. But just as [B] was a late insertion, so is this section, so late that it didn't get into Document E.2, but was appended to it later.

Finally, let's notice E.2.108-111, in which only the Elders are mentioned as having any authority.

If Section [B] was inserted late in the writing process, as is suggested by its similarity in content to E.2.141-52, then we find that throughout Documents E.1 and E.2 originally only the Elders were said to have authority over the Craft (indeed, the term "Elders" appears only in Sections in which the term "Craft" is used; only the term "coven" is used in [B], where "Priestess" is original). In a secondary overlay, the terms "Priestess" and "coven" have been worked in, to emphasize the Priestess's authority over the coven, as well as the coven's own authority balanced against that of the Elders.

So the demonstration is complete that the "Craft Laws" depend on the "Proposed Rules," and were worked up into the form represented by Documents E.1 and E.2 at some time after mid-1957, perhaps not until late 1959. Given that, let me develop a scenario that will explain how the "Craft Laws" were probably written.

After the two covens were formed in February 1957, there arose some sort of organizational problems that inspired Ned, as spokesman for the Elders, to write his "Proposed Rules" by about June, as a sort of written constitution for the organization.[59] The project did not achieve its original purpose; Robert told me he thought the "Craft Laws" were something gotten up by Doreen's coven, because they were never adopted by the original coven. But the idea of having such a document in the Book of Shadows apparently caught Gardner's fancy, and he began to work on the project.

Certainly he would have felt that the new document had to be in the sort of flowery, formal, and often archaic-sounding language in which most of the other documents had been written. He also wanted it to look and sound traditional in itself. Furthermore, he wanted it to have some theological content—to be concerned with how a coven is to work magic—not be just a set of organizational rules. In order to have raw materials for writing it, he combed through earlier writings—both the published books and various Book of Shadows documents—and gathered together passages that had some connection with the concept of a traditional collection of laws that defined and governed the "Craft." Given this collection of passages and the "Proposed Rules," Gardner then wrote Document E.1; and later, I now think in 1959, wrote Document E.2.

The fact that these were conceived as independent documents at first can be deduced from several different kinds of evidence. First, and most obviously, they were typed as separate documents. Second, the two contain a parallel structuring of their major content; that is, Sections [D], [E]-[G], [H], and [I] in Document E.1 exactly parallel the content, and often the wording, of Sections [K], [L], [Q], and [S] of Document E.2. Also, Document E.2 may have had its own preamble; Section [A] looks like a composite of two originally independent passages. Section [B] is a late insertion, and Document E.2 has many independent gemara stuck into it. Section [C] also parallels Sections [P] and [Q], but has been placed earlier. Finally, the two documents make sense as independent attempts to rewrite the same raw material, but are almost impossible to explain otherwise.

---

59 Doreen said in her 1985 letter to *Iron Mountain* that she had typed the "Proposed Rules." The typing matches that in her letter of 7/17/58 to Dafo.

Gardner retyped and tinkered with the resulting two documents until about 1960, misspelling the archaic words from the *OED*, and adding material. For example, why is Section [F] not in Johns or GLS? Probably because it was added by Gardner in his own copy, but was not in the copy that was ancestral to the version in Johns and GLS. The writing of the "Craft Laws" was certainly not finished until sometime in 1959, because they were not included in the documents that Florannis received in 1958 or 1959.

At some point, however, the attempts to coordinate these documents ceased, and they were simply strung together, duplications, warts, and all. Perhaps it was merely an accident that the result looks like a traditional document, in the sense that redundancies, inconsistencies, garbled passages, and odd lapses are typical of folk literature and of documents that have been repeatedly copied by hand. In any event, this appearance was certainly useful as part of the strategy of claiming the "Craft Laws" to be a traditional document; so, once created, it would have been left alone.

At this stage we need to ask whether the sort of religion Gardner proposed would have had such a document at all. What is peculiar and interesting about the "Craft Laws" is not that they are a rather ordinary set of organizational rules—for they are still just that, in part—but that they are an attempt to codify certain "laws of magic." But is this a concept from a pagan religion? We have genuine pagan magical writings in the literature of the Hellenistic period. They consist of recipes, myths, exhortations to virtue, polemics, rhetoric, and philosophizing—but nowhere do they attempt to offer a theoretical explanation of how magic works. The concept of a theory of magic, of laws of magic, is strictly an artifact of modern anthropology. It arises especially in the writings of Jane Ellen Harrison and of Sir James Frazer, with whose *Golden Bough*[60] Gardner and Valiente were, of course, familiar. In this sense, the Craft Laws are a very modern theological document.

The preceding analysis, by connecting the text of the various "Craft Laws" to their sources, ought to be more than adequate as proof that

---

[60] In fact, Frazer's concepts are mentioned in WT, p. 145, immediately after material on which Sections [G] and [A] are based.

Gardner wrote this document during the years 1957-1959. I am well aware that there are "orthodox" members of the Craft who are going to refuse to believe this argument, because it conflicts with what they want to believe. For example, some members of the New Wiccan Church, Inc., believe that their original copy of the "Ordains" (as they call the Craft Laws) was brought to California by a British war bride in the 1940s. There could have been such a person, but she could not have brought a copy of these "Craft Laws," since they did not exist before 1957 at the earliest.

There is a growing emphasis among the Orthodox Gardnerians on the Book of Shadows as a sacred book, not only in its role as a liturgical manual, but as consisting of documents that contain an implicit "Sacred History" of the Craft. They are thus operating with dilute forms of the Judaeo-Christian concepts of sacred scripture and of history itself as vehicles of salvation. Genuinely pagan religions have little use, and less regard, for writing, preferring the complexities of oral tradition.

(Doreen Valiente's response to my telling her about this was, "I have been very saddened by what you and others have told me about what is happening to the Old Religion in the USA. 'Orthodoxies' springing up—ye Gods! We'll be having heresy hunts and holy wars next." Yes, that is unfortunately starting to be possible.)

C.3. The Verse Charge (1961)

This document is an original, in Typeface I, on a sheet of white paper, about 16 lb., watermarked "Conqueror London 5." It is single-spaced, but with an extra half space between stanzas. The hand corrections are in blue ballpen, in Gardner's handwriting. Two holes are punched along the left edge, as on Documents C.6, B.7, C.13, and C.1; so it was probably typed about when they were. The sheet had been folded in half, then in thirds, apparently to fit into a small envelope for mailing. The outer corners are quite dogeared; so this apparently saw active use in a Book of Shadows.

I *the* Mother, darksome and divine,
Say to thee, Oh children mine,
        Mine the scourge & mine the kiss

The[61] Five point star of love and bliss
Here I charge ye in this sign

All ye assembled here tonight
Bow before my spirit bright
Aphrodite ,Arionrod,
Lover of the Horned God,
Mighty[62] Queen of Witchery and night

Astarte[63] Hecate Astroth Dioine
Diana ,Briged, Melusine
I am named of old by men
Artimis and Cerredwen
Hell's dark mistress ,Heaven's Queen.

Whenere trouble comes anoon,
Or ye would ask of me a boon,
Meet ye in some hidden shade,
Lead my dance by greenwood glade,
By the light of the full moon.

With the comerads alone
Dance about my altar stone
Work my holy Magistry[64]
Ye who are fain of sorcery

---

[61] The handwritten changes in this stanza merely bring it into conformity with the version in Document D.1, and so are probably merely corrections of typing mistakes.

[62] This word has been added in the righthand margin. It appears in GLS (p. 157), which gives a version with five-line stanzas, as does *Witch*; so we can infer that the four-line version in Document C.1 is the earlier one, even though the Farrars (1981, p. 41-42) still give the four-line version. Doreen Valiente has commented (1990) that she wrote the verse in quatrains, and doesn't see why anyone (i.e., Gardner) needed to alter them.

[63] Here "Astroth" was typed first, then "Astarte" typed above it.

[64] Here "Mystery?" has been typed to the left of the line, and this change then appears in GLS (p. 159). Doreen Valiente confirms that "Magistry" was her original word here.

I bring ye secrets yet unknown.

Whatere troubles come to thee,
No more shall ye know slavery,
    Who tread the round on Sabbat night,
    Come ye all naked to the rite,
In sign that ye are truley free.

I teach the *mystery*[65] of re-birth,
Keep ye my mysteries in mirth
    Heart joined to heart,and lip to lip,
    Five are the points of fellowship,
That bring ye ecstacy on Earth.[66]

I ask no offerings, do but bow,
No other law but love I know,
    By naught but love I may be known,
    All that liveth is mine own
From me they come to me they go.

The version of this verse in *Witch* must have been written before Florannis received it in August 1959; and so can be dated between February 1957 and July 1959. Hence this version must be somewhat earlier, but still must fall after February 1957, since Gardner would probably not having been rewriting Doreen's quatrains so freely if he had still been working with her in circle.

E.4. Casting and Charging (1961)

This document was typed in one-and-a-half spacing on 8" x 10" yellow foolscap in Typeface I. It is a single sheet of carbon copy, and is quite clean. It has never been folded, punched, stapled, or dogeared; that is, it shows no signs of ever having been used in a Book of Shadows. Paragraph [4] and the line above it are crooked, as if the carbon had

---

[65] Here "mysteries" had been typed. The hand correction is probably intended to avoid repetition of the word in the next line.

[66] The three preceding lines paraphrase the last few lines of verse in Document D.8, which therefore was probably written before this document.

slipped when the sheets being typed were reinserted into the typewriter for an addition to be made. It was almost certainly typed at the same time as Documents C.8, B.8, and C.13.

[1] Forming Circle. Light candles.[67]

1. Draw Circle with M[agic] S[word] or Athame.

2. Sprinkle with consecrated water.

3. Cense.[68]

4 Say "L Conjure Thee O Circle of Power that Thou beiest a Boundery and a Protection and a meeting place between the World of Men *and the realms of the Mighty Ones.*[69] A Guardian and a Protection that shall Preserve and contain the Power which we shall raise within Thee, Wherefore do I Bless and Consecrate thee.

5 Say "I summon, Stir, and Call Thee up,Ye Mighty Ones of the. (North, East, South, West, North.) To witness the Rites and to guard the Circle.[70]

[2] Closing Circle.

Say." Mighty Ones of the (East, South, West, North,) l thank you for attending ,and ere you depart for your lovely rehelms l say Hail and Farewell.[71]

[3] Consecration of Water and Salt.

[67] This "light candles" is actually the first instruction, and should logically have been numbered 1. However, this line does not appear in *Witch*; so it was added after the document was first typed.

[68] The censing, not mentioned in earlier drafts of the casting procedure, agrees with the HOGD Neophyte ritual and with the procedures of GKS (pp. 96-97).

[69] Inserted in Gardner's handwriting between the lines in blue ink with a broad-tipped fountain pen. These words do appear in *Witch*; so Florannis had a copy of Document E.4 that depended on this revision.

[70] This formula seems based on a procedure in GKS, p. 97. See Commentary on A.1.

[71] This is based on the "license to depart" of ceremonial magic. A different version of this formula appears on p. 296 of HMA.

Touch water with Athame, saying" l excorcise thee o Creature of Water that thou cast out from thee all the impurities and uncleannesses of the spirits of the World of Phantasm."[72]

ln the names of ;;;; & ———

Touching Salt with Athame say, "Blessings be upon this creature of Salt, Let all malignity and hinderance be cast forth hencfrom and let all good enter herein; Wherefore l bless thee that thou mayest aid me. ln the names of ——— & ———

[4] Drawing Down The Moon.

"l invoke Thee and call upon Thee. Oh Mighty Mother of us All, Bringer ofcall Fruitfulness.

'By SEED and Root, by Stem and Bud, by Leaf and Flower and Fruit, by Life and Love. Do We invoke Thee to descend' upon the body of Thy servent and Priestess ———

H[igh] P[riest] and other men give [Fivefold Kiss] women all bow.

This version of the basic Gardnerian ritual is intermediate between the versions in Documents D.1 and E.5. It is directly dependent on D.1, because we still have the sequence introduced in D.1 of censing the circle, followed by the redundant second casting of the circle, and then the invoking of the quarters. This is obviously not a full ritual, but merely notes on a few specific procedures, which would occur in the order [3, 1, 4, 2] during an actual ritual, as can be seen from Document E.5 and from the published sources. The writing of the document must date before August 1959, probably sometime in 1957 or 1958; but this revised typing of it dates to about 1960.

E.5. Forming the Circle

FORMING THE CIRCLE. [1] Must have a man and a woman.properly prepared.i.e naked.[73]

[2] Mark a circle nine feet across on the floor with chalk etc. The best

---

[72] This derives, via a little pruning, directly from GKS, p. 93.

[73] This prefatory line is new, typed onto the carbon later, and is addressed specifically to Charles Clark. Gardner is defining what he means by "properly prepared."

way is to get a string. *Tie 2* loops four foot six in[ches] apart.put one loop over a nail ir somthing in the centre. put chalk in the other and run it round. lf you cant make marks on the floor. put furnature etc.round to form it. Have a table.etc as an Altar.with all tools etc on it. have a bowl of water, and some salt.

[3] Place Athame on the bowl of water.say. "l excorcise thee O creature of Water that thou cast out from Thee all the impurities and uncleannn[ess]es of the Spirits of the World of Phantasm. in the name of """""""""" and """""""" ". But ever mind that Water purifies the body, but the [scourge] purifies the Soul."[74]

[4] Then place Athame on the salt.say. "Blessings be upon this crea[t]ure of Salt. let all malignity and hinderance be cast forth hensfrom, and let all good enter herin .W herefore l bless thee that thou mayest aid me.   ln the name of """""""""" ang """""""""" .

[5] Then Trace Circle on the lines[75] you have marked out. Starting at the East and returning to the East.[76](Alswys go round the circle with your Right hand to the Altar, Never go Widershins.) ~~Then sprinkle~~[77] Then put the Salt into the water. and go round the circle again sprinkling it to purify it. Then go round again censing it.(Everyone in the circle must be sprinkled and Censed.)

[6] Then go to the East,Sword or Athame in hand. Draw an invoking pentacle in the Air [drawing of pentacle], Starting at the top. and going to the left hand Corner. saying.

---

[74] This formula differs from that in earlier drafts by the addition of the final sentence, which also appears by itself twice in HMA (pp. 104, 298). This final version of the formula is quoted by Farrar (1971, p. 54, but the final sentence is tagged onto the formula for the salt) and by GLS (p. 117, where the sentence is also tagged onto the salt formula; so "salt" replaces "scourge"). Note that the final line in paragraph [3] occurs as a separate line of dialogue in HMA; it is added here to bolster the theological status of the scourging. That is, Gardner apparently inserted this line at different places on different copies of this ritual; this demonstrates that he continued to emphasize the scourging as much as possible even late in the writing process.

[75] Notice the plural here, contrary to the procedures in paragraph [2].

[76] See Commentary on A.1.

[77] Gardner had forgotten the salt wasn't in the water yet.

"L summon ,and call thee up. Oh Ye Mighty ones

of the East . to guard the Circle and witness our rites."then holding the point of sword or Athame upwards.do thesamet to the South.West and North,[78] and return to the Centre.to the south of the Altar.

[7] Then each girl should bind her man.Hands behind back.and cable Tow to neck. he shd kneel at altar, and [be scourged]. when all men are thus "Purified" they purifie the girls in turn. No one may be in the circle without being thus purified.[79]

[8] T*hen do whatever work wanted.*[80]

[9] When closing the Circle. The High Priestess, or whoever she tells to do it. saying. "Hail, ye mighty ones of the East. I thank you for attending. and Ere ye depart for your lovely rehelms, We say. Hail and Farewell."[81]

Commentary on E.5

This revision of Document E.4, which dates to about 1958, must have been done about 1959-1960, specifically to instruct new members. It expands Document E.4 into a clear set of instructions. Notice that the "rule" in the last sentence of [7] did not appear in Document E.4, and appears here for the first time. In other words, *the rule that "no one may be in circle without being thus purified [scourged]" WAS NEVER IN THE BoS OF THE ORIGINAL LONDON COVEN!*

Furthermore, notice that the sentences in parentheses in [5], "Always go round the circle with your Right hand to the Altar, Never go Widershins," meant *in context* "always cast the circle sunwise"—these instructions are for people who don't know how to cast a circle at all—and logically the casting *is* the one element of the working that could never be done withershins. That is, this procedure—the first to include the instruction about "Never go Widdershins"—was not written until about 1960, and was never used by Gardner's original coven.

---

[78] See Commentary on A.1.

[79] We now know what "properly prepared and purified" means.

[80] This is written on the carbon in blue ballpen; Gardner probably added it at the same time he typed on the new first line.

[81] Notice the indication here that the High Priestess is in charge of the proceedings.

It is precisely these sentences that American Gardnerians have generalized into a rule that forbids *all* withershins movements in the circle under any and all circumstances. This is an exact parallel to the way in which the Christian church took Paul's advice to the previously pagan women (whose idea of worship was probably very noisy) in the Christian synagogue at Corinth, and turned it into a universal rule that denied women all right to preach in any Christian church. There is no evidence that Paul intended any such thing, especially not when he praises the women ministers he knows; likewise, there is no evidence that Gardner intended to forbid withershins movements at any other point in the ritual, and thus to abandon half of the magical arsenal.

A careful comparison of the sequence of events here with that in the procedure for casting the circle given by the Farrars (1981, pp. 37-40; 1984, pp. 295-6) shows that the Farrars' procedure, and hence the procedure used by Patricia Crowther, is based on the one given here. The two differ in only three details, and the overall sequence is the same. In contrast, the Farrars' procedure differs from the one in "Ye Bok of ye Art Magical" and from the one described by Tanya Luhrmann (pp. 223-4) in many specific details, and the overall sequences are quite different.

A Final Commentary on the Weschcke Documents

We have now seen drafts scattered over more than a decade, from before 1949 to about 1960, of most of the contents of the Gardnerian Book of Shadows. We can identify many sources for these documents: Crowley; the HOGD rituals; the *Greater Key of Solomon*; Murray's *Witch Cult in Western Europe*; Leland's *Aradia*; and, more generally, Tantra Yoga and the works of the great Cambridge classicists (Harrison, G. Murray, Frazer, Cook, and Cornford). What we have NOT seen is any material that is more likely to have come from an earlier coven than from an identifiable literary source.

That these documents appear to have been written by Gardner is an accident caused by his having retyped and tinkered with them, and, indeed, one that confused me for several years. It is now clear that Doreen Valiente wrote most of these documents between 1954 and 1956. After the coven divided in two in February 1957, Gardner continued retyping and tinkering with the documents; and it was such copies that he sent to Clark in 1959 and 1960, as I know from Clark's letters in the file in Toronto.

At this point we have reviewed all the documentary evidence. The reader may now reread Chapter 3, and will be able to see that it is in fact the history supported by the evidence.

Chapter Nine

The Significance of Gardnerian Witchcraft as a Religion

The importance of Gardnerian Witchcraft as a religious movement is probably most obvious from its current size and rate of growth. As I mentioned in Chapter 2, in 1999, according to a survey sponsored by the Covenant of the Goddess, there were about 600,000 initiated Witches in America and therefore about 6,000,000 practicing Pagans. That is, this religion is clearly meeting some needs in American society that are not being met as well by other religions. Let me catalogue some of the needs to which the Craft movement offers a creative response.

First and foremost is the need for sacramental experiencing of sex. In theory this is possible within Christianity, but in practice such experiencing is not available to ordinary Christians; in practice Christianity continues to be oppressively antisexual. At best, it rates sex as harmless—as long as it takes place only under specific circumstances. The modern theologies that value sexuality as a revelation of the divine nature are taught in graduate seminaries—and then are kept more secret from the people than any "secret" in the Craft is. Andrew Greeley is, of course, the outstanding exception to this generalization; but there is no significant chance that the administration of the Roman Catholic church will pay any attention to him. Lady Epona said to me in 1987, "If the Roman Catholic church were actually as Greeley describes it, there would be no need for the Craft." (Of course, those from Protestant, Jewish, and other backgrounds have their own reasons for being attracted to the Craft.)

Second, the mainstream churches in America offer ordinary people no practical paths for personal spiritual development; traditionally, such development was reserved for the cloistered clergy or for elderly scholars. There was nothing for ordinary people, and that lack has not been repaired. The Western occult tradition has addressed that need, but in many ways it has been infected by the viewpoint of the Eastern religions, which are all at least mildly, and often strongly, opposed to the development of psychic or magical abilities, or at least to the use of such abilities for any purpose other than achieving (or helping others achieve) "enlightenment." The Craft rejects such an attitude as dualism, and asserts, in contrast, that the development and use of magical and psychic abilities *is* spiritual development. The Craft as currently practiced in America offers, at least potentially, a balanced and practical approach to development of a person's emotional, spiritual, intuitive, and psychic needs and abilities.

Third, the Craft's organization, based on the principle that every coven is autonomous, gives it a flexibility and viability that huge organizations lack entirely. Like the Jewish synagogue, the coven is inherently democratic; and in many covens, the democracy is kept from degenerating into irresponsibility and anarchy by the presence of a High Priestess whose authority depends upon her magical lineage, which is independent of the coven she leads and serves, just as the Synagogue can employ a Rabbi, but cannot itself ordain a Rabbi. (The analogy breaks down here, since the Craft movement generally recognizes the right of a coven to bootstrap itself into existence and to initiate its own priests and priestesses; but the balancing of responsibility between the Council of Elders and the High Priestess is still a valid structural parallel.) That is, the coven structure empowers its members, giving them control over their own religious practices and development.

The contrast with many of the Eastern religions and with the Roman Catholic church could not be greater. In many Eastern religions, the authority of the teacher is absolute; but Pagans tend to be extremely anti-authoritarian, and will not submit to arbitrary authority—and in the Craft (at least in most covens) they do not have to. Likewise, despite the rhetoric of the Second Vatican Council, ordinary Roman Catholics have no control whatsoever over their church. Theologians know that Christianity is inherently democratic, and that Christians have the right to elect their own ministers, priests, bishops, and so on. The founders of what is now Protestant Christianity rediscovered this fact during the Reformation. But no one in the Craft need worry that the Roman Catholic administration will soon relinquish the authority it has usurped over the centuries.

Fourth, the Craft is generally extremely anti-dogmatic in its approach. Although Witches do believe many things, belief is not a requirement for membership or initiation. Rather, the expectation in the Craft is that if a person goes through the training and experiences that the Craft has to offer with an open mind, then personal transformations will in fact happen—and "belief" as such will be unnecessary, since the person will know that he or she has been changed. As a result of this attitude, Crafters are not only open to modern science, but positively biased in favour of it—and so are rather well-equipped to live in the increasingly technological civilization of the future. In contrast, most varieties of Christianity, several varieties of Judaism, and many varieties of other "world" religions either try to ignore science or accept its results only if forced to; this sort of spiritual "laziness," as M. Scott Peck would characterize it, merely contributes to their ever-growing obsolescence. History is littered with the carcasses of religions that failed to evolve to meet changing circumstances, and big churches are a lot like dinosaurs—whereas the Craft is much more like the hot-blooded little mammals hiding in the thickets. Similarly, Crafters look with amazement and amusement at how New Agers generally seem devoted to swallowing entire truckloads of metaphysical horse-puckey.

Fifth, the Craft's polytheistic theology suits it for the future much better than the monotheistic or monistic theologies of most other religions do. The United States, and the world in general, is becoming more pluralistic. Given the immigration trends in the USA, our former WASP majority is rapidly losing its numerical and cultural dominance. The model for our future will no longer be the emotionless WASP male; rather, there will be no one model. Male and female, white, brown, or black, Asian or European, and free to feel our own feelings: we will all have the right to be different but equal. No longer will the most socially acceptable theology be, "There is only one God, and the rest of you better shape up, or else!" Nor will it be, "There are many gods, but they are all illusions," as many Eastern religions have taught. Rather, we will recall what the Jews knew when they were writing the Law and the Prophets: that God really is both one and many, both male and female, both father and mother, all things to all people, out of love. The respectable churches have failed to tell the people that for far too long—and so the Witches get to say, "Yes, the Gods are real, and magic is afoot."

Sixth, and last for now, the Craft is a religion dedicated to creativity, because it is a religion that Witches are creating for themselves continually. The only way to be a true follower of Gerald Gardner, my friends, is to have the guts to create a religion for yourself that meets your own needs. I think Witches love Tolkien especially because he teaches us that creativity is divine, that the nature of godhead is to be continuously overflowing with creativity like a fountain, and that we participate most completely in the divine nature when we ourselves are being creative. I think it deliciously ironic to know that Tolkien believed all that because he was truly a Roman Catholic theologian—and because his church has disowned him, as it disowns Andrew Greeley, it is up to the Witches to carry on his work and his vision.

"Lugh" and Disinformation

I need to deal here with the claims about George Pickingill that were raised by a writer known only as "Lugh," in a series of letters.[1] In order to evaluate Lugh's claims, we need to place them in the perspective of what looks like a purposeful policy of disinformation instituted by Gardner and carried on by some of his successors in the leadership of

---

[1] Lugh's first letters appeared in *The Wiccan* (a mimeographed British Craft periodical), issues 40/41 and 42, in 1974; later ones in *The Cauldron* Doreen Valiente said that, as Lugh's "stories became more and more preposterous . . . Michael Howard, the editor of *The Cauldron*, eventually stopped publishing them." The letters were reissued as a pamphlet, which was republished, along with other short Craft writings, in two volumes of the Garland Publishing series on new religions edited by J. Gordon Melton. Lugh disappeared from public view entirely, but he did write to me from Australia after the publication of *Crafting the Art of Magick, Book I,* to identify himself, and fill me in somewhat on the politics behind the "Lugh" articles. He is, literally, a relative of Alice in Wonderland and of S. L. McGregor Mathers.

the Craft movement. Doreen Valiente says there was never any such policy. Certainly there is no evidence that she ever had anything to do with such a policy, but there is evidence that Old Gerald was much more devious than Doreen ever wanted to believe, and that Lugh, for whatever reasons, was pursuing a course built on foundations laid down by Gerald.

Norman Moss's *The Pleasures of Deception* discusses the theory of hoaxes proposed by R. V. Jones, a physicist who was one of the most important members of British Intelligence during the Second World War, and indeed into the 1960s. In his paper "The Theory of Practical Joking," Jones proposed that the key to perpetrating a hoax is to gain control of all channels of communication, use them to feed false information to the audience, and thus distort their picture of reality enough that they make the desired false assumption and then the desired false move. This is easiest to do if there is only one possible channel of communication.

The application of his theory to the Gardnerian movement is this. Gardner, by writing his books, had created essentially a single channel of communication: the only possible source of information about "the Craft" was what he himself had devised. Since the religion had not previously existed, there was no need to worry about contradictory information coming from any other source, except perhaps from religious scholars—but scholars do not get interviewed on TV at Hallowe'en, and have no audience comparable in size to the one Gardner was aiming for.

Another technique used by Gardner is that of misdirection. He had claimed in *Witchcraft Today* that there was an earlier coven, that some information had come from it, that an older religious tradition had existed all along—that is, he used the sole channel of communication to create a false but plausible history. The misdirection then consisted in pointing backward to that history. As long as scholars and other curious people were looking back—to the 1930s or 1920s, or the 1890s or the 1880s, or any date at all—and trying to find information relevant to the Gardnerian claims, the misdirection was successful: because no such information had ever existed, it could not turn up; and Gardner could continue to claim that there was no evidence to disprove his story.

Once I had discovered that I could account for absolutely everything in the documents as being devised by Gardner, Valiente, and whoever else might have helped, there was no longer any reason to suppose there had been any earlier information, or coven, or sect at all—and then I realized that this misdirection was the key to the trick: it was the stage magician's technique of gesturing dramatically with his right hand, to grab your attention, while the left hand carries out the substitution that later seems so mysterious. Hence to accept the claim that there was any earlier tradition is epistemologically equivalent to buying the Gardnerian claims in full. Gardner could not have cared less what questions were asked, so long as attention was directed away from the 1950s.

For example, Elliot Rose, after considering the Book of Shadows material that is "quoted" in *Witchcraft Today*, goes on to say (pp. 204ff):

> *I would not like to exclude the possibility that the myth [of the descent of the Goddess] was originally composed . . . about the eighties; . . . A terminus a quo for the text quoted would be supplied by the first translation of the cuneiform tablets; . . . the nearest one could say is "about 1880" . . . at the earliest . . . I should ascribe the texts quoted, merely on literary flavour, to about the nineties; . . . I think we have someone raised on the last of the pagan Romantics [e.g., Swinburne] as the most recent Magus, not necessarily of the whole of British witchcraft, but of that part of it with which Mr. Gardner has come in contact.*

That is, Rose makes the strategic error of believing Gardner's claim that there had been an earlier coven, and so becomes lost in speculations about what sort of person might have been creating covens around the turn of the century, a point on which there can be no evidence *if there was no such person*—and it is Gardner who was obviously raised on Swinburne. But it does not seem strange that so able a scholar as Elliott Rose could have been thus misled when we realize that he was misled by precisely the techniques devised by the geniuses who worked in British Intelligence during the Second World War to mislead the Nazi war machine and make the Normandy invasion possible.

Gardner probably did not set out to deceive anyone; that's not how religious people think. He instead hit on the disinformation techniques by accident, while trying to make *Witchcraft Today* sound plausible, and only gradually realized how useful they were for getting the new religion accepted.[2]

However, I think "Lugh" (or perhaps the "elders" who Lugh claims were passing on to him the data he wrote up in his articles) was purposely creating a phony history in order to throw researchers off the trail.

Lugh claims that "Old George" was from a Hereditary "persuasion" of the Craft, had founded nine covens, had helped write the original rituals of the Hermetic Order of the Golden Dawn, and had initiated Aleister Crowley. He claims further that the coven into which Gardner had been initiated in 1939 was descended from a Pickingill coven, that Gardner had a copy of their Book of Shadows, that Crowley had written out from memory a second draft for Gardner of the Book of Shadows used by the Pickingill covens, and that Gardner had used these as a basis for his reform.

This story about Pickingill and Crowley seems to be an extrapolation on a paragraph in Chapter 4 of *Witchcraft Today*; in fact, Lugh mentions this passage specifically in his first letter.

> *The only man I can think of who could have invented the rites was the late Aleister Crowley. When I met him he was most interested to hear that I was a member, and said he had been inside when he was very young, but would not say whether he had rewritten anything or not. But the witch practices are entirely different in method from any kind of magic he wrote about, and he described very many kinds.... certain expressions and certain words... smack of Crowley; possibly he borrowed things from the cult writings, or more likely someone may have borrowed expressions from him.*

Having looked at drafts of Gardner's documents from 1946 to 1960, we can see how very devious Gardner is being here: Crowley, being dead, cannot deny any of this; the witch practices are based directly on

---

[2] Still, I think Gardner did persuade other writers he knew, such as Cottie Burland and Robert Graves, to include materials that would support Gardner's claims in their books. None of Graves' comments about the survival of Witchcraft that seem to support Murray's thesis were in the first edition of *The White Goddess*; they were all added in the second (1956) and third (1963) editions.

Crowley's methods; Gardner himself borrowed wholesale from Crowley; and Valiente rewrote this material to disguise the borrowing. If Gardner had had a Book of Shadows that had been written for him by Crowley (as Francis King claimed), he would not have needed to undertake the drafts and rewritings that we have been looking at.

I presume that Gardner simply made up the claim that Crowley had been a witch when young. There is no corroboration of this anywhere in Crowley's writings, and Crowley kept no secrets about anything.

Lugh's claim that Crowley wrote Gardner's original Book of Shadows—he is no doubt building on the similar claim by King (p. 180)—cannot possibly be true: nothing that could be called a Book of Shadows existed while Crowley was alive. Furthermore, Lugh seems to be ignorant (or is pretending to be ignorant) of the true role of Doreen Valiente in writing the Book of Shadows.

But there is a way to demonstrate directly that the letter is a scarlet herring. At one point it states: "The Pickingill-led covens have commemorated a cardinal tenet of the Old Religion. All of our rites are conducted in toto by a woman. This derives from the Scandinavian and French models," which are purely imaginary. As we have seen, before 1957, the dominant figure in Gardner's coven had been the High Priest, Gardner himself, just as we expected for a "re-creation" of witchcraft based on Margaret Murray's descriptions. Lugh's argument is specious, since it is based on the Gardnerian party line, adopted *after* 1959, that only the priestess could conduct the circle. Lugh goes on:

> *The Horned God was always served and honoured by women in Scandinavia. The Mother Goddess could only be served and honoured by men. . . . only the priestess approved by the God could call upon him to descend into the body of a man chosen as his living representative. Only a priest consecrated to the Goddess could call upon her to descend into the body of a woman chosen as Her living representative. . . . In many Traditionalist covens the Lady calls down the sun on the Magister, and the Magister reciprocates by Drawing Down the Moon on the Lady.*
>
> *I can find no published reference to substantiate our claim the "Old George" Pickingill devised the basic format of the Gardnerian rituals.*

We have also seen the ritual of "Drawing Down the Moon" evolve through several stages; but even in 1957 Gardner was not clear on whether the arms-crossed position represented the God or the Goddess.

We can see that Lugh is proposing an elegant bit of theologizing: the Priest is the Priest *of* the Goddess, but incarnates the God; the Priestess is the Priestess *of* the God, but incarnates the Goddess. But none of this could have predated the rituals that we now know were created in the 1950s; so all of Lugh's statements are similarly groundless.

I had wondered why Doreen Valiente, who helped write these rituals in the 1950s, quotes Lugh[3] as if he were a reliable source of historical information. She responded, "I really don't know what to think about him. As I said in *[The Rebirth of Witchcraft]*, nothing checks out. At the same time, I didn't like to call the man a complete imposter. I tried to take a charitable view—did he have some hidden motive in telling all these years? If so, what was it?" Ms. Valiente's wanting to be charitable to Lugh goes along with her continuing to believe that there was some sort of Craft tradition before 1939. My own answer to her question is, yes, he did have a hidden motive: the covert purpose of his letters was to take advantage of Rose's speculations about someone at the turn of the century, and to give a name and a face to the person Rose had guessed at, in order to divert attention away from the 1940s and 1950s.

To confirm this, notice that Chapter 4 of *Witchcraft Today*, just after the passage about Crowley quoted above, goes on to mention the founders of the Hermetic Order of the Golden Dawn (ca. 1885), Napoleon, Francis Barrett (ca. 1800), Sir Francis Dashwood, the Hellfire Club, and the Cabalists of the 1790s as possible authors of the rituals; all of these are dismissed as unlikely, but the misdirection consists in the suggestion that the true carriers of the witchcraft tradition during this period were not well-known public figures.

George Pickingill is a historical figure, mentioned by Eric Maple, but all the evidence is that he was a garden-variety folk-magic witch and a home-grown Satanist. Such persons can be found in the working-class neighbourhoods of any metropolitan area; they are not evil, but they are also not very sophisticated by middle-class standards. Lugh seems

---

[3] In her 1978 book on pp. 15-20, and in Chapter 12 of *Rebirth of Witchcraft.*

to be aware that the argument about Pickingill is flimsy, and insists that a "conspiracy of silence" has for 125 years suppressed the true status of a man who, Lugh also asserts, gloried in publicity and extravagant public statements. Alan Moonbloode, a private detective who was a member of a NROOGD coven, once tried to track down some of these statements, and could find no trace of them, nor of any of the supposedly published articles that Lugh cites as evidence. I think we are being fed a tall tale that is simultaneously a conspiracy theory and an argument from silence—impressive in its way.

At the point in my thinking (about 1974) when I thought that Gardner might have had two separate, original documents on which the Craft Laws were based, I found Lugh's assertions, that Gardner had two different Books of Shadows from two covens that he had been initiated into, to be quite exciting: here was a possible source for those documents—and I went to Toronto hoping to find those original books. But they weren't there. Having now concluded that Gardner compiled the Craft Laws himself, I see that this argument, unlike a string, can be pushed as well as pulled. Suppose we ask, "What information must Gardner have gotten from these alleged Book of Shadows rather than from somewhere else?" The answer is, "None." It merely complicates life to suppose that Gardner had gotten the Masonic, Golden Dawn, magical, etc., raw material that he worked with at second hand, via these supposed Pickingill covens, rather than directly from the available sources.

Lugh also alleges that Crowley had used bits and pieces of Pickingill's rituals in his own writings. He apparently wants his readers to think that the passages from Crowley which Gardner quotes are the ones that Crowley was quoting from Pickingill. Likewise, his allegation that Pickingill was the source for various unspecified elements of the Golden Dawn rituals is intended to encourage his readers to think that the identifiable Golden Dawn elements in Gardner's rituals may therefore instead be from the Pickingill tradition. Hence this is all special pleading.

Lugh also capitalizes on statements by Buckland and others that they had seen a Book of Shadows in Crowley's handwriting on display in Gardner's museum. Doreen Valiente says that, to the contrary, there was no such book in Gardner's collection, and that the Book of Shadows in question is in fact "Text A," which she owns.

What about Lugh's claim that Pickingill devised the basic format for rituals that was inherited and used by Gardner? As we have seen, the order of events in a basic Gardnerian ritual are:

(1) casting the circle;
(2) invoking the guardians of the four quarters;
(3) invoking the Goddess or the God;
(4) working magic, or an initiation, or both;
(5) having the "little feast" of cakes and wine;
(6) dismissing the guardians, and closing the circle

We have seen that Gardner was painfully working his way through drafts of (1), (2), and (6) in the 1940s, working directly from such sources as the *Greater Key of Solomon*, and again in the late 1950s. No doubt he would have been happy to have readymade procedures for all this—but he didn't. Any number of sources could be suggested for (5), but Gardner clearly didn't know a standard procedure for this. The only thing left that Pickingill could have contributed, therefore, is the basic idea of combining the working circle of the magicians with the shamanistic procedures of witches. If there is any closer similarity between the Gardnerian rituals and those of Lugh's "persuasion," this merely proves that Lugh's are dependent on Gardner's, not vice versa.

This situation might also explain why Gardnerians appear to have done very little over the years to dispute the claims of interlopers, no matter how blatant. As the Farrars also argue in their 1981 and 1984 books, Alex Sanders' copy of the Book of Shadows was derived from that written by Gardner and Valiente; he certainly did not inherit it from his grandmother. There is also a letter in the Toronto files, to Gardner from Pat Kopanski, giving the date and other details of Sanders' initiation in 1963; this correlates with Sanders' admission to Johns (p. 62) that he was unaware of the existence of any other witches before 1963.

Now, the Gardnerians could easily have proved Sanders a liar several times over without detracting anything of significance from the general Gardnerian story; so why haven't they?[4] Probably because the annoyance

---

[4] Actually, Valiente does so in the Farrars' 1984 book; but I think hardly anyone has noticed this.

caused by Sanders' grandiose claims was more than offset by the usefulness of his claim to descend from the "old religion" independently of the Gardnerians. After all, if you have two cousins, then their common grandparent must really have existed. That is, Sanders' claim blurs the trail to the 1950s, and reinforces the misdirection tactic, by also pointing back to the 1920s.

Precisely the same is true of Ms. Jessie Wicker Bell, who, under the name of "Lady Sheba," published a version of the Book of Shadows that she had probably gotten from an Alexandrian coven, and claimed that the Craft had existed in her family in the Ozarks; and of Sybil Leek, who claimed the Craft as her family's religion. Again, this reinforcing of the misdirection would have more than made up for any annoyance these ladies caused.

However, Doreen Valiente pointed out to me that I was being unfair, and was unaware of some of the facts concerning Sanders. She wrote,

> *To my knowledge, various Gardnerians did try to expose Sanders as a phony, but as I said in* The Rebirth of Witchcraft, *the media simply didn't want to know. For instance, Pat Crowther sent a letter to one newspaper attacking Sanders' claims—and the newspaper sent it back to her, saying that they couldn't publish it because Sanders might sue them for libel! Actually, in my opinion, the situation was that Sanders was supplying the media with colourful stories that sold newspapers, and that was all they cared about. . . . On another occasion certain Gardnerians, again to my personal knowledge, agreed to appear on a television programme only on condition that Sanders was not on it. They were given verbal assurances to this effect; but when the programme appeared, there was Sanders strutting his stuff as usual. They protested, only to meet with the usual bland reply that 'it had been a misunderstanding.' What could they do about it?*

I agree that it must have been a difficult situation. It's hard to see from this side of the Atlantic how radically different British journalistic standards are from American ones—British tabloids, for example, make the *National Enquirer* and other rags sold with the Twinkies look pompous and conservative. The fact is that the newspaper Pat Crowther sent her letter to could have gotten away with saying anything it liked about Sanders, and its declining to publish her letter for fear of being sued was simply an astonishing piece of bare-faced mendacity.

Aesthetics and Religious Creativity

What we have seen in this book is that Gerald Gardner, with occasional help from others, invented a plausible history for his new religion, and created documents to support that history. If he had been doing this for the sake of fame, wealth, or power, we could call what he did forgery—but he was not. It is (or at least ought to be) notorious that the Gardnerians have from the beginning refused to allow their movement to be used to make money for anyone. This sort of ethical stance is taken only by persons whose motivations are genuinely religious. Gardner was engaging in what is actually a well-known sort of religious behaviour: the inventing of a new history for one's community is a way of searching for meaning and authenticity. What he did is not so very different, after all, from what the scribes of the school of Ezra did in assembling legends and fragments of history into the new, unified history of Israel we have in the Law and the Earlier Prophets.

The new magical religion that Gardner, Edith Woodford-Grimes, and Doreen Valiente helped to create is utterly different in nature from the kind of folk-magic witchcraft that we looked at in Chapter 2 and that they may have started from. As a viable system, it began to grow, to take on a life of its own, and to display the assimilative voracity typical of living systems. (Folk religions, in contrast, are continuing to die out.)

One body of information the Gardnerian movement began to assimilate was the "White Goddess thealogy" invented by Robert Graves, although this only becomes visible in the late 1950s. Murray emphasizes the Horned God, not the Goddess. I think Gerald was responsible for introducing the Horned God and Goddess as *equals*, but even in *Witchcraft Today* that is often obscured by references to "the Gods" in general, since that sounds like a reference to the Greco-Roman pantheon, rather than to this "duotheistic" concept. It was only gradually that the Goddess came to be more important in practice than the Horned God (and later came to be of sole importance in some covens in the USA), and that the High Priestess came to be more important than the High Priest. The period of this shift in emphasis apparently coincides roughly with the period of Doreen's tenure as High Priestess of the London coven; so I tended to think that she must have had something to do with forcing Gardner to see the importance of Graves' White Goddess concept, and to make it the focus of the reform. However, she insists that she cannot take the credit for that. Whoever was responsible for this, it was a stroke of genius, for it is the Goddess concept that seizes the hearts of those who are drawn into the Craft movement.

No one before now has given Gardner, or especially Valiente, credit for what measure they have of creative genius—but, then, they could not claim such credit as long as they maintained the stance that they were merely reviving and carrying on an older tradition. The critical perspective I introduced in Chapter 2, of understanding the Craft as a new religion, and hence as evolving according to the same laws that apply to any other social institution, means that we can apply the same standards to it as to any other movement. Especially, if we understand the creating of a new religion to be a *creative* activity, then we can think about such activity in terms of artistic criteria.

When I apply aesthetic criteria to new religions, I find the Gardnerian Witches to be far more interesting than many other new religions. In saying this, I am not stating a simple preference. Rather, I am making a complex judgment about the quantity and quality of the creativity that has gone into the movement and that its members routinely display, about how accurately its founders assessed needs that the established churches were not meeting, about how effectively the movement has been structured to meet those needs, about how its peculiar perspective reorganizes the raw materials of theology into a coherent and novel worldview, about how well it enables its members to proceed with their own maturation, and so on. It is fair, and not very subjective at all, to compare religions in general in these terms. In contrast, I find a "new religion" that is merely another literalistic, elitist Christian sect, or merely an Eastern religion transported wholecloth to America, to be not very new, not very creative, and therefore not very interesting.

Moreover, my intuition tells me that the Gardnerian movement is far more important than most other new religions, far more important than perhaps any of us now realize. Why? I keep turning back to study the movement, trying to explain that intuition to myself, trying to justify it to others.

Perhaps someone might be stubborn enough to say at this point, "Well, if this Witchcraft movement is a new religion, then you are admitting that Gardner did just make it all up, that he was some sort of well-meaning fraud." No, that is not what I am saying, because that is not how religion works. Can you say, "The Buddha just made it all up"? Or "Homer just made it all up"? Or on the other hand, can you give me an example of a religion that was not made up by human beings? If that mysterious factor, creativity, is needed in order to write a poem, it is very much more needed to found a religion. Gardner could be written off as a charlatan if his work had been unsuccessful—but then who would ever have heard of him? The fact that the Craft movement has grown so rapidly in a few decades is proof enough, indeed, the only relevant proof, that Gardner was doing something right.

It may well be that Gardner, even though he appears to be a first-class dissembler, and even though he was also trying to meet his own sexual needs, did in fact think that what he was doing was reforming an older religion—because founders of new religions usually seem to think that they are merely putting an old religion on a firmer foundation by introducing a few new elements into it. Zoroaster began his reform of Iranian religion at almost the same time that Gotama was reforming what was still almost the same religion in India, and at the same time that Hilkiah was reforming Israelite-Canaanite religion. Christianity began with what was, I think, an attempt to establish a reform movement in Judaism. Mohammed intended to reform not only native Arab religions, but also Judaism and Christianity as he understood them. Numerous less-famous religions—Jainism, Manichaeism, those of the Druse and the Sikhs, Bahá'í, to name just a few—have resulted from this same process.

Anyway, whatever Gardner's intentions may have been, he did found a new religion, entirely different in structure and functioning from what had gone before it. That the Gardnerian Craft still shares many elements with the Old Religion of Europe as described by Murray and others, and with other folk religions, does not change the situation. The sharing results merely from the fact that human creation is never *ex nihilo*; it begins from the available materials. A poet may sometimes coin a new word, but he does not invent a new language; he uses the resources of the language that everyone around him speaks. Likewise, a religious reformer starts from the religion that he knows; Gotama, by an extraordinary feat, could invent Buddhism, but he could not have invented Christianity.

In fact, the Gardnerian Craft is so different from the kinds of religions, past and present, that have been called witchcraft that it is not very logical to call the members of these very different religions by the same name. If Gardnerians are Witches, then they are the first true Witches in history; if those other people back then were Witches, then Gardnerians are not.

Anthropologists, medieval historians, and various other scholars generally agree that in their fields the term "witch" refers to a person believed to worship the principle of evil, to work malevolent magic against enemies, and generally to lack all redeeming social qualities. If so, why do the members of the Gardnerian movement choose to call themselves Witches? Why do they choose to explain over and over again to cub reporters, weekend TV announcers, and graduate students in religious studies, that they, like all the witches in the past, worship only a pleasant goddess of bunny rabbits and flowers, perform only faith healing and fortune telling, and have regular nature walks and dances in field and grove to the sound of pipe and timbrel?[5] Why? Well, for one thing, calling yourself a Witch gets you free publicity at Hallowe'en; calling yourself a Goddess-worshipper would not. But there is a far more important reason for the choice. To see it, we need to look briefly at the nature of the movement.

Gardner's claim that in September 1939 he had been initiated into one of the last surviving covens in England, a coven whose ancestry went back through the Burning Times and ultimately to the Stone Age, serves,

---

[5] The Craft generally does have an innocuous "party line" like this to be given out to the media. The Craft's actual activities are far more serious, and not nearly so innocuous; else it would not have much to offer its adult members, of whom there are many.

as I have said, as the foundational myth of the Gardnerian movement. It establishes continuity, and therefore solidarity, with all those persons—as many as 9 million, in some estimates—who died in the first Holocaust. The meaning of a myth, after all, does not depend on its historicity. Why is this important?

Only during and after the Second Vatican Council has the Roman Catholic Church offered an apology, and the beginnings of an attempt at amends, to the Jewish community at large for its slander and persecution of Jews during the preceding 1640 years. The world Jewish community seems to still be deciding whether the apology is sincere, and whether the amends proposed might be adequate. I mention this only so that I can go on to make the point that neither the Roman Catholic Church, nor any other Christian church, has ever offered any apology, or attempted to make any amends, for the murder of those millions of "witches" and "heretics" from the 12th through the 17th century. Worse yet, the office of the Inquisition still exists! That it still exists is a scandal. That its name has been changed, to the "Congregation for the Doctrine of the Faith," but not its nature, is an insult. The man who held the position of the Grand Inquisitor, Joseph Cardinal Ratzinger, was responsible for the harassing of Fr. Charles Curran, and of Fr. Matthew Fox, whom he accused of heresy. Why? Because Fox hired Starhawk (and Luisah Teish, a Voudun priestess) to teach at Holy Names College in Oakland, California. Ratzinger did force Fox out of the Dominican Order; Fox has decided to become an Episcopalian rather than give up being a priest. That is still how the Roman Catholic administration treats its most creative members.

When Starhawk or Gardner or anyone else says, "I am a Witch," that says, "You Catholics did not stop persecuting people until we took the power to persecute people away from you by force. You claim, in your Vatican II documents, that you do not intend to persecute anyone again. *So why do you still own all the machinery of the Inquisition?*" And in 1987 I realized that I had no answer.

I also realized that from the Witches I was hearing the same voice of prophecy that cried out against injustice, against corrupt power, against privilege that destroys our ability to feel compassion, that cried out through Amos, and Hosea, and Jeremiah, and Jesus. And that voice is the gift of the Spirit.

Let me extend to you the Witches' invitation: "If you, dear reader, can no longer stomach being in communion with Cardinal Ratzinger—or whoever the Chief Son-of-a-Bitch of your particular persuasion may be—then come circle with the Witches. We offer you liberty, fraternity, and equality."[6]

[6] I wrote this passage back in 1990, when Ratzinger held the office of Prefect of the CDF, long before he became Benedict XVI. Hence I find myself in the embarrassing (or ironic) position of having apparently insulted the Pope in public, in writing. I hope the reader can understand that I was attacking the office he held, not the man himself. Benedict is a brilliant theologian, but politically is ultraconservative. I continue to believe that the CDF should be abolished, as I advocated in every talk I gave in the 1980s, as part of my Quixotic program to democratize the Roman Catholic Church. I wish the Cardinals had elected a more liberal Pope, and I hope that Benedict may yet carry out the reforms mandated by the Second Vatican Council, reforms that, by the way, meet all the criteria for infallibility laid down by the First Vatican Council.

Appendix A.

Toward a General Theory of New Religious Movements

Many people tend to suspect that any new religious movement (NRM) is probably antisocial in some way, or that the very existence of a NRM is evidence of some sort of social pathology. This tendency often results from assuming a "Golden Age" model of religion, that is, from assuming that once upon a time God or the Gods handed down the perfect religion to mankind, and that everything has been downhill ever since. In this sort of Platonic model, perfection is changelessness; hence any change must be away from the original perfection. Obviously, a NRM is a change, and so it must be for the worse.

There is an old joke about a borrowed vase. A man is hauled into court, charged by a neighbour with breaking a borrowed vase. In his defence, the man argues to the judge, "Your honour, I want to make three things clear. First, I never borrowed the vase. Second, it was already broken when I borrowed it. Third, it was in perfect condition when I returned it."

This joke is really about the psychology of denial, and it applies to the study of NRMs as follows. A person who assumes a Golden Age model of religion will tend to deny the existence of NRMs, and will surely resist the idea of purposely going out to look for them: "people don't purposely start new religions; they're just being immoral; you can't study something that no one is doing." That is, there are no organized phenomena to study; there is only random noise. That is, I never borrowed the vase.

Next, confronted with sufficient evidence of the existence of a NRM, the person will deny its importance: "that's not a real religion; it's a parody of religion; only a few nuts believe in that; that's all just superstition, occultism, bad mental health; there's nothing there worth studying." That is, something is going on, but it is not religious. That is, the vase was already broken.

Finally, when it becomes obvious that the NRM will not go away, that it is performing some useful social functions—this is usually just about when people stop calling it a cult and start calling it a church—then our person will want to argue that the NRM is merely a minor variation on the mainstream religion, or on some long-known and well-understood religion. That is, there is nothing new here to study. That is, I returned it in perfect condition.

And notice the assumption implicit in these last two stages: if it's religious, it can't be new; if it's new, it can't be religious.

Current liberal, mainstream Christian thought understands "church" to be not a collection of persons who have acquired special privileges, but rather a missionary enterprise: "our primary purpose is to carry the message to those who still suffer," for example. But as a missionary, I will run into other churches, other religions, not merely old established ones, but new ones. If I have dualistic tendencies, I will be tempted to attribute these new religions to the forces of evil—as the early Church fathers did—but such a position cannot be maintained very long. These NRMs do work, they do their members much good, by ordinary standards; and much creativity has gone into establishing and maintaining these new religions. Now, Christians cannot attribute such goodness and creativity to the forces of evil: that would be Manichaeism, not Christianity. A strict monotheist must believe that all good things, all creativity, come from the one source of goodness, that is, the one God. Hence these other religions must be gifts of the same Holy Spirit that has created and maintained his or her own church. But this creates a dreadful problem: if the revelation to my church was complete, why is the Spirit creating other churches? As W.H. Auden put it, "I know that we are here to serve others. Why the others are here I have no idea."

Having contemplated that argument, perhaps we can leap to the realization that our problem lies precisely in assuming that there is something wrong with NRMs as such. But what if there isn't? What if the creating of new religions is a normal function of human social life? If it is, what is it good for? Obviously I cannot answer such questions by means of a classical, Platonic model of a sort long banished from the natural sciences and many of the social sciences. Instead let us consider a more modern model for understanding NRMs, specifically, an evolutionary model, and let us therefore quickly review how biological evolution works.

First, there is a source of change, which creates variations in the characteristics of offspring, so that some of them will differ from their progenitors in one or more ways. We know now about genes and mutations; Darwin did not have that advantage.

Second, most mutations—changed characteristics—are harmful or useless; they don't make the offspring more likely to survive. But one of every so many mutations is helpful: the offspring with the resulting characteristic has a little bit better chance to survive and to reproduce than its peers have.

Third, if the population remains in the same environment, descendants of the individual with the helpful characteristic will slowly increase as a percentage of the overall population.

Fourth, however, if the characteristic enables individuals who have it to survive in a new (nearby, etc.) environment, in which individuals who lack the characteristic cannot survive, then descendants of the former will populate this new environment exclusively. This new environment is what we now call an "ecological niche."

Fifth, when descendants of a common ancestor have acquired so many divergent characteristics that they can no longer interbreed and produce fertile offspring, then they are considered members of separate species.

To the preceding, let me add two philosophical or theological observations. First, there is no evidence of spontaneous generation. As far back into the past as we can look, living creatures are spawned only by other living creatures.[1]

---

[1] I am not here trying to deal with the problem of how this process got started, but we have archaeological evidence of religious behaviour from tens of thousands of years ago, before we had finished evolving into this species of Homo sapiens. It seems relevant that new religions are often - perhaps usually - begun with the idea that they are merely reforms of an older religion; that is, they claim to be that older religion, only a better version of it. I don't think anyone has understood the reasons for this pattern.

Second, those who wish to preserve the role of God in all this can easily do so. Modern liberal theologians believe that the first two chapters of Genesis were intended to be a theological statement, not a biology textbook. These chapters assert that God created all things and all life, including human life; they were not intended to give details of how he did it. Hence one can suppose that biological evolution is the process that God created in order to create life. One need not suppose that God created the universe, then had to interrupt himself in order to invent human beings.

That, in an outrageously oversimplified form, is the theory of evolution and some of the theological issues it touches on. Let's apply it to the question of NRMs and see what happens.

First, there is a source of new religions in human creativity. In this sense, every tiny new sect, of a few people, is like a creature with a mutated gene. I don't have to explain how this creativity works, anymore than Darwin needed to know about genes; I merely need to point out that the behaviour exists.

Second, most new religions, like most mutations, don't have much survival value, and in fact most don't survive very long. But one of every so many NRMs does have survival value: it meets the needs of its members a little bit better than any of the other possible choices does.

Third, so long as a NRM continues to meet people's needs at least as well as the other available religions do, it will continue to survive and grow.

Fourth, however, if the NRM is meeting needs that the other religions are failing to meet, then it will probably grow rapidly, at the expense of those religions. This is the equivalent of exploiting a new ecological niche. In fact, because humans operate cognitively, perception of needs that are not being met is, of course, a major reason for the creating of a NRM. To be able to perceive an unmet social need, and to be able to propose creative solutions that would meet it, a person does have to have special talents. Such talents have traditionally been considered to be gifts of the Spirit, and part of the gift of prophecy.

Fifth, when two religious movements have diverged so much that their members no longer celebrate festivals on the same dates, then they are considered members of separate churches. (But notice that choosing a date for a festival different from that of the others is an effect of a schism, not a cause.)

To the preceding, let me add two philosophical or theological observations.

First, there is no evidence of spontaneous generation. As far back into the past as we can look, religions are spawned only by other religions, that is, by humans with religious beliefs.[2]

Second, for those concerned to preserve the role of God in all this, I still think there is no problem. If one can suppose that biological evolution is the process that God created in order to create life, then one can just as easily suppose that social evolution is the process that God created in order for us to acquire law, order, religion, community, and other social goods. If God did not need to interrupt his creating of the universe in order to invent human beings, then we also don't need to suppose that He created us as culture-bearing social creatures, then had to interrupt himself in order to create churches and religions.

Having come up with this new viewpoint, I am in danger of behaving like a man with a new hammer: I may be going around banging on things, looking for nails. Nevertheless, as I mentioned in Chapter 2, all five major world religions began as NRMs, at dates which we know fairly precisely. For Islam and Buddhism, this is obvious. Hinduism as we have it must be considered a sibling of Buddhism, since it resulted from an acceptance of some, though not all, of the Buddha's reforms. Judaism, as the state religion of Judah, dates from 621 B.C.E.[2]; but Christianity and Judaism as we have them are siblings, arising together from the ashes of Jerusalem, which was destroyed in 69 C.E. The important issue here is that if all religions begin at some time and place as new religions, then the study of NRMs is not the study of fringe sects, epiphenomena, and so on. Rather, it is the study of characteristics central to all religions.

Still, this evolutionary model is merely an hypothesis, not a theory. It is provocative; it may prove to be controversial; and it may prove to be testable, because it immediately raises other questions.

---

[2] See II Kings 22

For example, are NRMs created steadily, spasmodically, only under certain conditions, or what? Biological mutations occur at a steady rate, but a new species arises only when there happens to be a new ecological niche to be exploited. If this parallel holds true, we would find that NRMs are created steadily, but are noticed only when they have grown to a certain size.

Although people write poems, paint pictures, and exercise artistic creativity in whatever ways are available to them simply as a part of being human, this does not create a steady flow of art. It is easily recognized that there are periods of greater or lesser productivity, at least in terms of what survives until later times. The periods of greater productivity, such as that of Periclean Athens[3], Renaissance Italy, Elizabethan London, are often called Golden Ages, and those of little productivity Dark Ages.

The same sort of pattern exists for religious creativity. The most noticeable "Golden Age" in religion was a world-wide phenomenon: between about 650 and 500 B.C.E. there appeared Hilkiah in Judaea, Zoroaster in Iran, Gotama in India, Lao-Tzu and Confucius in China, and Pythagoras in Italy, to mention only the brightest lights.[4] Another important period was the Hellenistic (in the broadest sense), which saw a great many religions founded, beginning with the Mysteries of Isis in the early third century B.C.E., and ending with Mani in the third century C.E.

A Golden Age model assumes that NRMs will be rare, unusual, on the periphery, occurring only when there is an unfortunate coincidence of breakdowns in the central system. The evolutionary model proposes that NRMs will be created more or less steadily at all times and places, and that

---

[3] In examining the phenomenon of Periclean Athens, Alfred Kroeber proposed that human beings with high I.Q.s are born at a steady rate, but are recognized as geniuses only when their culture provides them with a new intellectual niche to exploit. The alternative explanation - that dozens of persons with extraordinary abilities were born within a short period - violates parsimony: we cannot explain why or how such a statistical anomaly could occur.

[4] I do not know why so many of the world's most long-lived religions should have been founded almost simultaneously and certainly independently; but surely this fact merits an explanation.

variations in the rate of creation will be caused by local circumstances. How could we test the veracity of this proposal?

As we look at historical records, there do seem to be vast differences in the numbers of NRMs being created at various times and in various places, but are these differences real? That is, do they represent a real difference in the rate at which NRMs are being created, or merely a failure to record and preserve data about NRMs? It is probably almost always the latter. Why? Because established churches, established power structures of any sort, will obviously want to oppose new organizations that pose a counterclaim against their established authority. They might oppose NRMs by denying their arguments, or by denying their importance, or by denying their existence; this last option, the most effective of all when it is feasible, would imply suppression of all data about the existence of NRMs. Hence we could suppose that data about NRMs would appear in the historical record only when the existing religious establishment was unable to ignore it. We can also suppose that whenever we have sufficiently detailed historical records, we will find new religions being created at a fairly steady rate.

This is what we seem to see in Book I of Irenaeus's *Detection and Refutation of Knowledge Falsely So-Called*: he is describing the flurry of NRMs—usually called collectively the Gnostic movements—during the period 130 to 180. Other Church Fathers describe similar NRMs during the following century. During this period the "mainstream" Christian churches were still illegal in the Roman Empire, and therefore could not mount a political offensive against such movements.[5] The rate of formation of NRMs appears to decline rapidly after the Christian church became the only legal religion, but this may result only from suppression of data.

If so, this would create a different emphasis in Gnostic studies. First, there would be no need to explain why these NRMs were arising at that time, since their arising would be the normal state; only their survival for some length of time would need explaining. Second, there need not be

---

[5] The best single source of information about these NRMs is still Book I of Irenaeus, although this is usefully supplemented by the data in other Church Fathers and in the now-standard Robinson anthology.

only a single mechanism to explain all these NRMs. Some may have arisen from the schismatic Johannine communities, as Raymond E. Brown has proposed. Some may have been older dualistic sects, ultimately Persian in origin, that adopted Christian trappings in order to proselytize, as Hans Jonas proposed. Some may have developed out of Greek philosophical / religious movements, as Hippolytus proposed. And so on. This model would make our perception of that period richer and more interesting, not less so.

Similarly, we find another flurry of NRMs beginning during the tenth century, the nadir of Roman administrative corruption and of central authority in Europe. The mounting of internal crusades against heretics, and the founding of the Inquisition, were the reactions of the established church against these NRMs, which it could not exterminate completely because its power was curtailed by the struggle between the Papal and Imperial feudal systems for supremacy.[6] If the Waldensians, the Albigensians, the Brethren of the Free Spirit, the "witches," and all the variety of messianic and reformist movements during this period can be understood as NRMs, then they must also be understood as gifts of the one Spirit. In that case, what do we make of those who fought them, persecuted them, massacred them? Do we not have to admit that that first Holocaust was an example of sheer evil, like the Nazi holocaust against the Jews, like our bombing of Nagasaki, like the genocide in Cambodia? It is surely hypocrisy to attempt to explain it away, minimize it, or justify it as necessary. In other words, following the profound insights of Walter Niggs in *The Heretics,* I do believe that the Spirit of God was on the side of the "witches" and heretics who were murdered, and that the Roman Catholic church acted as the agent of the forces of evil. Persons who oppose NRMs now therefore risk perpetrating the same great evil.

A third example is provided by religious history within the United States. Ahlstrom provides an elegant documentation of the more or less steady creation of NRMs in the USA that has been allowed by the *Laissez faire* attitude toward religion guaranteed by the First Amendment. Curiously, many of these American NRMs have reinvented systems of belief and practice that, according to Iraenaeus, Clement, and Hippolytus,

---

[6] Lea's data about the Cathars make it obvious that they were a NRM according to the criteria I am assuming here.

had already been invented by NRMs during the second and third centuries; that is, they seem to be filling similar ecological niches.

Questions About New Religious Movements

What might be some of the right questions to ask about NRMs? And what methodology is needed in studying NRMs? The answers offered here are partly deductive, and partly impressionistic, based on data that is anything but exhaustive. But at least it is a place to start.

A Golden Age model and an evolutionary model will point toward very different concepts about NRMs. First, a Golden Age model will assume that NRMs are symptoms of social pathology, and represent a condition that must be somehow cured. The evolutionary model is not 180 degrees different on this point, but it does not assume that NRMs are inherently "wrong." Rather, it proposes that NRMs will be created whenever existing religious structures are failing to meet individual or social needs. This proposal is not testable, at least not directly, because the only reasonable test would be to look for a NRM that was created when no one felt any need for it. Obviously, this would be like looking for a square circle. It seems reasonable to suppose instead that the creating of a NRM is itself evidence that those who are creating it feel that their needs are not being met.

A Golden Age model tends to assume that "real" religions have always existed, and certainly are not created by mere human beings; and that "false" religions, in contrast, ARE created by mere human beings, usually by a heresiarch who, desiring power for his own selfish and sinful reasons, will seduce a certain percentage of the faithful away from the One, True Faith by lying to them, pandering their base weaknesses, and generally misleading them.. The evolutionary model implies that a NRM will begin with a very few people, perhaps only two or three, and grow at some rate that might depend on very many different factors. (It's certainly worth noting that NRMs do not grow by luring members away from the established churches; rather, almost all of their members come from the "unchurched," those who have not recently been members of any church, and whose religious needs were not being met at all).

A NRM grows as a social organization, not at the whim of any individual. That is, the laws of its growth are sociological in nature, not psychological. At some point the NRM will become large enough to be noticed by people who have reasons to oppose its growth or existence, usually members of the existing religious power structure. At this stage political battles or polemics will begin, and these negative descriptions by political enemies are usually the earliest historical record of a NRM. Positive accounts of the NRM by its adherents may appear in the records only much later, if at all.

Obviously the very early stages of the evolution of NRMs, before they have been noticed by outsiders at all, are the most crucial ones, the ones in which the greatest amount of pure creativity is exercised, the ones that set the direction in which the NRM will almost certainly continue to grow. These are also the stages that are rarely if ever documented; often all we know about them comes from the anecdotes, inflated by folklore, of the second (or a later) generation. (Perhaps one permanent value of this book will be that it documents the Gardnerian movement from its own documents, and thus sheds light on how one NRM did in fact evolve.) A major problem for contemporary students of NRMs must be, therefore, how to locate an NRM early enough in its evolution that one can observe and record the phenomena associated with its founders and first-generation members.

One of the first crisis points in the evolution of a NRM will occur when its central decision-making body (often smaller than the entire active membership) becomes too large to function any longer as a small group, that is, by means of unwritten rules, and must instead create some sort of written charter for itself, along with some sort of rules for electing or choosing decision-makers, defining classes of membership and their attendant duties and privileges, and so on. Some percentage of NRMs do not survive this social rite of passage.[7]

---

7 For example, the NROOGD, which began in October 1967, reached the size that demanded a written charter in March 1973; and upon reaching the next crisis point in its growth in 1976, when those entitled to serve as decision-makers would have needed to elect an Executive Committee from among themselves, they instead voted to disband the movement's formal organization, leaving its local units autonomous and free to enter into ad hoc alliances with other local units in the Craft movement.

In contrast to a Golden Age model, the evolutionary model implies that NRMs should be common, ordinary, and so relatively easy to locate—and this is indeed the situation, at least now, in the USA. The evolutionary model also implies that the rate of formation of NRMs should be directly proportional to population density, that is, highest in metropolitan areas, lowest in rural areas, and this seems to be borne out by actual counts of NRMs (e.g., Melton, 1984, pp. 472-3). It is a commonplace observation that small towns tend to be socially and culturally conservative; in contrast, pressures toward conformity are much weaker in cities for any one person. Hence innovations in religious matters, just like innovations in art or science or business or any other field, are easier to carry out in cities.

There are few adherents of the current Pagan movement among genuinely rural people, those who have been born and raised in the countryside or small towns, and who live and work there, surrounded by a network of relatives and neighbours that extends backward for generations. Rather, Pagans are to be found among those people whom Spectorksy labeled the exurbanites, city folk who have moved out into the countryside for aesthetic or religious or otherwise noneconomic reasons.

Exactly what part of the urban population would be most likely to create NRMs? A Golden Age model would attribute the founding of NRMs to the least socially acceptable members of society: habitual criminals, the mentally ill, perverts, the uneducated, the weak, the powerless, the poor, the undesirable, the unwashed. In contrast, the evolutionary model proposes that the kind of persons who carry out innovations in religion will probably be the same kind of persons who do so in other fields: middle-class intellectuals, largely, with a scattering of persons from other backgrounds. Hence wherever we find a clustering of people characterized by good education, creative interests or abilities, and sufficient wealth to have discretionary time, we are likely to find people who are interested in studying, joining, or creating NRMs. In most cities we will find such a clustering at the local university, as well as in certain types of businesses that attract intellectuals: publishing, computers, advertising, journalism, research, and so on. Hence we should, and do, find a clustering of NRMs around New York City, the San Francisco Bay area, and the Los Angeles area.

Where in cities could one find NRMs that are still small, creative, growing rapidly, and open to new members? One of the best ways is to look for community bulletin boards in bookstores that specialize in non-Christian religious literature (and perhaps various kinds of psychic and magical supplies.) NRMs of most of the eight family types distinguished by Melton (1984) will occasionally post discreet notices on such boards, to inform interested "seekers" of an "open" event—a picnic, a holiday family gathering, a lecture, a ritual or liturgical drama—at which all parties can size each other up. Another pathway is to seek out the local "bulletin board" for Pagan groups on the Internet. As of the year 2007, there are thousands of covens, groves, and other kinds of Pagan groups maintaining websites, and events open to newcomers are routinely posted on these.

A first-generation NRM will continue to function as a "small group" in the sociological sense as long as its central decision-making body consists of about a dozen people, and certainly not more than two dozen. An observer in a group this size cannot be an "outside" observer; he or she will be tolerated as a member of this "central committee" only if he or she does a fair share of what the group defines as the work that needs doing. That is, he or she will constitute some 5 or 10 percent of the entire group, and so of the group's activities, decisions, and so on. In studying NRMs at this stage we are therefore confronted with the theological form of Heisenberg's Indeterminacy Principle: in religious studies we are always ourselves part of the phenomena we are attempting to study. Since you cannot study a group of this size without being an active member of it, you will usually have to pick one that, at least, does not violate your sense of ethics, and preferably one whose methods and goals you can positively support. It is not particularly unusual for a new member to be accepted into such a group even though (or sometimes because) he or she admits the primary motive for joining is to study the growth process of a NRM, since many NRMs are made up largely of people who are also interested in doing precisely that.

Perhaps one of the most curious and most important characteristics of our human religions is that they work for us even when we know, or think we know, how they work. If that were not so, no one would ever have been able to devise a NRM. Many of us professional intellectuals will find that we personally have much more in common with the kind of amateur intellectuals who start NRMs than we do with most of the very nice people who belong to mainstream churches, whom we may love very deeply, but with whom we often find that we have nothing of mutual interest to talk about.

Training Religious Creativity

During the last decade or two in America, the pattern of religious creativity has itself begun to exhibit increasingly more creativity. We find religious creators who know and assert from the very beginning that what they are attempting to create will be new, not a variation, improvement, or "correction" of something old; who have a sense of humour and build it into their religious systems; who disclaim anything like oracular infallibility; and who argue, proclaim, and insist that "religious truth" is and has always been available by direct experience to anyone who makes the effort to seek it out, that it is not monolithic but different for every person, and that every human being has a right to develop a religious system of his or her own.

A Golden Age model assumes that every aspect of the Perfect Religion is God-given, and must therefore be accepted without question. An evolutionary model proposes instead that every aspect of a NRM is shaped by human hands and minds, and that all the doubts, criticisms, false start, flashes of inspiration, hard work, and breakthroughs normal to the creative process are necessary for this sort of creativity also. What this means is that a NRM need not be, and usually is not, created by any sort of True Believers. Rather, it is created by people who, whatever their intellectual and creative gifts, are essentially ordinary human beings attempting to meet their ordinary human needs, working out their salvation in fear and trembling, very much hampered by however much of a Golden Age model they are themselves carrying about, and hence intensely self-conscious about what they are doing.

The evolutionary model enables us to think about NRMs in a new way: if they are creative, and therefore a type of artform, can we evaluate them by means of artistic criteria? That is, we don't have to consider all NRMs to be equally "good," any more than we must with art: there is both good art and bad art. It is not an accident that Starhawk teaches a course on the creating of rituals as an artform in the Institute for Culture and Creation Spirituality at Holy Names College. It is not an accident that the New, Reformed, Orthodox Order of the Golden Dawn began as a project for a course on creating rituals taught by the poet James Broughton in the Creative Arts department at San Francisco State. All of the reforms made in the Roman Catholic liturgy since the 1960s look incredibly stodgy compared with the ritual and liturgical discoveries made, and still being made, by the current Pagan movement.[8]

Many people react to the idea of creating a ritual that is intended to have genuinely religious effects, with something approximating horror: "How can you do that? That's tampering with people's lives! That's irresponsible!" Such vehemence apparently results from, again, assuming a Golden Age model: if the rituals or liturgies we have now were instituted by God himself, then any change, any innovation, must be for the worse. But of course our present liturgies were created by people at some time and some place. A Golden Age model, with its tendency toward dualistic interpretations, tends to overblow the ethical dimension. In contrast, an evolutionary model help keep ethics in perspective. If a new ritual works better for some people than the old one did, if it gives them a religious experience or dimension they had been lacking, then it represents a step in the right direction, and is a gift of the spirit. How great the step is, is a different question.

People write poetry all the time, but some poems are better than others, and some poems are more popular than others. As T.S. Eliot pointed out, one can tell whether a poem is good or not by strictly literary standards, but one cannot tell whether a poem is great by strictly literary standards. Eliot was here talking about two different problems. First, the popularity of a poem is unpredictable, partly because popularity need

---

[8] Sometimes people reinvent the wheel, sure, but my point is that most people don't realize that it is possible to invent anything in this field.

have no relationship to literary merit, partly because one never knows what might seize people's hearts. Second, literary standards are necessarily based on what has already been created, and a great poem will usually be so radically new that it will burst through the bounds of those standards, and therefore be unjudgeable in terms of them.

Instruction on versecraft is an old discipline, at least as an adjunct to learning a foreign language. Roman schoolboys were taught how to construct precisely correct measures. Only in recent decades have teachers of English seen that the major virtue of a poem lies in its originality, and that the basic craft and techniques needed in order to write an original poem can be taught, as they are now in college creative writing programs.

Now, suppose we generalize Eliot's dictum, thus: One can tell whether a religion is good or not by strictly religious standards, but one cannot tell whether a religion is great or not by strictly religious standards. That is, the popularity of a reformed or newly founded religion will be unpredictable; and a radically new religion will likely burst through the bounds established by all previous religions.

Since human beings create religions at least as enthusiastically as they create art, it would be reasonable to establish a training programme in the craft of creating religions. The disciplines involved would, naturally, be as much spiritual and artistic as academic, but so they are already in any good school of the arts or ecumencial seminary. Teachers of such a programme could realistically expect to teach any reasonably intelligent student how to create a good, original religion, with "goodness" being judged by extrapolation from known religious standards; and they could hope, although not expect, that some student would discover how to create a great religion.

Such a programme would have two related social benefits.

First, whereas a bad poem merely bores people, a bad religion can harm them severely. For example, people who believe that their religion is the One, True, Right, and Only Way have had, throughout history, a bad habit of killing other people who decline to agree with them. And if a religion is based on ordinary madness, rather than on the divine madness, the pathology it institutionalizes can also lead directly to death:

the Manson cult, Jonestown, but also a father who allows a child to die because he believes a flying saucer, or the Messiah, or some other *deus ex machina* is coming with miraculous medicines. If such a training programme could teach that creativity can be cultivated and enhanced, that religious inspiration is a fairly common experience among human beings, that every human being can be his or her own prophet and need not follow anyone else, it might do more to reduce the sum of human misery than any governmental programme aimed at mere social targets could.

Second, a person who has learned how to create a good poem is far more likely to create a great poem than a person who has had no training at all. Likewise, a person trained to create a good religion is more likely to create a great religion than the untrained amateur.

Anomie is the inability to experience meaningfulness in life; and it is a lethal disease. Religion is precisely what supplies meaningfulness in human life. A religion would need to work in completely unprecedented ways to supply that meaningfulness for a world civilization without strangling it to death. Any effort which increases the probability that such a religion will be created is therefore a step toward the greatest social benefit for mankind that I can imagine.

Appendix B

Rex Nemorensis.

Shortly after Gardner's death in 1964, there appeared a pamphlet entitled *Witch*, by "Rex Nemorensis," the pseudonym of Charles Cardell. The pamphlet claimed to be an expose of Gerald Gardner and Doreen Valiente, and contained many documents—indeed, almost the entire Book of Shadows—of the same type as the Weschcke documents. As we will see, these Cardell documents were from exactly the same period as those that Gardner sent to Charles Clark.

Witch was first reprinted in *Earth Religion News*, vol. 3 (nos. 1-3), 1976, but with a large portion left out by mistake. I have a xerox (kindly sent me by Margot Adler) of the second edition, dated December 1964. It is typewritten and self-published. The name on the title page is "Rex Nemorensis"—that is, the "King of the grove at Nemi" who guards Diana's sacred bough in Frazer's 13-volume work—but a notice about Gardner's recent death on the next page is signed "Charles and Mary Cardell."

Aside from interstitial material and illustrations, the contents fall into four major sections.

1. An introductory statement by "Rex" on pp. 1-10 (*ERN*, 155-57).
2. A section titled "Here be Witchcraft" that reproduces documents essentially identical with the Weschcke documents on pages numbered 1-43 (*ERN*, 158-69).
3. A section titled "Florannis Speaks," pp. 44-56 (*ERN*, 169-73).
4. A final statement by "Rex" entitled "Aftermath" on pages that should be numbered 59-62 (*ERN*, 173-74); it was added in the second edition.

The first section is given the grandiose title, "Nemesis: Rex Nemorensis Draws His Sword." It begins,

It was a wild night, the rain was lashing down with the wind blowing it fiercely . . . in my sound-proof consulting rooms in London . . . I sat in peace. For over forty years I have been a confidential Psychologist, specialising in trying to unravel the tangle and jumble created in the minds and emotions of unfortunate people who have dabbled in the occult in some form or other.

In what follows he paints himself as an occult Sherlock Holmes. Out of the storm, there arrives a young woman who informs "Rex" that she has been initiated by Gardner, because of whose "beastliness, superstition, and sheer downright roguery" (which are not explained by any further details), her "sensitive nature" has suffered a "complete breakdown." So next we read:

On that stormy night in 1957, Rex Nemorensis woke from his sleep and, drawing the Sword of the Water City, set forth to do battle with one more slimy serpent of the bogus occult world, leading a small band of people who dedicate their time and money to protecting the innocent from these money grubbing ghouls, who pretend to occult powers.[1]

After giving some opinions about Gardner and Doreen Vlachopoulos, whose marriage certificate is reproduced and whom he identifies as "Ameth" (Doreen commented to me, "Cardell's venom against me was occasioned by the fact that he tried very hard to recruit me into his coven, and I wasn't having any. Neither was Ned."), he says, if I may paraphrase, that he sent in "Florannis" (whose name was actually Olive Green) as a ringer to be initiated so that she could get her hands on Gardner's rituals. In Section 2 of the pamphlet, Cardell prints those rituals, which are virtually identical to the Weschcke documents, and so are of some help in understanding the chronology of the various drafts of Gardner's rituals.

In her statement in Section 3, Florannis describes how she got hold of the rituals. She attempts to paint Gardner as a simple-minded old pervert, but instead manages to portray him as a rather kindly and gullible eccentric. Doreen has written to me, "I was told some years later by Jack Bracelin that all the business about Florannis having a `private initiation'

[1] This sort of grandiosity appears many times in this brief pamphlet. It seems to be not merely literary, but a symptom of poor mental health.

was occasioned by the fact that the others had never liked her and never wanted her in Gerald's coven; but poor old Gerald was so infatuated with her that he wouldn't listen to any warnings. I can believe this. It was typical of him, unfortunately, and just the sort of thing that our `Proposed Rules' had been intended to prevent."

Facing page 10 in Section 1, we find a letter from Gardner, typed in Typeface II, and reproduced by photo-offset. It reads,

> *Castlerown 28.8.59.*
> *My dear Olive*
> *Now, the main thing l have to say is, "Yousay l Stink." Well, l do not think that this is so, And l do not think l am frightned either. But, lf you think "l STINK." l do not think it is worth saying anything more.*
> *Yours sincerely*
>
> *May you be blessed.*
> *Gerald [handwritten]*

"I SENT A LETTER TO MY LOVE"!

In most of this letter, Gardner typed lower-case ells instead of capital eyes, as was his habit. If the letter to which Gardner is replying is anything like the letters from Olive Green in the files in Toronto, then it was evil-tongued indeed. I do not have specialized knowledge of "poison-pen" letters, but certainly Ms. Green's letters are the most malevolent and vicious writing I have ever seen. Doreen has written me, "Gerald showed me some specimens of Florannis's letters, after we got together again. It takes something to shock me; but I was genuinely shocked. It is possible, however, that they were actually dictated by Cardell." Gardner's letter is rather calm and compassionate for a man who has been betrayed by a young woman whom he had loved and trusted. It certainly does not square with the story Florannis tells in her statement, nor with Cardell's claim that the Gardnerians proceeded to cast curses at him—something that is strictly against Gardnerian ethics in any case. Why was this letter included at all? Apparently Cardell could not see that it damaged his claims. Fortunately for my purposes, the letter gives us a "last possible date" for these events, and so for the documents reproduced in Section 2, and therefore for the Weschcke documents they correspond to.[2]

The story Cardell tells here does not square at all with the facts in Doreen's letter to Dafo, nor with the fact that the Cardells were teaching Witchcraft classes during this period. I see no reason to doubt the veracity or authenticity of Doreen's letter; so I must suppose that Cardell is lying, as is also indicated by his grandiosity. I have therefore been even more cautious than usual in making use of data from this pamphlet; only the data in the documents he reproduces, since they can be authenticated by comparison with documents from other provenances, can be safely used.

Cardell asserts that Gardner had begun searching for witches in 1944, but had not found any by 1951. When he met Doreen Vlachopoulos [Valiente],

> *...realising that there were not any witches in Britain, they hit on the idea that people might be persuaded that there were. So together they wrote and compiled... WITCHCRAFT TODAY, in which... Gardner... stated that he had discovered witches in Britain...Our own investigations... have proved conclusively that there was no suggestion of modern witchcraft in Britain prior to the advent of Gerald Brosseau Gardner and Doreen Vlachopoulos. Until then, witches were merely characters in children's fairy tales...[p. 7] the complete witchcraft ritual, with its initiations and ceremonies, has been pieced together by [G.B.G and D.V.] from ... many different sources... odds and ends of Folk-lore, Barrett's "Magus", Rites of Isis, and much actual [quoting] and paraphrasing of "Aradia"...There are even ideas from the Catholic Mass.*

All that seems true enough to me, but Cardell knows nothing about *High Magic's Aid*, Dorothy, Dafo, and Gardner's work during the decades before he met Doreen. Cardell then goes on to claim that the Gardnerian covenstead at the nudist club near St. Albans was merely for "hoaxing the National Press." Having heard a history of that covenstead from Robert, who has met his coven in it regularly for the last quarter-century, I know better. Cardell also calls almost all of Gardner's followers "psychologically

---

[2] There is no exact correspondence to the reprint in ERN, whose editors managed to lose everything from p. 4 to p. 16, thus collapsing the first- and second-degree initiations together.

unbalanced," but that, I suspect, is projection. In other letters in the Ripley's files in Toronto, Gardner's friends report to him that Cardell is teaching witchcraft classes, and charging hefty fees for them, using the documents that Florannis had gotten her hands on. Cardell's desire to get those documents seems to provide a simple and sufficient explanation for the facts related by Doreen, and for those inadvertently revealed in his own pamphlet.

Let us now assess the documents in Section 2. In the Glossary on the last page, Cardell says that "the rituals... are exactly as written by G. B. Gardner, including diction and spelling"; i.e., Cardell did have some scholarly traits. He then goes on to explain the symbols for the first, second, and third degrees, the scourge, and the fivefold kiss, and gives "Kerunnos" and "Arida (a corruption of Aradia) later changed to Arianrod" as the secret names of the god and goddess. As I said earlier, he probably thus forced the Gardnerians to "change the locks."

The documents are as follows.

a. Pages 1-5; "First Initiation"' this is essentially Document D.6, but there has been some revision of wording.

b. Pages 6-7; virtually identical to Document D.2, with only slight revisions.

c. Pages 8-9; The Warning; essentially as printed in *Witchcraft Today,* but the wording is closer to that in Document E.1. Since this passage from *Witchcraft Today* was incorporated into the Craft Laws, and would not have been included separately in a Book of Shadows after the Craft Laws had been promulgated, "The Old Laws" must not have been typed before about September 1959.

d. Page 10: "Invocation"; differs only slightly from Document D.13.

e. Pages 10-11: "The Goddess Speaks": essentially the same as Document E.3.

f. Pages 12-18: "Second Degree"; *word-for-word* identical with Document D.7, except that a few lines have been added to the Narrator's penultimate speech.

g. Pages 19-21: "The Charge"; *word-for-word* identical to Document D.2, except for leaving off its first two lines.

h. Pages 22-24: "Third Initiation"; *word-for-word* identical to Document

D.8; two new opening lines were later typed onto Document D.8, a carbon copy, of which Florannis probably received the original.

i. Page 25: "Of Spells"; included in Chapter 6 as Document D.11.

j. Pages 25-26: "The Witches' Chant"; essentially the same as Document D.9.

k. Pages 26-27: "Cakes and Wine"; included in Chapter 6 as Document D.3.

l. Pages 28-31: "To Gain the Sight"; *word-for-word* identical with Document D.14, a carbon copy, of which Florannis probably received the original.

m. Page 31: a diagram of the eight paths.

n. Page 32: "The Scourge and the Kiss"; included in Chapter 6 as Document D.12.

o. Pages 33-35: "The Eightfold Paths"; yet another minor revision of Document D.5a and b; not interesting enough to reproduce yet again.

p. Pages 36-43: the Sabbat rituals; essentially the same as Document D.4, but leaves out the winter solstice and Candlemas.

Reviewing the list shows that all but four of the Weschcke documents are represented here. The missing four are: an earlier draft of "The Amalthean Horn," which is included here; D.1, which had already been rewritten into the form included here; and C.10 and E.4, which appear to have been typed up especially for Charles Clark. Florannis therefore did receive everything in the Gardnerian Book of Shadows in 1959, as far as I can tell. Indeed, for four of the Documents, she seems to have received the originals of which Charles Clark later received carbon copies.

A Final Comment on *Witch*

The pamphlet certainly did not discredit the Gardnerians, if that is what it was intended to do. It does allow us to see what was in the Gardnerian Book of Shadows in early 1959, and it was right (for the wrong reasons) in attributing everything in the Book of Shadows and the movement to the creative work of Gardner and Doreen Valiente. But in what it reveals about its own author, it must be classified, coolly though compassionately, with the sort of crank religious pamphlets that Gardner was in the habit of collecting.

Bibliography

I include here all works that I refer to, plus some others that I have found especially useful, but I am not attempting to survey all the worthwhile books that concern the Craft or that are relevant for understanding it. For some books, I list the original date of publication, but page numbers in citations are those in the editions listed here. I use square brackets to indicate authors of works that were published anonymously or pseudonymously.

Abbreviations used in citations:

AAR	American Academy of Religion.
ANET	Pritchard, *Ancient Near Eastern Texts.*
ANF	*Ante-Nicene Fathers.*
BAM	Gardner, "Ye Book of ye Art Magical."
GKS	Mathers, *The Greater Key of Solomon.*
GLS	Bell, *The Grimoire of Lady Sheba.*
GW	Murray, *God of the Witches.*
HMA	Gardner, *High Magic's Aid.*
MW	Gardner, *The Meaning of Witchcraft.*
OED	*The Oxford English Dictionary.*
WCWE	Murray, *The Witch-Cult in Western Europe.*
WT	Gardner, *Witchcraft Today.*

Adler, Margot. *Drawing Down the Moon.* Viking, 1979. Beacon Press paperback, 2d ed., 1987.

Ahlstrom, Sydney E. *A Religious History of the American People.* Yale University Press, 1972; Doubleday Image, 2 vols., 1975.

Alfred, Randall H. "The Church of Satan." In Glock and Bellah, pp. 180-202. An excellent example of participant observation of a NRM.

Ante-Nicene Fathers. Eerdmans, 10 vols., 1950 (reprint of the 1895-8 American edition).

Barrett, Francis. *The Magus, or Celestial Intelligencer; being A Complete System of Occult Philosophy*. London: Lackington, Allen, 1801. Citadel Press, 1967. [Bell, Jessie W.] *The Grimoire of Lady Sheba*. Llewellyn, 1972.

Bonewits, P. E. I. *Real Magic*. Weiser, 3d ed., 1988.

Bracelin, Jack. *Gerald Gardner: Witch*. Octagon House, 1960. Fred Lamond told me that this was actually written by Idries Shah, who then decided he didn't want his name on it.

Bromley, David, and Philip Hammond, eds. *The Future of New Religious Movements*. Macon, GA: Mercer Press, 1987

Brown, Raymond E., S.S. *The Community of the Beloved Disciple*. Paulist Press, 1979. Presents Brown's central concepts on the origins of the Gnostics from the Johannine communities.

Buckland, Raymond. *Witchcraft from the Inside*. Llewellyn, 1971; rev. 3d ed., 1995.

Burland, C. A. *Echoes of Magic: A Study of Seasonal Festival Through the Ages*. Peter Davies, 1972. Burland was a member of the Gardnerian inner circle in the late 1950s.

Cardell, Charles [Published under the pseudonym "Rex Nemorensis."] *Witch*. London: Privately published, 1964.

Carmichael. *Carmina Gadelica*. Edinburgh: Oliver & Boyd, 1900.

Cavendish, Richard. *The Black Arts*. Putman, 1967.

———. *A History of Magic*. London: Weidenfeld and Nicolson, 1977.

Clement of Alexandria. *Miscellanies*. In *ANF*, vol. V.

Colquhoun, Ithell. *Sword of Wisdom: MacGregor Mathers and the "Golden Dawn."* Putnam's, 1975.

Crowley, Aleister. *Magick in Theory and Practice*. Castle, n.d. [ca. 1930]

Crowley, Vivianne. *Phoenix from the Flame: Pagan Spirituality in the Western World*. Thorson's, 1994.

------. *Wicca: The Old Religion in the New Age*. Aquarian Press, 1989.

De Givry, Grillot. *Witchcraft, Magic, and Alchemy*. Trans. J. Courtenay Locke. Houghton Mifflin, 1931. Dover reprint, 1971.

Dewar, James. "Masonic Ceremony." In Tiryakian, pp. 101-109.

Dumezil, Georges. *Camillus*. University of California Press.

Duncan, *Masonic Ritual.* 1844.

Eliade, Mircea. *Shamanism: Archaic Techniques of Ecstasy.* Trans. by W. Trask. Princeton University Press, 1964.

———. "Some Observations on European Witchcraft." *History of Religions*, 14, no. 3 (Feb. 1975), 149-172.

———. *Yoga: Immortality and Freedom.* 1954. Trans. by W. Trask. Princeton University Press, 2d, rev. ed., 1969.

Ellwood, Robert S., Jr. *Religious and Spiritual Groups in Modern America.* Prentice-Hall, 1973.

———. *Alternative Altars: Unconventional and Eastern Spirituality in America.* University of Chicago Press, 1979.

Farrar, Stewart. *What Witches Do: The Modern Coven Revealed.* Coward, McCann, 1971.

———, and Janet Farrar. *Eight Sabbats for Witches.* London: Robert Hale, 1981.

———. *The Witches' Way.* London: Robert Hale, 1985. (These two volumes are available in the U.S. in paperback, under the title *A Witches Bible*, from Magickal Child.)

Farren, David. *The Return of Magic.* Harper and Row, 1973.

Fontenrose, Joseph. *The Ritual Theory of Myth.* University of California Press, 1948. Among other things, a devastating criticism of Frazer.

Frazer, James. *The Golden Bough.* Macmillan, 3d ed., 13 vols., 1912.

Galbreath, Robert. "The History of Modern Occultism: A Bibliographical Survey." *Journal of Popular Culture*, V, no. 3 (Winter 1971), 98-126.

Gardner, Gerald B. "Ye Book of ye Art Magical." Unpublished MS., written between about 1945 (or earlier) and 1953, formerly owned by Ripley's International, Ltd., now owned by Richard James of the Wiccan Church of Canada in Toronto.

———. *A Goddess Arrives.* Hinton, WV: Godolphin House, 1997. Original ed by M. F. Robinson & Co., England, 1938(?).

———. *High Magic's Aid.* Michael Houghton, 1949.

———. *The Meaning of Witchcraft.* Aquarian Press, 1959.

———. *Witchcraft Today.* Jarrolds, 1954.

Gibson, Ian. *The English Vice: Beating, Sex, and Shame in Victorian England and After.* London: Duckworth, 1978.

Ginzburg, Carlo. *Ecstasies: Deciphering the Witches' Sabbath.* Trans. Raymond Rosenthal. Random House, 1991.

Glanvil, Joseph, and Henry More. *Saducismus Triumphatus: or, Full and Plain Evidence Concerning Witches and Apparitions.* London: Lowndes, 3d ed., 1689. Scholar's Facsimiles, 1966. One of Murray's major sources of information.

Glass, Justine. *Witchcraft, the Sixth Sense — and Us.* Spearman, 1965.

Glock, Charles Y., and Robert N. Bellah, eds. *The New Religious Consciousness.* University of California Press, 1976.

Grant, Robert. *Gnosticism and Early Christianity.* Columbia University Press, 1966.

Graves, Robert. *The Greek Myths.* Pelican, 2 vols., 1955.

———. "An Appointment for Candlemas." *Magazine of Fantasy and Science Fiction*, Feb. 1957. The existence of this story proves that Graves was part of Gardner's disinformation campaign by 1956.

———. "Witches in 1964." *Virginia Quarterly Review*, XL (1964), 550-559.

———. *The White Goddess: A Historical Grammar of Poetic Myth.* 1948. Noonday, 3d, rev. ed., 1966. Few of the references to Murray's theories about witchcraft were in the 1948 edition; they were all added after Gardner and Graves had linked up.

Greeley, Andrew. "Implications for the Sociology of Religions of Occult Behavior in the Youth Culture." In Tiryakian, pp. 295-302.

Green Egg. Journal of the Church of All Worlds. Otter Zell, ed.

Harrison, Jane Ellen. *Prolegomena to a Study of Greek Religion.* Cambridge University Press, 1908.

———. *Themis: The Social Origins of Greek Religion.* Cambridge University Press, 1912.

———. *Epilegomena to a Study of Greek Religion.* Cambridge University Press, 1922.

Harvey, Graham, and Charlotte Hardman, eds. *Paganism Today: Witches, Druids, the Goddess and Ancient Earth Traditions for the Twenty-First*

Century. Thorson's, 1995.

Heselton, Philip. *Gerald Gardner and the Cauldron of Inspiration.* Capall Bann, 2003.

Hippolytus of Rome. *Refutation of All Heresies.* In ANF, V, 9-153.

Hobsbawm, Eric, and T. Ranger, eds. *The Invention of Tradition.* Cambridge University Press, 1983.

Howe, Ellic. *The Magicians of the Golden Dawn: A Documentary History of a Magical Order,* 1887-1923. Routledge Kegan Paul, 1972; Weiser, 1978.

Hutton, Ronald. *Triumph of the Moon.* Oxford University Press, 1999.

Irenaeus of Lyon. *Detection & Refutation of Knowledge Falsely So-Called (Against Heresies).* In *ANF*, I, 315-567.

Iron Mountain: A Journal of Magical Religion. Edited by Charles Clifton and Mary Currier-Clifton. Artemisia Press.

Johns, June. *King of the Witches: The World of Alex Sanders.* Coward McCann, 1969.

Jonas, Hans. *The Gnostic Religion: The Message of the Alien God and the Beginnings of Christianity.* Beacon, 2d ed., 1963.

Kelly, Aidan A. *Crafting the Art of Magic, Book I: A History of Modern Witchcraft, 1939-1964.* St. Paul, MN: Llewellyn, 1991.

———. "Looking Reasonably at Outrageous Religions: Satanism as a Normal Phase of Religious Maturation." Paper delivered to a session of Philosophers for Social Responsibility at the Pacific Division meeting of the American Philosophical Association, Los Angeles, March 1986.

———. "The Invention of Witchcraft: Uses of Documentary and Oral-Historical Materials in Reconstructing the History of the Gardnerian Movement." Paper given to the Religion and Social Science Section of the AAR, in San Francisco, December 1981. *Zetetic Scholar* #10, 1981.

———. "In the Season of Scarlet Herrings: Some Rather Personal Observations on Methodology in Religious Studies." In *Devils, Witches, Pagans, and Vampires: Studies in the Magical World View* (*Fort Hayes Studies*, Third Series, Humanities, No. 5., 1985). [This essay subsumes a paper I gave to the Women and Religion Section of the

AAR/West in Pasadena, March 1981, entitled "Observations on Some Systemic Methodological Problems with Theories of Ancient Female Monotheism."]

———. "An Update on Neopagan Witchcraft in America." Paper given to the GNRM of the AAR, Boston, Dec. 1987. Revised version published in James R. Lewis, ed., *The New Age in Perspective* (SUNY Press, 1993).

———. "Textual Criticism and the Craft Laws." *Gnostica*, Sept 1974.

Kenyon, Theda. *Witches Still Live.* 1928.

King, Francis. *Ritual Magic In England, 1887 to the Present.* Spearman, 1970.

Kroeber, Alfred. *Anthropology.* Harcourt, Brace, 2d, rev. ed., 1948.

Lea, Henry Charles. *A History of the Inquisition of the Middle Ages.* Harper & Bros., 3 vols., 1888. On the Cathars see vol. I, Chapters 3 & 4, especially pp. 91-107.

Leek, Sybil. *The Complete Art of Witchcraft.* World, 1971.

Leland, Charles Godfrey. *Aradia, or The Gospel of the Witches of Tuscany.* Trans.Mario Pazzaglini and Dina Mazzaglini. Contributions and commentary by Chas Clifton, Stewart Farrar, Robert Matheisen, and Robert E. Chartowich. Blaine, WA: Phoenix Publishing, 1998. David Nutt: London 1899

Lethbridge, T. C. *Witches: Investigating an Ancient Religion.* 1962. Citadel, 1968.

Lewis, James R., ed. *Magical Religion and Modern Witchcraft.* State University of New York Press, 1996.

Luhrmann, T. M. *Persuasions of the Witch's Craft: Ritual Magic in Contemporary England.* Cambridge, Mass.: Harvard University Press, 1989

Marty, Martin. "The Occult Establishment." *Social Research*, XXXVII (Summer 1970), 212-230.

Mathers, S. L. MacGregor, ed. and trans. *The Greater Key of Solomon.* De Laurence, Scott, 1914.

Melton, J. Gordon. "Modern Alternative Religions in the West." In J.R. Hinnells, ed., *A Handbook of Living Religions* (Viking/Penguin, 1984), pp. 455-474.

———. *Encyclopedia of American Religions.* Detroit: Gale Research, 4th ed., 1994.

———. *Magic, Witchcraft, and Paganism in America: A Bibliography.* Garland, 1982; 2d ed., 1992.

———. *The Cult Experience: Responding to the New Religious Pluralism.* Pilgrim Press, 1982.

———. "Origins of Modern Sex Magick." Paper delivered to the Society for the Scientific Study of Sex, Midcontinent Region, Chicago, June 7-9, 1985.

Metzger, Bruce M. *The Text of the New Testament: Its Transmission, Corruption, and Restoration.* Oxford University Press, 1964.

Midelfort, H. C. Erik. "Recent Witch Hunting Research, or Where Do We Go from Here?" *Papers of the Bibliographical Society of America*, LXII (1968), 373-420. Lists 509 items, almost all published since 1940, some of which are relevant to the Gardnerian Craft.

Miller, David L. *The New Polytheism: Rebirth of the Gods and Goddesses.* Harper and Row, 1974.

Moore, Virginia. *The Unicorn: William Butler Yeats' Search for Reality.*

Moss, Norman. *The Pleasures of Deception.* Reader's Digest Press, 1977.

Murray, Margaret A. *The Witch-Cult in Western Europe.* Oxford University Press, 1921. Oxford paperback, 1962.

———. *The God of the Witches.* Oxford University Press, 1934. Doubleday Anchor, 1960.

Needleman, Jacob, and George Baker, eds. *Understanding the New Religions.* Seabury, 1978.

Nugent, Donald. "The Renaissance and/of Witchcraft." *Church History*, XL (March 1971), 69-78.

———. "Witchcraft Studies, 1959-1971: A Bibliographic Survey." *Journal of Popular Culture*, V, no. 3 (Winter 1971), 82-97.

Oxford English Dictionary. Oxford University Press, 2 vols. (compact ed.), 1971.

Pritchard, James B., ed. *Ancient Near Eastern Texts Relating to the Old Testament.* Princeton University Press, 3d, rev. ed., 1969.

Rabinovitch, Shelley, and James R. Lewis. *The Encyclopedia of Modern*

Witchcraft and Neo-Paganism. Citadel Press, 2002.

Randolph, Paschal Beverly. *Eulis: Affectional Alchemy*. Quakertown, Pa.: Beverly Hall, Confederation of Initiates, 5th ed., 1930.

Randolph, Vance. *Ozark Superstition.* Columbia University Press, 1947. Dover reprint, under title *Ozark Magic and Folklore*, 1964.

Regardie, Israel. *The Golden Dawn: An Account of the Teachings, Rites, and Ceremonies of the Order of the Golden Dawn. 1937-1940*. Hazel Hills, 2d ed., 1969.

———, ed. *Gems from the Equinox: Selected Writings of Aleister Crowley.* Llewellyn, 1974.

Robbins, Rossell Hope. *The Encyclopedia of Witchcraft and Demonology.* NY: Crown, 1959. Lists virtually everything published about any kind of witchcraft up to 1958.

Roberts, Susan. *Witches USA.* Dell, 1971; Phoenix House, 2d ed., 1974.

Robinson, James M., ed. *The Nag Hammadi Library in English.* Harper & Row, 1979; 2d ed., 1988.

Rose, Elliott. *A Razor for a Goat: A Discussion of Certain Problems in the History of Witchcraft and Diabolism.* University of Toronto Press, 1962.

Russell, Jeffrey B. *A History of Witchcraft: Sorcerers, Heretics, and Pagans.* Thames and Hudson, 1980.

Ryall, Rhiannon. *West Country Wicca: A Journal of the Old Religion.* Custer, WA: Phoenix Publishing, 1989.

Schad-Somers, Suzanne P. *Sadomasochism: Etiology and Treatment.* Human Sciences Press, 1982.

Seims, Melissa. *Charles Clark -- Gardnerian High Priest and Child of the Wica.* Circle, issue 93, Spring 2005.

------. *He Casts the Circle*. The Cauldron, no. 120, May 2006.

------. *The Scottish Roots of the Wica* -- the Early Gardnerian Craft in Scotland." Pagan Dawn, no 159, Beltane 2006..

------. *Doreen Valiente and the Golden Dawn*. The Cauldron, no. 123, February 2007.

---------. .Home for Some of the Wica: www.thewica.co.uk

Seth, Ronald, ed. *In the Name of the Devil: Great Witchcraft Cases.*

Jarrolds, 1969; Arrow paperback, 1970.
Shah, Sayed Idries. *The Secret Lore of Magic: Books of the Sorcerors.* Muller, 1957; Citadel paperback, 1970.
Starhawk [Miriam Simos]. *The Spiral Dance: A Rebirth of the Ancient Religion of the Great Goddess.* Harper & Row, 1979; 2d ed., 1989.
———. *Dreaming the Dark: Magic, Sex, and Politics.* Beacon Press, 1982.
Tiryakian, Edward A., ed. *On the Margin of the Visible: Sociology, the Esoteric, and the Occult.* Wiley, 1974.
Truzzi, Marcello. "The Occult Revival as Popular Culture: Some Random Observations on the Old and the Nouveau Witch." Paper presented to the Ohio Valley Sociological Society, Akron, May 1, 1970. *Sociol. Quarterly*, 13 (Winter 1972), 16-36. Excerpted in Tiryakian, pp. 215-222.
———. "Towards a Sociology of the Occult: Notes on Modern Witchcraft," in Zaretsky and Leone.
Valiente, Doreen. *Where Witchcraft Lives.* Aquarian Press, 1962.
———. *An ABC of Witchcraft Past and Present.* St. Martin's, 1973.
———. *Witchcraft for Tomorrow.* St. Martin's, 1978.
———. Letter to the Editors, *Iron Mountain*, vol. 1, no. 3 (Fall 1985), pp. 3-6.
———. *The Rebirth of Witchcraft.* London: Robert Hale, 1989.
Zaretsky, I. J., and M. P. Leone, eds. *Religious Movements in Contemporary America.* Princeton University Press, 1974.

Other titles available from Thoth Publications.

TEUTONIC MAGIC
by Kveldulf Gundarsson

Tales of Teutonic magic have thrilled the world for centuries. Now bringing together the dark stuff of sagas, Kveldulf Gundarsson reveals the personal magical path behind the legends and explains the practical techniques of the Northern Tradition. Gundarsson is a well known expert on the esoteric lore of the Teutonic people. This, his first book Teutonic Magic brings a lifetime's worth of expertise to the subject. Blending historical lore with practical experience of esoteric skills, Gundarsson presents the reader with a spiritual path walked by the ancient and dark age Germans.

He explains the magical writings of the Teutonics, including the uses of each of the runestaves, the laws of magic in the Northern tradition. He provides the key to unleash the awesome might of the Northern magical tradition.

This is not a dry academic book. Gundarsson's writing flows like the sagas themselves, covering subjects such as Norse deities and rituals. It describes the structure of the spiritual realms in which the Norse Magician would walk. It is no wonder that this book is considered the classic text book of anyone who would study Runes or the Northern Tradition.

ISBN 978-1-870450-22-5

PRIESTESS: THE LIFE AND MAGIC OF DION FORTUNE
by Alan Richardson

In the meantime I had my dream of moon-magic and sea-palaces and day by day I lived more in another dimension where I had that which I knew I should never have on earth, and I was very happy.

Dion Fortune was the pen-name of Violet Firth, one of the most luminous and striking personalities of the twentieth century, Womanhood's answer to Aleister Crowley, and quite possibly the Shakti of the Age.

This new, revised, expanded and beautifully-written edition tells the full story of a woman who hid behind a veil of secrecy and who became a cult figure in the years after hew death in 1946. A brilliant writer and pioneer psychologist her whole life was devoted to living out an eternal Myth in a story that can be told in terms of Virgins and Dragons, Moons and Oceans, and the spirit of the land itself.

As a powerful psychic and medium, obsessed with the study and practise of Magic, and a high-grade initiate within the Hermetic Order of the Golden Dawn, her career was never entirely in this world, and her companions not always human. In her own eyes at least she was a Priestess, a channel for the Great Goddess, an exponent of the time-lost Mysteries of Women long before the present generations of feminists and goddess-worshippers where ever born.

From her birth in Llandudno, through her years in the drowned lands of Somerset, Alan Richardson unfolds the luminous and very moving patterns of her life: her early career as a psychoanalyst, her nervous breakdown, her time as a Land Girl and her developing psychism; her memories of past lives on Atlantis and relationships with Inner Plane beings who have an evolutionary interest in our world; her romance with a man she believed to be non-human and her fraught marriage to a doctor whom everyone knew as Merlin; the foundation of her own group devoted to bringing through the Western Mysteries at a time when few people knew that there was such a thing; her occult battles against the Nazis and fellow magicians – and the start of her long, hard, and always stormy journey into the Otherworld, toward the heart of the Goddess that she saw as sleeping within the Earth itself, and who needed awkening…

ISBN 978-1-870450-11-9

PATHS OF WISDOM
by John Michael Greer

Acclaimed as an instant classic on its original publication and eagerly sought by students of magic ever since, *Paths of Wisdom* is a comprehensive introduction to the theory and practice of the magical Cabala, as practiced in the Hermetic Order of the Golden Dawn and most other contemporary Western occult traditions. Engaging and accessible, yet packed with material found in few other books, it illumines the Cabalistic underpinnings of today's Hermetic magic as never before.

From the fundamentals of Cabalistic philosophy, through a detailed examination of the Spheres and Paths of the Tree of Life, to the magical disciplines that bring the symbolism to life as a potent toolkit for self-knowledge and esoteric attainment, *Paths of Wisdom* is you guide to the principles and practices of the magical Cabala.

John Michael Greer is the author of more than a dozen books on magic and alternative spirituality and a long-time practitioner of the Golden Dawn system. Also active in Druidry, he currently heads the Ancient Order of Druids in America (AODA) as its Grand Archdruid. He lives in the mountains of southern Oregon, USA.

ISBN 987-1-870450-25-6

CPSIA information can be obtained
at www.ICGtesting.com
Printed in the USA
LVHW091208101120
671260LV00003B/15

9 781870 450584